Jekyll on Trial

ELYN R. SAKS

with Stephen H. Behnke

Jekyll

New York University Press

NEW YORK AND LONDON

Multiple

Personality

Disorder

on Trial

and

Criminal

Law

NEW YORK UNIVERSITY PRESS
New York and London

Material in this book has been adapted with permission from:

"Multiple Personality Disorder and Criminal Responsibility," *U.C. Davis L. Rev.* 25 (1992): 383, © 1992 The Regents of the University of California.

"Does Multiple Personality Disorder Exist?" *International Journal of Law and Psychiatry* 17 (1994): 43-78. © 1994 Elsevier Science Ltd.

"Integrating Multiple Personalities, Murder, and the Status of Alters as Persons," *Public Affairs Quarterly* 8 (1994): 169-85, © 1994.

"The Criminal Responsibility of People with Multiple Personality Disorder," *Psychiatric Quarterly* 66 (1995): 119-31, © 1995 Human Science Press, Inc.

Library of Congress Cataloging-in-Publication Data
Saks, Elyn R., 1955-
Jekll on trial : multiple personality disorder and criminal law /
Elyn R. Saks, with Stephen H. Behnke.
p.   cm.
Includes bibliographical reference and index.
ISBN 0-8147-8042-3 (cloth : acid-free paper)
1. Multiple personality. 2. Forensic psychiatry. 3. Multiple
personality — Law and legislation.   I. Behnke, Stephen H., 1958-
II. Title.
RA1152.M84S25   1997
614'.1 — dc20   96-35676
                    CIP

New York University Press books are printed on acid-free paper,
and their binding materials are chosen for strength and durability.

Manufactured in the United States of America

10 9 8 7 6 5 4 3 2 1

For My Parents

Contents

Acknowledgments

I am deeply grateful to many people for their help in the writing of this book. I thank Dean Scott Bice for helping ensure that the University of Southern California Law School maintains its scholarly atmosphere and for providing extraordinary support to us all in our academic endeavors. I thank Albert Brecht for administering such a responsive and helpful library at USC. I also thank the librarians who helped with this project, particularly Laura Cadra. I thank Rosemary Hendrix for her wonderful secretarial assistance. And I thank Shirly Kennedy for her helpful contributions to the preparation of the manuscript.

I would like to thank the individuals who helped me to develop a rich, clinical feel for multiple personality disorder (MPD). Marlene Steinberg shared one hundred hours of videotapes in which individuals suffering from MPD and other disorders were interviewed on the Structured Clinical Interview for DSM-IV Dissociative Disorders (SCID-D). Seeing these videotapes enormously enriched my sense of what it is like to suffer from MPD. It also gave me an appreciation of the immense value of the SCID-D in diagnosing dissociative disorders. Walter Young and Steven Frankel kindly facilitated my meeting and interviewing patients at Del Amo Hospital. I would like to thank the patients themselves; I admire their courage in coming to terms with terrible histories and a sometimes crippling disorder.

I would like to thank two clinical and forensic experts on MPD,

Judith Armstrong and Stephen Marmer. Our work together has been extremely helpful in refining my thinking on how MPD should be handled at different stages in the criminal process, and I am enormously grateful to them for the insights they have shared with me.

Many people generously gave of their time in reviewing and commenting on the manuscript. I am especially grateful to Scott Altman and Judith Armstrong for their thoughtful comments on multiple versions of *Jekyll on Trial*. I would also like to thank in this regard Gerald Aronson, Sherry Colb, Richard Craswell, Michael Dorf, Joshua Dressler, Alon Harrell, Thomas Lyon, Alexander Meiklejohn, Daniel Ortiz, Michael Otsuka, Michael Shapiro, Larry Simon, Christopher Slobogin, Marlene Steinberg, Nomi Stolzenberg, Charles Weisselberg, John Young, and Walter Young.

Many individuals helped in ways both large and small by doing research. While they are too numerous to name individually, I do want to single out Lisa Barrett, Joseph Dung, Linda Ferry, Laura Frye, Steven Kim, Lois Perrin, Rebecca Reynolds, Maria Ronchetto, and Jonathan Schwartz.

The staff at NYU Press were enormously helpful. I am especially grateful to my editor, Niko Pfund, for his many wonderful suggestions and his unfailing patience as I struggled with bringing my first book to press.

I now turn to people to whom I owe a debt of a different sort. Two of my college professors, John Lachs and Paul Elledge, first excited me about thinking and writing. I never knew how wonderful the life of the mind could be before I met them. I am also deeply grateful to my professors at the Yale Law School who increased my love of learning and sensitized me to the plight of those less fortunate. I think especially of Stephen Wizner in this regard, truly one of the gems of the Yale Law School. I would like to thank Joseph Goldstein, whose precision and rigor forced me and my classmates to think more carefully than we ever had before. I am also grateful to Lea Brilmayer, Jay Katz, and John Simon for their kindness, generosity, and support. I am extremely appreciative of all my colleagues at USC who so generously nurtured me during my junior years on the faculty. Most noteworthy are Richard Craswell and Michael Shapiro for their extensive support of my early scholarly endeavors.

I am blessed with too many close friends to thank each individually, but I am eternally grateful to all. I would like to mention Stephen

Behnke and Kenny Collins in particular. They have added a depth and richness to my life for which I am enormously grateful, and have been with me through good times and bad. Each has meant the world to me. I also wish to thank William Vinet for his special friendship and support.

A deep and profound debt goes to the late Martha Harris, Stanley Jackson, and Melvin Lansky. My life as I know it would not be possible without them.

Finally, I thank my family: my brothers, Warren and Kevin, their families, and my parents, Barbara and Bert Saks. I dedicate this book to my parents as a small token of my love for them. I could not begin to thank them enough.

A Note on How This Book Was Written,
with a Special Thanks to Stephen H. Behnke

I wish to give a special thanks to Dr. Stephen H. Behnke for his extraordinary help on this project. Steve recrafted this manuscript, from beginning to end, in order to give it its present form. The book is much more accessible to readers as a result of his efforts.

While the ideas and arguments in this book are mine, Steve brought many of these positions to life through rich and colorful examples in his rewriting of the manuscript. Ironically, Steve's thinking about MPD and the criminal law is much at odds with my own, and his participation in this project should not be taken to imply that he endorses the views presented in this book. Far from a burden, however, our theoretical and clinical differences have served to crystallize and clarify each of our positions in this complicated and interesting area. I very much look forward to the thoughtful contributions on MPD and the law that Steve is now in the process of preparing, and hope they will inspire a more general public debate.

Steve, as always, was a pure delight to work with. Our days of collaborating date back to the Yale Law School, and I look forward with great joy to collaborating with him on many projects in the future.

1. Introduction

MULTIPLE PERSONALITY DISORDER has long captured the public's imagination. *Three Faces of Eve* and *Sybil* share the field with books and movies such as *Invasion of the Body Snatchers, Total Recall,* and *Alien* that trade on MPD themes. From *Sixty Minutes* to *Baywatch* to *Oprah* to *One Life to Live,* audiences debate the fate of multiples who, divided against themselves, wreak havoc in the lives of others.

Why is MPD so fascinating? Perhaps because this strange disorder raises universal fears and fantasies of being more than one person. Indeed, each of us is aware of dividedness within ourselves — we act one way on the job, another with family members, a third with friends and lovers. At times discrepant parts of our personality take hold: we act wholly out of character and, later, not understanding why, explain our behavior with a naively simple "I just wasn't myself" or "That wasn't me." Over and above such mundane experiences undoubtedly lies a fantasy that deep within our psyche lie hidden parts — people — waiting to make themselves known, a fantasy that is the source of both hope and dread. A brilliant scientist or creative genius may emerge. Or, yet again, a Jeffrey Dahmer — after all, many MPD experts hypothesize that possession is actually MPD dressed up in religious garb. Unconscious fears of being possessed ("The devil made me do it") are common in today's parlance.

Literature is replete with MPD themes, in various genres. Walter Young (1986a) explores how comic strips have depicted heroes who, arising from an epic trauma, are split between a super- and a subhuman self. Superman, for example, originates in the cataclysmic explosion of his world, Krypton, and is sent to earth as an orphan. While mild-mannered Clark Kent is impotent and devalued, Superman, virtually invincible, carries the memory of his traumatic past in the form of the one threat to his invulnerability — kryptonite. Other writers look to the more macabre. Norman Bates, perhaps the most famous multiple in American popular culture, believes his mother to be alive, well, and living with him at the Bates Motel. Norman is aghast when he discovers that his "mother" has murdered a young woman, and he makes desperate efforts to conceal the deed. Other stories, such as that of Dr. Jekyll and Mr. Hyde, explore whether multiples are morally responsible for their crimes. Dr. Jekyll commits suicide when Hyde, no longer dependent upon Jekyll's goodwill to emerge, can prowl the streets of London at will. The popularity of *Superman, Psycho,* and *Dr. Jekyll and Mr. Hyde* illustrates how powerful we find the themes inherent in a divided self.

That MPD is fascinating is not, however, the sole or even primary reason for my writing this book. My interest in writing on MPD stems from my research and teaching about psychiatric illness and criminal responsibility. Perhaps my interest is best explained by a brief discussion of why traditional notions of criminal responsibility are problematic when applied to MPD.

To understand the classic definition of criminal responsibility, one must start with the two elements of a crime—a "guilty mind" and a "guilty act," more commonly known by their Latin names, *mens rea* and *actus reus*. Without both a mens rea and an actus reus there can be no crime, hence no guilty party. Thus if a man breaks into his neighbor's house in order to abscond with an expensive painting, there is both a guilty act and a guilty mind, and so a crime. If, however, he enters the same house because he reasonably believes someone inside is in dire need of medical attention, the mens rea necessary for a crime is absent. When you have what *appears* to be a guilty act and a guilty mind — a crime — what serves to vitiate mens rea or actus reus? Traditional legal doctrine has formulated the defense of insanity to apply to those situations in which mens rea is lacking, while involuntariness applies to situations in which an actus reus is lacking.

Insanity doctrine is based on the more common mental illnesses such as schizophrenia and manic-depressive disorder, the defining characteristics of which are disturbances in thought or mood. The American Psychiatric Association classifies schizophrenia, for example, among the psychotic disorders, disorders defined in part by hallucinations and delusions. Manic-depressive disorder, on the other hand, is classified in the *Diagnostic and Statistical Manual of Mental Disorders, 4th Edition (DSM-IV)* as a mood disorder, a disorder that has "a disturbance in mood as the predominant feature" (APA 1994, 317).

With such mental illnesses in mind, the law has formulated tests for insanity that focus on cognitive and volitional impairments at the time of an agent's act. Certain tests, such as the M'Naghten rule, are more oriented toward cognitive disturbances — disturbances in an actor's capacity to understand or appreciate the nature of what he is doing. Daniel M'Naghten, after whom the test is named, had killed the secretary of the British prime minister, whom he believed to be the prime minister himself. At the time of the murder M'Naghten was laboring under the delusion that the Tories intended to harm him and that the only way to save himself was by such an act. The rule based upon this case states that the party committing the act is insane, if, as a result of mental illness, he did not know "the nature and quality of the act he was doing; or, if he did know it, that he did not know he was doing what was wrong" (*M'Naghten's Case* 1843, 722).

The balance of tests for insanity generally look to a combination of cognitive and volitional impairments to establish insanity. The American Law Institute test states that a person is insane who, as a result of "mental disease or defect . . . lacks substantial capacity either to appreciate the criminality [wrongfulness] of his conduct or to conform his conduct to the requirements of the law" (ALI 1985). Marmion Pollard, a police officer whose wife and daughter were killed by a drunken neighbor, committed a series of bank robberies after the murders. At trial, the psychiatrists were in agreement that Pollard, because he had failed to protect his family, "suffered from severe feelings of depression and guilt; that . . . he had an irresistible impulse to commit criminal acts; an unconscious desire to be apprehended and punished; and that he geared his behavior to the accomplishment of this end."[1] After a lengthy legal process Pollard was acquitted of his crime because of his inability to conform his conduct to the requirements of the law.

The problem with traditional tests for insanity is that none were formulated with MPD in mind. Unlike many people with mental illnesses, those suffering from MPD are intact, both cognitively and volitionally, for the vast majority of the time. Put another way, on any given afternoon an individual with MPD will know what she is doing and will be able to act in a goal-directed manner. Unlike M'Naghten, who labored under the delusion that the Tories were after him, or Pollard, who was unable to follow the strictures of the law, people with MPD may know exactly what they are doing and be quite able to control their behavior. The classic rules for insanity seem not to apply to the case of MPD.

An actus reus is the second element of a crime and, like mens rea, is necessary before criminal responsibility can be established. An actor is not guilty — there is no actus reus — when his act is involuntary. Examples of involuntary acts include reflex actions, sleepwalking, and acts performed under hypnosis or posthypnotic suggestion. Like insanity, involuntariness, as it has historically been understood, provides a poor fit with MPD.

The doctrine of involuntariness is actually a compilation of theories brought under one umbrella. Unlike insanity, there is no single formulation for or understanding of what renders an act involuntary. One theory is that an act is involuntary if, during the act, the agent is unconscious. Mrs. Cogdon, for example, murdered her daughter with an ax. At trial it was held that because Mrs. Cogdon was sleepwalking — not conscious — when she committed the murder, the killing was involuntary; it was not *her* act (*King v. Cogdon* 1950). Another theory is that an act is involuntary if it is not under the agent's control. Mr. Martin was physically lifted from his home into the street and subsequently charged with public drunkenness. The court held that the act of being inebriated in a public place was involuntary, since forces not under Mr. Martin's control had taken him there (*Martin v. State* 1944).

These applications of the involuntariness doctrine do not work for MPD. Individuals suffering from MPD are no more often the victims of external forces than are any other group of people, and unconsciousness is hardly a greater problem for people with MPD than for others. In short, the doctrine of involuntariness fits MPD no better than does the doctrine of insanity.

Despite the uneasy fit between traditional doctrines and MPD, there are substantial reasons for thinking that many individuals suffering from MPD should not be held responsible for their crimes. Of course, the overwhelming majority of multiples do not commit crimes. But *when* they do, people with MPD may manifest a dividedness that, in many cases, is inconsistent with viewing them as single agents. It is indeed as if one body housed more than one person, each with his or her own wishes, dreams, fears, and goals. *The Diagnostic and Statistical Manual of Mental Disorders* gives as one of three defining characteristics of the disorder "the presence of two or more distinct identities or personality states," each of which has "its own relatively enduring pattern of perceiving, relating to, and thinking about the environment and self" (APA 1994, 487). The identities may, within the same individual, show striking psychological and physiological differences from one another and, as the second *DSM-IV* criterion holds, "recurrently take control of the person's behavior" (APA 1994, 487). Alter personalities can thus act autonomously, with or without the consent, cooperation, or even knowledge of the other alter personalities. Imagine taking Mrs. Cogdon's problem — she was unaware of what she was doing — and multiplying that problem times the number of alter personalities. Can anyone seriously deny that certain multiples ought not be held responsible for their crimes?

The dividedness of MPD thus creates a problem for the law. The problem is that none of the traditional ways of thinking about and addressing mental illness and criminal responsibility speaks to the radical dividedness found in individuals who suffer from MPD. If the reader takes one point away from this book, I would like it to be just that — the law has a problem, and the problem will not go away unless new and creative ways of thinking are brought to bear.

In this book I would offer the law a way of conceptualizing criminal responsibility in the context of MPD. In formulating this conceptualization I draw upon traditional doctrines. My focus is not so much on how those doctrines have been applied — indeed, I think classical applications do not speak to MPD — but more on the reasons behind the doctrines. The spirit of the insanity and involuntariness doctrines — that we punish only those who are blameworthy—*does* speak to MPD. The singularity of MPD, however, calls for a unique analysis.

I begin by outlining some basics about MPD — its phenomenology and etiology. (I discuss more technical issues-assessment, empirical studies, and treatment — in an Appendix.) The purpose of this brief review is to provide the reader with a sufficient clinical sense of the disorder to proceed to the more theoretical questions. I next discuss the controversy over the existence of MPD. MPD has not been embraced by the entire mental health community; indeed, some — -whom I shall refer to as skeptics — -dispute that MPD is even real. Some skeptics claim that MPD is an artifact of therapy, a wish to please one's therapist with an exciting and exotic disease, while others argue that fascinated therapists, by inducing suggestible patients to assume the role of multiple personalities, are themselves responsible for the phenomenon. Still others claim that MPD patients are nothing more than malingerers. I set forth the skeptics' claims as precisely as I am able and discuss each in turn. I then focus on the meaning of this controversy for the law.

I next turn to the most clinically central aspect of MPD: alter personalities. There is nothing else in nature like alter personalities or, as they are often called, alters. In many respects alters are like people, yet in many respects they are not. Apparently more than mere parts of people, alters lack a body, long considered an essential aspect of personhood. My treatment of them is, by necessity, philosophical. Drawing upon definitions of personhood, I ask how well such definitions describe alter personalities. I then explore what ontological status we should accord alter personalities if they are not people. The discussion arrives at no definitive conclusions; its purpose, rather, is to establish what alternatives we have available in terms of categorizing these strange entities.

Criminal responsibility is my next subject. During the fall of 1977, a string of rapes and robberies terrorized the campus of Ohio State University. After a careful investigation, the police believed they had found their culprit, a man named Billy Milligan. Intending to apprehend Billy, the police broke into his apartment, only to be greeted by a dumbfounded young man who had no idea what was going on. As it turned out, one of Billy's alter personalities had been present when the police arrived. Billy, the original personality, had been banished from consciousness for many years because of his suicidality—the other alters had moved to provide for the safety of the multiple as a whole. The perpetrators of the rapes and robberies, as the psychiatrists would discover, were Adalana and Ragan, two of Billy's other alter personalities. Ironically, Billy Milligan was the last to learn that he was the "person" who had committed these terrible crimes. The Billy Milligan case illustrates as well as any the radical dividedness inherent in MPD. How we think about this dividedness depends upon how we conceptualize alter personalities, and so hearkens back to our previous discussion. Are Adalana and Ragan people? Centers of consciousness that are like people? Mere parts of a person? And what implications for criminal responsibility flow from each of these three conceptualizations? This last question forms the bulk of my discussion of criminal responsibility. I put forth a set of rules to govern the responsibility of individuals suffering from MPD — based on the unfairness of punishing people who have innocents within them — and contrast those rules to existing case law.

In the penultimate portion of the book I explore a series of legal questions having to do with competency to stand trial, civil commitment, and the sentencing of multiples. Once again, the radical dividedness found in MPD creates new problems for the law. Who, for example, is the true defendant? Whose recommendation should the lawyer follow when alters cannot agree on what to plead? Can we hold a multiple competent for execution? That multiple agencies exist in a single body adds an entire level of complexity to already difficult questions.

Finally, I examine other dissociative disorders in the context of criminal responsibility. Other dissociative disorders are weaker versions of MPD, and the case for criminal nonresponsibility is correspondingly less potent. Nevertheless, psychogenic amnesia or psychogenic fugue, two examples, are often reactions to extreme trauma and can result in a person being divided against herself. I compare this dividedness to the dividedness of MPD and ask what relevance the difference has for the criminal law.

A disorder new to the law calls for new ways of thinking, and it is precisely such ways that I wish to explore in this book. I urge the reader to see this work as an exploration into the nature of MPD and the legal consequences that follow. I fervently hope it provokes responses, however strong they may be. Research, like the law, lives and breathes, and cannot grow in a vacuum.

2. What We Know about Multiple Personality Disorder

T HE AMERICAN PSYCHIATRIC ASSOCIATION first recognized multiple personality disorder in the third edition of its *Diagnostic and Statistical Manual of Mental Disorders* (DSM-III), published in 1980.[1] Significantly more women than men appear to suffer from MPD as it is defined by the DSM; estimates of the ratio have ranged from between three and nine females to one male. While most often the diagnosis is given in one's third or fourth decade, MPD is thought to begin in early childhood, and at least one study has found the symptom picture of children to be consistent with that of adults (Hornstein and Putnam 1992). MPD does not usually present in a florid state and is often confused with other disorders at the outset of treatment; on average, MPD patients receive 3.6 diagnoses over 6.8 years before being properly diagnosed (Putnam et al. 1986). Coons has concluded that MPD is not a culture-bound phenomenon, although currently it is found most often in North American countries (Coons et al. 1991). Prevalence estimates for the general population range from one in ten thousand (Schafer 1986) to one in a hundred;[2] most commentators agree with the 1 percent figure, although Putnam argues that we lack sufficient information to speculate in any meaningful way about prevalence rates in the population at large (Putnam 1989). Prevalence estimates for identified psychiatric populations range from 1 percent (Steele 1989) to 10 percent (Bliss and Jeppsen 1985). Such differences notwithstanding, there is general agreement that the preva-lence of MPD has increased sharply in the past two decades, a phenome-non I discuss at greater length in the following chapter. In the present chapter I review the psychiatric literature on MPD by discussing its phenomenology and etiology.[3]

PHENOMENOLOGY

The *Diagnostic and Statistical Manual* categorizes MPD among the dis-sociative disorders, disorders characterized by "a disruption in the usually integrated functions of consciousness, memory, identity, or perception of the environment" (APA 1994, 477).[4] MPD, the most severe of the five dissociative disorders, has three essential elements:

1. The presence of two or more distinct identities or personality states (each with its own relatively enduring pattern of perceiv-ing, relating to, and thinking about the environment and self).
2. At least two of these identities or personality states recur-rently take control of the person's behavior.
3. Inability to recall important personal information that is too extensive to be explained by ordinary forgetfulness. (APA 1994, 487)

Central to these elements are two concepts: first, that of personalities that "recurrently take control of the person's behavior" (alter personali-ties); and second, that of the "inability to recall important personal information" (amnesia).

Just what is an "alter personality," the sort of which is found in individuals suffering from MPD? Ross (1989, 109) defines alter personal-ities as "highly stylized enactments of inner conflicts, drives, memories, and feelings," while Putnam conceptualizes alters as "discrete states of consciousness organized around a prevailing affect, sense of self (in-cluding body image), with a limited repertoire of behaviors and a set of state-dependent memories" (Putnam 1989, 103). Braun and Kluft see an alter personality as "an entity with a firm, persistent, and well-founded sense of self and a characteristic and consistent pattern of behavior and feelings in response to a given stimuli," having "a range of functions, a range of emotional responses, and a significant life

history (of its own existence)."[5] Another of Kluft's definitions is somewhat more elaborate:

> The mental address of a relatively stable and enduring particular pattern
> of selective mobilization of mental contents and functions, which may
> be behaviorally enacted with noteworthy role-taking and role-playing di-
> mensions and sensitive to intrapsychic, interpersonal, and environmen-
> tal stimuli. It is organized in and associated with a relatively stable (but
> order effect dependent) pattern of neuropsychophysiologic activation,
> and has crucial psychodynamic contents. It functions both as a recipi-
> ent, processor, and storage center for perceptions, experiences, and the
> processing of such in connection with past events and thoughts, and/or
> present and anticipated ones as well. It has a sense of its own identity
> and ideation, and a capacity for initiating thought processes and action.[6]

Mental health professionals seem clear in their thinking that personality
in this sense is not the same as person. Putnam (1989, 103) says that
"whatever an alter personality is, it is *not* a separate person," while
Colin Ross (1990b) lists under his twelve cognitive errors about MPD
the idea that alter personalities are distinct people. So entrenched is
this way of thinking that some professionals deny that alters are even
personalities.[7] Braude (1991) underscores the irony here — each commentator quoted earlier is clear that alter personalities are *not* separate
persons, yet these definitions certainly *sound* as if they are.

How do patients talk about their alter personalities?[8] Many speak
of alters as if they are separate people. One, a mental health professional
herself, sees alters "as other people. I've always thought of them as
other people. . . . I know it's only supposed to be one person per body
. . . but that's not what it feels like to me."[9] Another patient expressed
the same experience in a slightly different way: "They're not me and
I'm not them. It's like you and me."[10] A third, when asked whether
her alters feel like separate people, replied, "Oh yea, I mean they're, oh
yea . . . *we all* feel separate; I'm included in that."[11]

Interestingly, the reality testing of multiples appears to remain
largely intact. One explained that "the bottom line is there's one body
. . . the logic is one thing, the reality is another . . . the reality is there
is only one body . . . but I feel like and they feel like they're different.
They're not me and I'm not them. They're separate, except that there's
only one body, so that it doesn't make sense."[12] Others rely on metaphor to convey the complexity of their experience: "All those little
pieces, they all fit into one big, huge puzzle, but . . . they all feel like

when they're on the floor . . . they're all separate from each other";[13]
"It's kind of like a shamrock, different leaves based in the same
stem."[14] To the question of whether the alters are separate persons to
these patients, the answer appears to be not yes *or* no, but yes *and* no.
Judy Armstrong (1991b) has written about the postformal logic that
MPD engenders.

Multiples report a wide range in the number of their alters. The
average has been described as fifteen; women tend to have more than
men, and adults more than children. While most patients have certain
categories of alters such as child, protector, and persecutor,[15] each
multiple has her own unique number and type. Many cannot be classified in simple terms. There is often overlap — there may be groups of
alters that share many similarities as, for example, the "scared children."
Some alters may be quite well-rounded, displaying a wide range of
emotions, significant versatility in cognitive processes, and a complex
personality style. Empirical studies have found that such alters differ in
striking ways from one another in their physiology, psychology, and
memories (see Appendix). Other alters are more fragmentary, characterized by a single emotion or job. Such alters are referred to as
"fragments."

The "host personality" is an alter personality that is sometimes
accorded special status. The host is defined as the personality that is in
control most of the time during a given period of time. The host is not
necessarily the original, or birth, personality. Nor is it necessarily the
personality that presents for treatment (the "presenting personality").
While one might have thought the host had most claim to be the
person, the notion of host is wholly quantitative. As a consequence,
the host personality of a multiple can change numerous times over the
course of a multiple's life.

The differences between alters in personality styles and skills are per-
vasive and striking. One multiple described the personalities of her different alters: "Sarah is vicious and Terry is mean. . . . Frank, my friend,
told me, 'Just let me know when Sarah arrives. She has a black belt in
karate and I don't want to deal with it.' I mean, how can your friend tell
you that you have a black belt, and I don't even know karate? I'm not
very athletic either" (Steinberg 1995, 257–58). Another remarked, "Sarah
likes partying and drinking, Elizabeth cross-stitching, Ann reads a
lot."[16] A third explained that while "[s]ome people . . . see me . . . as a
wimp crying in the corner, . . . [others see me] doing public speaking

about disability rights . . . a really effective attorney and advocate. They're both me, just radically different."[17] Such experiences obviously hold disconcerting possibilities, as more than one multiple has discovered: "I found myself doing things I didn't know how to do";[18] "suddenly I could not do basic math . . . , and then a couple of years later, I was getting an 'A' in calculus."[19] Some individuals with MPD actually describe hallucinating differences between their alters — they literally *see* a different body. One young man recalled looking at himself in the shower and seeing a wholly different body; so anxiety-provoking was his experience that he ran out screaming.[20] Other multiples just imagine the differences — as one summed up, "Obviously my body doesn't change, but I don't know . . . that it doesn't change."[21]

The classic, florid presentation of MPD involves personalities taking control in turn. Nevertheless, alters can influence the patient in less overt ways. As one example, patients speak of passive influence experiences — feelings that their behavior and thoughts are being controlled by other personalities. Many multiples hear voices of alters speaking among themselves or to the patient. While patients may be hard-pressed to put into precise words the difference between the voices of alter personalities and their own thoughts, most are emphatic that they can easily distinguish between the two.

Patients describe differing degrees of consciousness among alter personalities. Some personalities are present and "listening in," while others are out and evident to people who may interact with the multiple. One patient explained that, when coconscious, "it's like sitting in the back seat, someone else is driving, and I'm in the car" *(Del Amo interview)*. Other alters seem to have quite different experiences — they may know only that other personalities exist, although even this is not always so. In the latter instances the multiple may realize that she "loses time," or that other people call her by different names, but most likely concludes that she is crazy, not that she has MPD.

Multiples vary in their ability to switch among personalities and to control the behavior of different alters. For some multiples, alters switch only in response to environmental triggers; for others, especially those advanced in treatment, alters may take over on cue or of their own accord — "they control when they come out . . . or I ask for help."[22] Struggles between the alters are by no means unheard of — as one multiple put it, "All of them were fighting to see who would get out first."[23] It is often not immediately clear who will win the struggle: "I went to go and attend [the meeting], and I went to walk into the room . . . my body turned around and walked out."[24] Another put the matter a bit more dramatically: "Sometimes I want to say something and I'm not able to. Something's stopping me . . . something's scream-ing out to say something or screaming for help . . . and I can't."[25] Another speaks to the intensity of the struggle:

> That person wants to come out. . . . He struggles, struggles with me. And this guy must think I'm nuts, if I'm gonna let him out. If I let him out, I'm never gonna let myself back in. And that's what scares me most. . . . [The struggle] is like a tug of war. Pulling, pulling the rope, pulling, you keep pulling and pulling, and he pulls you back and you pull it forward, and you want to say, "Hey,man. Take the damn thing." And I keep pulling that rope, and he keeps pulling it back, and I pull it again. (Steinberg 1995, 222)

Despite experiencing their alters in vastly different ways, all multi-ples, by definition, house more than one personality. Likewise, by definition, all multiples suffer from amnesia. Many, if not most, report "losing time," presumably when other personalities are in control. Time lost ranges from minutes to years and is likened to "a black space . . . like going to sleep and then all of a sudden it's morning."[26] There is an eerie consistency to how patients describe their amnesia: "[There were] chunks of school work where I couldn't figure out how it got done";[27] "It's the Sunday paper, and I thought it was Friday";[28] "I'll be driving along, and I won't have any idea of . . . where I'm going, or why I am in the car."[29] Such fugue-like experiences are understandably disorienting: "[I] found myself in an airport — I didn't know what airport it was or what state I was in, or if I was getting on a plane or I had been on a plane, or how I got there."[30] More commonly patients describe being recognized by people they do not recall meeting and finding things in their possession they do not recall purchasing.

In addition to alter personalities and amnesia, individuals suffering from MPD often display a constellation of other, mostly dissociative, symptoms. Marlene Steinberg's SCID-D has brought to light the impor-tance of depersonalization and derealization. Steinberg portrays the different dissociative disorders by examining the extent to which each entails symptoms clustered in the areas of amnesia, depersonalization, derealization, identity confusion, and identity alteration. Multiples dis-play symptoms at the highest level in all five areas. Dissociative pathol-ogy often makes understandable symptoms that may have led naive treaters to other diagnoses. Auditory hallucinations, a case in point, may be used as a basis for a psychotic diagnosis but may actually be personalities "talking" to one another. Self-destructive behavior may be a function of one personality attempting to harm or even kill another. Affective, somatoform, and post-traumatic stress disorder (PTSD) symptoms are common; interestingly, MPD patients report more "first-rank" symptoms of schizophrenia than do schizophrenics themselves (Kluft 1986a, 1987b).

The phenomenology of MPD is highly complex, no doubt explaining, at least in part, the diagnostic confusion. To make matters even more complicated, alter personalities can vary in their level of psychopathology. Some may be quite psychotic, while for others reality testing may be intact; certain personalities may suffer from affective disorders, while others may exhibit no pathology in this regard. The complexity of MPD affects its assessment and treatment, issues I discuss in the Appendix. For now let us turn to theories about the etiology of MPD.

ETIOLOGY

Theories about the etiology of MPD can be categorized in three general ways: first, that MPD is a clinical entity in its own right; second, that MPD is a variant of some other disorder, most likely borderline personality disorder; and third, that MPD is either a factitious disorder or malingering. I address the third way of understanding MPD in the following chapter.

Many, if not most, theories which hold that MPD is a clinical entity in its own right attribute a large etiological role to childhood abuse. Perhaps the most well-known theory in this category is Kluft's "Four-Factor" theory:

> Multiple personality disorder occurs when a child with the capacity to dissociate (factor 1) is exposed to overwhelming stimuli (factor 2) that cannot be managed with less drastic defenses. Hence the capacity to dissociate is enlisted in the service of the defense. Dissociated contents become linked with one of many possible substrates and shaping influences for personality organization (factor 3). If there are inadequate stimulus barriers and restorative experiences, or an excess of double-binding messages that inhibits the child's capacity to process his experience (factor 4), multiple personality disorder can result. (Kluft 1987a, 366)

Braun (1984a) has proposed a similar model in which predisposing factors for MPD include a family environment permeated by stress, inconsistency, and abuse, accompanied by the patient's inborn capacity to dissociate. Precipitating factors include a stressful event that overwhelms the individual's defenses, the activation of dissociation, and the subsequent creation of personalities whose function it is to deal with the stress. Perpetuating factors include recurrent family stress and abuse that lead to repeated dissociations, which, over time, lead to personalities developing a life history.

Putnam (1989), drawing on developmental psychology, claims that the switches alters undergo are similar to the transitions infants undergo when they change from one affective state to another. One of the developmental tasks of growing up involves consolidating self and identity and learning to modulate transitions across behavioral states. Children, by nature, are prone to enter into dissociative states and have a significant capacity for fantasy that often manifests itself in the ability to project "personality" onto inanimate objects. Putnam suggests that repeated trauma may engender profound state changes in the child at the preoperational level of cognitive development. The child fails to develop a unified self across state changes, which failure permits the persistence, and tolerance, of the separated states. As Putnam sees it, recurring trauma creates a situation in which it is adaptive for the child to magnify the separation of behavioral states in order to compartmentalize the trauma. Thus the genesis of MPD.

Others who believe that MPD is a clinical entity in its own right have quite different views about its etiology. Bliss (1983, 1984a), for example, holds that MPD is the unwitting abuse of self-hypnosis,[31] while Kihlstrom, Glisky, and Angiulo (1994) propose that dissociative tendencies such as hypnosis, absorption, and fantasy proneness are diatheses for the dissociative disorders. Price (1988, 233), proposing a transactional analysis interpretation, sees MPD as representing the "end of a continuum of possible outcomes that result when the child employs dissociative splitting of the self into more or less independent part selves because of overwhelming environmental circumstances." Barratt (1994, 123), on the other hand, discusses dream characters as analogous to MPD alters: "Dreaming may also be a more literal precursor, whose physiological mechanisms for amnesia and the projection of dissociated identities get recruited in the development of MPD. . . . Extreme early trauma may mutate or overdevelop these dissociated parts and call upon them to 'wake up' and function in the external world." Ross and Gahan (1988) interpret MPD in terms of cognitive principles, while Sternlicht and his colleagues (1989) provide a neuroscience and cognitive perspective on MPD.[32]

Perhaps the most elaborate theories about the etiology of MPD are found among psychoanalytic writers. Like other theorists, most psychoanalysts attribute MPD to early trauma. In their explanations for how childhood trauma leads to MPD, psychoanalytic theorists tend to look to the primitive quality of the defenses, ways in which the ego remains split, how dissociation is used to defend against intolerable affects, and how part-objects are internalized and remain unintegrated from the rest of the psyche. Psychoanalytic theorists have different emphases; while Brende and Rinsley (1981), for example, see the theme of abandonment as playing the most prominent role in the psychodynamics underlying MPD, Reis (1993) sees annihilation anxiety and fears of nonbeing as central. Others, such as Marmer (1991), address the intense and complex transference-countertransference paradigms.[33] Marmer (1980) has also addressed the role of splitting of the ego and use of the self as a transitional object in understanding MPD.[34] These psychoanalytic theorists, like the other theorists discussed earlier, all hold that MPD is a clinical entity in its own right, and should be thought of and treated as such.

The second way in which MPD has been understood contrasts with the first; according to theories in this category, MPD is considered a medical phenomenon yet not a clinical entity in its own right. Put in other words, MPD is neither a supraordinate nor even a coexisting disorder—it is a variant, or complication, of another medical disease.[35] Supporting this position is the comorbidity of MPD symptomatology with other mental disorders such as borderline personality disorder,[36] PTSD,[37] affective disorders,[38] eating disorders,[39] somatic disorders,[40] schizophrenia,[41] epilepsy and other seizure disorders,[42] Munchausen's syndrome (Toth and Baggaley 1991), chemical dependency (Kolodner and Frances 1993), and obsessive-compulsive disorder.[43] Chu (1991) notes that the differential diagnosis of MPD from a variety of other disorders may be extremely difficult. This difficulty has led certain writers to conclude that the symptomatology of MPD is, in reality, an associated feature of some other pathology.

Perhaps the most intensely debated controversy in this regard is the relation between MPD and borderline personality disorder (BPD). While the position that MPD is actually an eating or affective disorder, for example, has not held great sway, many in the field believe that MPD could well be a variant of BPD. The debate, complicated to begin with, is made even more so because some commentators claim that MPD is a form of borderline personality *organization,* while others say that MPD is a form of borderline personality *disorder.* To put the matter as simply as I can, borderline personality organization refers to a level of personality organization in which primitive defenses such as splitting and projective identification predominate. Borderline personality disorder, on the other hand, is a narrower, descriptive concept. The DSM describes this disorder phenomenologically in terms of features such as impulsivity, inappropriate anger, unstable identity, and volatile interpersonal relationships.[44] Those in the former camp—who see MPD as a form of borderline personality *organization*—understand MPD as an essentially pre-Oedipal phenomenon.[45] Among those who see MPD as a form of borderline personality *disorder* are Clary, Burstin, and Carpenter (1984), Pohl (1977), Buck (1983), and Kirsten (1990), who sees MPD and BPD as having the same etiology, symptoms, and course. Kirsten proposes that MPD should be classified on Axis II as a variant of BPD.

The problem with the view that MPD is actually some form of BPD is theory and research indicating that the two can be differentiated. Perhaps the most thoughtful treatment of the relationship between MPD and BPD is that of Marmer and Fink (1994), who argue that while the two disorders can be confused with one another from the DSM phenomenological perspective, they are actually distinct conditions with different process, structure, and dynamic features. Marmer and Fink first describe such differences between MPD and BPD, and then address differences in their superficially similar presentations.

In terms of process, structure, and dynamic features, the writers note that, while borderline splitting is a "low-tech" defense that polarizes good and bad, MPD splitting is a "high-tech" defense that, because it compartmentalizes memory and affect in order to erect stimulus barriers against overwhelming trauma, preserves the ability to complete developmental tasks.[46] Marmer and Fink liken the "architecture" of the borderline to a warehouse with little differentiation, lacking adequate temperature control: it is all either too hot or too cold. The "architecture" of the multiple, in contrast, is like a library or archive with enormously differentiated spaces: one vault can be freezing, the neighboring vault steaming. The structure of BPD is thus low-tech, while that of MPD is high-tech. Marmer and Fink go on to point out that borderline dissociation is dreamy, "spaced-out," and absent—as if the borderline were in a hypnotic trance. Dissociation experienced by the multiple, on the other hand, is a complex hierarchy of nuanced dissociated states, each involving an elaborate fantasy element—as if the multiple were living in a waking dream. Moreover, multiples, unlike borderlines, are capable of high degrees of symbolization, perhaps explaining their greater capacity for self-soothing. Multiples may use their alters as transitional objects, which allows them to tolerate an experience of being alone. Borderlines lack this capacity and must depend on others to soothe them or bring them out of dysphoric states. Similarly, while multiples suffer from what may be called "stable instability," borderlines suffer from "unstable instability": the former's decompensation is generally predictable once the architecture of the system is known, while the latter's is not. Finally, unlike the defenses in MPD, BPD defenses seem to be more a consequence of developmental arrest than of trauma. Borderlines seem unable to move toward true object constancy; "stuck" in splitting-style defenses, they are unable to progress to higher, repression-style defenses. In the words of Marmer and Fink (1994, 753), "BPD is more like rickets, whereas MPD/DID is more like a series of many repeatedly broken bones. As such, MPD/DID patients suffer not from too few defenses, but from too many. They possess too much structure, whereas BPD patients possess too little."

Turning to the phenomenological overlap between MPD and BPD, Marmer and Fink begin by pointing out that while both multiples and borderlines suffer from identity problems, for the borderline the "is" in *who she is* remains unclear, whereas for the multiple the "who" is unclear. While the borderline experiences "affect storms," suffers from an unstable polarity of affects, and modulates affect according to part-object phenomena, the multiple's affect, which covers a full range, tends to be overcontrolled and changes according to triggers and internal conflict. Marmer and Fink explain that while the borderline's impulse control problems are linked to affect intolerance, the multiple's impulse control problems are linked to dissociation: because impulsive actions are a product of state changes or switches, often accompanied by amnesia, they are unpredictable to the patient. Similarly, suicide attempts and repeated self-injury in the borderline are related to a perceived absence or rejection by a primary object, which mobilizes aggression. In the multiple, self-harm is employed for its symbolic meaning: it is a disguised way to tell about the past or to express internal conflict over whether it is safe to tell one's history. In terms of interpersonal relationships, borderlines seek external objects to complete internal stability. When the object is frustrating or unavailable, the BPD patient may react with rage and devaluation, or may temporarily adopt a more schizoid position. Multiples are wary of objects at the outset yet, at the same time, are desperately object-seeking. As Marmer and Fink (1994, 763) put it, "MPD/DID patients are introverted in the original sense of the term, seeking data from within to affirm the safety of the outside world and the people who populate it. BPD patients are extroverted, seeking stability in external perceptions of the behavior of others to know how to feel and how to relate."

Research has supported the conclusion that BPD and MPD are distinct disorders. Fink and Golinkoff (1990), for example, compared multiples and borderlines on a variety of measures. Finding that the multiples and borderlines differ in many clinical features, the authors conclude that "while there were 'borderline' tendencies in our MPD group, few MPD patients would have been diagnosed with the disorder" (Fink and Golinkoff 1990, 132). Kluft (1992, 145) argues that "although it remains commonplace to attempt to understand MPD as a borderline variant, and . . . MPD patients often behave in ways that resemble those of borderlines, . . . there is ample evidence that many MPD patients are without borderline features, . . . and that dissociative phenomena are easy to mistake for those of primitive character pathology."[47] In unpublished research, Kluft (1992) has found that the chaos of MPD often generates a phenocopy of borderline phenomena but that many of the patients are not actually borderline. Only ten of thirty apparently borderline multiples remained borderline after their MPD was resolved. Gabbard (1989, 1236), who believes that MPD and BPD are different disorders, proposes several guidelines to help in their differential diagnosis:

1) The split self-representations seen in the borderline patient usually do not appear as distinct personalities but rather as different aspects of one core personality. 2) The borderline patient has good recall of each self-representation and regards the contradiction with indifference or bland denial. 3) The predominance of a particular self-representation in the borderline patient depends more on the immediate object relational context than do the various personalities of the patient with multiple personality disorder.[48]

While there is a plethora of views on the relation of MPD to BPD, the most subtle and careful thinking to date appears to view the two as distinct disorders.

As is often the case with MPD, discussions about etiology are permeated by profound theoretical differences. One position is that MPD is a clinical entity in its own right, a position supported by an extensive literature, much of which is psychoanalytic in orientation. A second position, just sketched out, is that MPD is a variant of some other disorder. While a panoply of other mental illnesses has been suggested to lie behind what appears to be MPD, the most likely candidate is BPD. Ample research and theory, however, have been able to distinguish the two. The best evidence, then, suggests that MPD is a disorder in and of itself, not merely a form of some other mental illness. What, though, of those who say that MPD is neither a disorder in its own right nor a variation of another entity—who say that MPD does not exist at all? It is to this third and final position we now turn.

3. Is Multiple Personality Disorder "Real"?

ULTIPLE PERSONALITY DISORDER has attracted wide skepticism, even hostility, within the mental health profession. Some skeptics express their disbelief in MPD privately, while others are quite public about their positions. Tozman and Pabis (1989, 709) are perhaps the best example of the latter:

> We regard MPD as a dissociative phenomenon of exceedingly rare occurrence if it occurs at all. Unsurprisingly, it seems related to hypnotizability. The accentuation and "epidemic" of this rare, iatrogenic disorder does no justice to scientific psychiatry, generating media and literature distortions and misinformation. It distressingly often provides untenable and flamboyant legal defense maneuvers for serial killers and others of ill repute. Psychiatry should not reinforce the mystical and bizarre.

Aldridge-Morris (1993) has written that the apparent increase in diagnoses of MPD can be likened to an increase in sightings of UFOs. Others go as far as to interfere with the treatment of MPD patients. Dell (1988), for example, found that half of the practitioners who treat MPD patients had encountered deliberate interference with clinical care and repeated acts of harassment against the patient and/or therapist. In a study of 207 mental health professionals, Hayes and Mitchell (1994) found that inaccuracy in diagnosing MPD in a case vignette was predicted by skepticism about MPD. Interestingly, Hayes and Mitchell also found knowledge and skepticism about MPD to be inversely related, suggesting that those who are skeptical about MPD do not know a great deal about the disorder.[1]

What forms does skepticism over MPD take? To start off, the skeptics can hardly mean that there are not people who present as if they have two or more identities, each with its own memories, personality characteristics, preferences, and goals — clearly there are such people in the world. The most mild form of realistic skepticism, then, holds that the prevalence of MPD is much lower than MPD experts believe.[2] According to these skeptics, MPD is exceedingly rare and the increase in prevalence is illusory. Nevertheless, *some* MPD is real and should be treated so by the law. A second form of skepticism — which I also see as a mild skepticism — looks to the phenomenology of MPD. This brand of skepticism claims that there are no personalities, or independent systems of control.[3] I refer to this position as mild because many MPD experts themselves doubt the reality of alter personalities — to deny that alter personalities are real is not, however, to deny that individuals manifesting such personalities suffer a real disorder. A third form of skepticism claims that MPD is a culturally specific metaphor, not a universal disorder,[4] while a fourth claims that cases of MPD are actually misdiagnoses of other disorders, such as schizophrenia, manic-depressive disorder, or borderline personality disorder.[5] A fifth form of skepticism claims that MPD is iatrogenic,[6] a variant of which sees MPD symptomatology as the consequence of implicit or explicit suggestion.[7] Finally, other skeptics understand MPD on the basis of social role theory (Zalewski 1991); as a social construction consisting of goal-directed and social behavior geared toward perceived expectations (Spanos 1994);[8] or as the result of individual choice, conscious role-playing, and personal convenience in problem solving.[9]

To determine whether MPD is a disease might lead to a deep philosophical discussion into the nature and existence of diseases, a discussion made more complex because MPD is a *mental* disease. Even having the discussion would generate debate — a pragmatist would say that a disease exists if it is useful to act as if it exists. I intend to avoid all such controversy. The question I want to pose is whether MPD exists regardless of one's theory of disease. To give an example, if MPD is malingered, it is irrelevant to ask whether diseases exist independently of our minds.

Skepticism about the reality of MPD — what I call "radical skepticism" — can be reduced to three views: first, that MPD is an artifact of therapy — that it is an iatrogenic disorder; second, that MPD is the result of unconscious simulation; and third, that MPD is the result of conscious simulation. The question before us is whether any of these views is convincing in its denial of MPD's existence. The question is not whether prevalence rates are unduly inflated, nor whether some clinical entity is present, albeit one other than what we have labeled MPD, but whether multiples suffer from a genuine clinical entity. If our answer is no, MPD ceases to be of concern to the law — no legal consequences would turn on an unreal psychopathology.

The first of the skeptics' three claims is that MPD is not real insofar as its etiology is iatrogenic. MPD is iatrogenic either in the sense that doctors misread as MPD the ordinary dividedness which every individual displays or in the sense that they misread mild dissociation as indicating the presence of alter personalities. Doctors, according to this view, do not create alter personalities but see as alter personalities the ordinary, or perhaps slightly exaggerated, parts of everyone's personality. Now, clearly, doctors who make false diagnoses can cause all sorts of harm. A doctor who mistakenly diagnoses a patient with cancer may cause that person to feel extreme distress and to become preoccupied with ailments having nothing to do with cancer. Similarly, the person with ordinary, or slightly dissociative, dividedness may suffer much iatrogenic harm when diagnosed with MPD, such as feeling distress and shame, taking more sick days off from work, even going to the hospital. These consequences are real — but his MPD, the claim goes, is not.

The problem with this interpretation of the iatrogenesis claim is that it does not afford a plausible account of the current state of affairs. Some generally normal, or slightly dissociative, behavior may be overread as MPD. Certain commentators believe that overreading accounts for a significant portion of the high incidence of MPD. But other MPD behavior is so florid that no one believes it to be simple dividedness overread as something more. Florid symptomatology is something different — something abnormal. It could be, of course, that normal, or perhaps slightly dissociative, dividedness, once misread as MPD, comes to take on a life of its own and then grows into florid MPD. But then it is the transition into floridness that counts as the iatrogenesis of MPD — the insubstantiality of the diagnosis itself ceases to be the issue.

The etiology of MPD can be understood as iatrogenic in another sense — that the disorder is brought about, created, by doctors. The problem with this understanding of the iatrogenesis claim is that MPD is no less real simply in virtue of being brought about or created by a treater. Modern treatments may produce any number of disorders that are surely real — exposure to infectious agents during surgery may lead to infections that, while clearly iatrogenic, are just as clearly real.

Perhaps the iatrogenesis claim could be made more substantial if read to say that the etiology of MPD is *solely* iatrogenic — that unlike infections, which can have many origins, MPD would not exist in the world were it not for psychotherapeutic interventions. The iatrogenesis claim now reads that MPD is not a naturally occurring disease entity. MPD is a product of people's (therapists') interactions with the natural environment. This understanding of the iatrogenesis claim fails as well. Many diseases are the products of humans interacting with the environment. Certain cancers, for example, may never have occurred had it not been for the introduction of man-made chemicals into the environment, and no one would find themselves in an emergency room with a bullet wound had other people not participated in some fashion. That a condition is nonnatural, insofar as it is the product of human activity, does not make it any less real.

A final version of the iatrogenesis claim is that therapists produce MPD — unlike infections contracted during surgery — by means that are not physical or biological. This final version of the iatrogenesis claim, like its predecessors, is not persuasive. The idea that diseases must have physical antecedents is quite limited. Virtually no one dismisses post-traumatic stress disorder because the stressor may have been psychological in nature. While the psychological sciences are increasingly biological — the days of tracing most disorders to childhood are waning — neither theory nor practice warrants the view that *only* conditions with biological causes are true diseases. [10] A twist on this version of the iatrogenesis claim is that doctors unwittingly create MPD by giving suggestible patients the tools to enact the MPD role. At this point, however, the iatrogenesis interpretation merges with the skeptics' second and third claims: that patients are unconsciously or consciously playacting when they present with the symptoms of MPD.

The skeptics' second claim is that MPD is unconsciously produced or unconsciously simulated. The problem with saying that MPD is unconsciously produced is that many mental disorders arise from *precisely* such origins. Obsessive-compulsive disorder, for example, may well be the result of unconscious, intrapsychic conflict, yet no one denies that it is real. The etiology of many neurotic disorders, recognized as clinical entities by the American Psychiatric Association, is thought to reside in the unconscious — most likely unconscious conflicts. The claim that MPD is not real because it is unconsciously *simulated* is more complex, yet no more compelling. Factitious disorders, of which Munchausen's syndrome is the most well known, are mental disorders whose raison d'être appears to be the satisfaction of an unconscious need to be cared for, given attention, or loved. Although the symptoms of factitious disorders are unconsciously simulated, they are nevertheless recognized by the APA as clinical entities in their own right. Of course, there is *something* unreal about phenomena whose origins are purely intrapsychic — hysterical blindness will not be evident on physiological tests. But patients are no more able to see — nor do they suffer any less — simply because their symptoms have an etiology in unconscious simulation. In this sense, their illnesses are every bit as "real" as a broken leg. That its symptoms may be produced and maintained for unconscious purposes and by unconscious processes hardly seems to disqualify MPD as a disease.

The claim that MPD is the result of conscious malingering does indeed have force. A person who pretends to have whiplash in order to collect insurance does not really have whiplash; and if "whiplash" occurred only when people feigned neck pain in order to collect insurance, we would strike whiplash from the roster of diseases. That malingered diseases are not true diseases seems clear — malingerers are perpetrators of fraud, not sufferers of a disease that warrants study and treatment. Thus "malingered MPD" should not be understood as a psychiatric disorder. The skeptics, the American Psychiatric Association, and I are in complete agreement here — the DSM correctly classifies malingering as a condition brought to the attention of mental health professionals that is not a mental disorder.

The arguments of the skeptics, reduced to three claims, are that MPD is iatrogenic, that MPD is simulated unconsciously, and that MPD is simulated consciously. The first two are not persuasive in showing that MPD is not real; illnesses are no less real in virtue of their iatrogenic etiology, and unconscious production, maintenance, or simulation of symptoms is the defining — as opposed to disqualifying — feature of a number of disorders recognized by the American Psychiatric Association in the DSM-IV. The final claim — conscious simulation — is quite persuasive. Malingered MPD is not MPD at all but a sham. Not even the most radical of skeptics, however, has claimed that *all* MPD is consciously malingered.

ARGUMENTS AND EVIDENCE FOR AND AGAINST THE EXISTENCE OF MPD

Skeptics point to six empirical observations to support their claim that MPD does not exist: first, many experienced therapists have never seen a case of MPD,[11] while a small number of therapists seem to have seen many;[12] second, the prevalence of MPD has risen dramatically in recent years;[13] third, the symptoms of MPD have changed over time[14] — in early cases, for example, patients had very few personalities, usually only two or three, while in more recent cases they appear to have many, even up to one hundred, and formerly few MPD patients recounted histories of childhood sexual abuse; fourth, many MPD patients report bizarre "memories" of satanic ritual abuse that, insofar as they are probably false, cast doubt on the validity of their other reports;[15] fifth, MPD appears to be a largely North American phenomenon, with cases practically unheard of, for example, in Britain;[16] and sixth, the interview procedures, hypnotic[17] and others, that are used routinely to diagnose MPD are extremely leading and provide patients with all of the information needed to enact the MPD role.[18] These observations are used to support one, or more, of the views skeptical of MPD's existence. For example, the observation that a small number of therapists see and treat the vast majority of MPD cases — while many therapists have never seen a single one — suggests that therapists who so often find the disorder may actually be creating MPD through their interventions. That MPD patients report occurrences very likely to be false, such as satanic ritual abuse, calls into question their credibility on other matters — they may be feigning MPD, consciously or unconsciously. Reliance upon leading interview techniques suggests that MPD may be both iatrogenic and feigned, in that therapists are inducing MPD by informing patients how to simulate its symptomatology.

The skeptics' first observation, that a small number of therapists see a large number of cases while the vast majority of therapists see none at all, may simply be wrong. It may be that only a few clinicians report on MPD cases, while a large number of other clinicians send those cases to MPD experts.[19] Few treaters see and report on individuals suffering from Tourette's or Asperger's disorders, yet there seems little dispute that both of these are legitimate clinical entities. Moreover, the inequity between prevalence and clinicians seeing cases may be due to misdiagnosis. Most multiples do not present in a florid state; recall that, on average, individuals suffering from MPD receive more than three diagnoses over a period of nearly seven years before being correctly diagnosed. It seems quite likely that many multiples *never* receive the correct diagnosis of MPD—thus explaining why many therapists never "see" this disorder.

The skeptics next point out that the number of MPD cases has risen dramatically. The observation can be explained by improvements in diagnosis or by changing conditions in our culture. In terms of the former, one commentator has suggested that the diagnosis went out of favor with the introduction of the term "schizophrenia" in the early twentieth century—many multiples were misdiagnosed as schizophrenics (Rosenbaum 1980). In terms of changing societal conditions, a number of factors may explain the increased prevalence of MPD. Feminism, for example, has brought about an increased sensitivity to child abuse and its consequences, and there seems to be general agreement that our culture is becoming increasingly fragmented. The prevalence of other disorders has risen as well — consider that only a few decades ago borderline personality disorder was unheard of, that obsessive-compulsive disorder is far more often diagnosed today than in the past, that infectious diseases are increasing precipitously, and that breast cancer is on the rise in the United States. Is anyone about to argue that borderline personality disorder, obsessive-compulsive disorder, infectious diseases, and breast cancer are not real?

The third observation of the skeptics is that the symptoms of MPD have changed over time. Symptoms of somatoform disorders have changed dramatically over time as well — cases of conversion disorder are exceedingly rare in the 1990s — yet they are no less real as a result. MPD symptomatology may be more florid because child abuse — in both prevalence and intensity — appears to have increased in the last several decades. Treaters may also have become better, and more sophisticated, in describing the true nature of MPD; improvements in the diagnosis and treatment of schizophrenia dramatically changed how that disease was described. Changes in symptomatology may be due to a variety of factors; in and of themselves, changes hardly show that MPD does not exist. Moreover, such changes are inconsistent with the simulation hypothesis, which would suggest that the symptom picture, because it is being mimicked toward the end of appearing real, would remain relatively stable over time.

The skeptics' fourth observation, that patients sometimes report bizarre histories, such as having been the victim of satanic ritual abuse, certainly casts doubt upon their credibility. Yet this very bizarreness makes it more, rather than less, likely that they suffer from some form of psychopathology. It would indeed be strange were someone to argue that an individual with a rich, detailed, and textured description of being abducted, examined, and inseminated by aliens from another planet were free from psychopathology because his story could not possibly be true.

The skeptics next point out that MPD is confined largely to North America. Note the "largely"; MPD *has* been found in other countries. Moreover, cultural conditions in North America, combined with hostility to the diagnosis in other countries, may account for the difference in prevalence rates. An astute observer could object that I am missing the point here — human beings are much the same all over the world, at least physiologically, and therefore a true disease ought to be universally present. Yet this is a limited view of the concept of a disease. Many diseases differ in different areas, and some are confined to circumscribed areas — neurosis was once thought prevalent only in industrialized societies, amok occurs primarily in Malaya, and even AIDS was once confined mostly to Africa. Martínez-Taboas (1991) has argued forcefully that cultural factors necessarily complicate the presentation of diseases yet do not detract from their status as diseases. He gives some striking examples of mental disorders confined to a particular time or place:

(a) alcoholism, drug abuse, and suicide become major mental health problems during periods in which traditionally oriented populations are modernized rapidly

(b) anorexia nervosa and bulimia, well-known psychopathologies in the Western world, are nearly non-existent in many Oriental and Asian countries

(c) the clinical course of schizophrenia is markedly better for patients in the less developed countries, and worse for those in the industrially most advanced countries

(d) numerous studies of depressive symptomatology in non-Western cultures allude to the reduced frequency or absence of psychological components of depression and the dominance of somatic aspects. (Martínez-Taboas 1991, 129)

The variable presentation of a disorder over time and place seems a poor basis for calling it nongenuine.

The skeptics' sixth and final observation, that clinicians use "leading" interventions that provide patients with all the information they need to enact MPD, is perhaps their strongest argument. Spanos, Weekes, and Bertrand (1985) found that experimental subjects, asked the same questions as the "Hillside Strangler," readily enacted multiple personalities. Of the experimental subjects receiving the "Hillside Strangler" treatment, over 80 percent reported there was another part of themselves unknown to the examiner and adopted a name for that part. Most subjects then admitted to guilt for a crime committed when they were the "other person"; spontaneously reported amnesia for the hypnotic occurrences; scored differently on two psychological tests while in the different "personalities"; and read a text slower than would be expected upon a second reading, as if to suggest amnesia for the first reading. While the evidence is powerful enough, it is also more complicated than it may first appear. Patients, it would seem, can learn to enact the role of *any* mental disorder if appropriately cued and rewarded — if an experimental subject were asked whether or not he was commanded by God to commit his crime, an acute case of command hallucinations would most likely appear. Schizophrenia would be no less real as a result.

The skeptics may argue that leading interviews are the norm when it comes to MPD. Does the evidence support this claim? Most diagnostic interview procedures — from routine mental status examinations to standard forensic evaluations — pose questions designed to elicit relevant symptoms, questions that may "lead" suggestible or clever patients. Moreover, there is evidence that "leading" occurs in many psychotherapeutic interventions as well; patients in Kleinian analyses tend to give associations that suggest preoccupations with "good breast/bad breast" material, while patients in Freudian analyses tend to give associations that suggest castration anxiety. And many patients in maintenance treatment are routinely educated — instructed — about their disorders. It would seem highly likely that, over time, some, many, or most patients would notice and report symptoms consistent with those disorders. My point is that diagnosticians and treaters may play a much larger role in patients' reports of symptomatology than they would comfortably admit, whether the disorder at issue be schizophrenia, manic-depressive disorder, or MPD.

In order to establish that multiples are more likely to simulate as a result of "leading" treatment techniques, we need objective studies comparing the diagnosis and treatment of MPD with other disorders. Such studies would ask whether MPD therapists lead more than therapists engaged in intensive therapies with non-MPD patients; how often patients in nonintensive psychotherapy are instructed about symptomatology typical of their disorders; whether patients exposed to information about their disorder, through either subtle interpretation or explicit instruction, tend to produce symptom pictures in greater conformity with their diagnoses; and whether patients in leading interviews and treatments tend to produce reports that are open to doubt on other grounds. Until such questions are answered, the claim that the diagnosis and treatment of MPD is more role-informing than the diagnosis and treatment of other disorders is suggestive at best.

That symptomatology may conform to the nature of an intervention, whether the intervention be treatment or diagnosis, neither proves malingering nor disproves the existence of a disorder. Patients may simply come to focus on what seems more relevant in a confusing array of symptoms. Should MPD therapists be more role-informing than others, this means only that MPD patients are provided readier means to malinger, not that they are necessarily malingering. Moreover, from a purely pragmatic standpoint, other psychopathologies seem far easier to malinger than MPD, where one would have to portray a range of personality styles, each with its own affective tone, way of viewing the world, and characteristic likes and dislikes. To feign schizophrenia, for example, one need only voice delusions, pretend to listen to voices, and act fearfully. Our index of suspicion for malingering, especially in the forensic context, should always be high; whether it should be higher for MPD than for other disorders is unclear.

A final point is in order here. The skeptics make six observations in support of the claim that MPD is not real. Consider how these six observations would have applied to another disorder: first, a small cadre of specialists treated this rare disorder; second, the disorder was increasing over time; third, because of people's behavior, new infections overcame patients with this disorder, thus changing the symptom picture; fourth, confused and sometimes inaccurate memories occurred in patients with dementia related to this disorder; fifth, the disorder was largely confined to a single continent; and sixth, caregivers were likely to have informed patients about this disorder so that they might better care for and monitor themselves. These observations, of course, describe the epidemiology of AIDS fifteen years ago.

Do MPD proponents have evidence to bolster their claim that MPD is indeed a recognizable clinical entity in its own right? Proponents make four observations. They first point out that MPD patients almost uniformly present with a history of childhood physical and sexual abuse. While histories can certainly be falsified, there is a growing body of evidence corroborating histories of abuse,[20] as well as a literature that speaks to the sequelae of childhood abuse.

Widespread agreement over the phenomenology of MPD is a second factor that appears to support its existence.[21] Even quite subtle signs and symptoms appear from study to study — the symptomatology, taken in its entirety, is not one that patients could produce simply by thinking through what it might be like to have alter identities. While this observation might be consistent with the iatrogenesis claim, it seems hard to square with malingering. Unless we suppose that MPD patients all acquaint themselves with the most recent scientific research, the consistency of nonobvious signs and symptoms seems to support the reality of MPD.

A third observation that appears to support the existence of MPD is that specialized instruments developed to screen for and diagnose MPD, such as the SCID-D, are equally reliable and valid as diagnostic and screening instruments for other, concededly real, mental disorders, such as schizophrenia and manic-depressive disorder.[22] Skeptics will be quick to point out that skilled actors could produce the symptom picture of a disorder without being genuinely ill. True, of course, but true *for all psychiatric disorders, not just for* MPD. We have no independent way of checking the diagnosis of, say, schizophrenia — there is no schizoccocus bacteria. Reliability and validity are the best we can do, and we can do that as well for MPD as for schizophrenia.[23] We should ask no more of MPD than we ask of other psychopathologies.

A fourth observation that weighs in favor of MPD's existence is that a particular form of treatment — one that integrates alter personalities — appears to have some efficacy. In contrast, therapies that ignore patients' multiplicity or that address other, comorbid conditions seem less effective in treating MPD.[24] Of course, this sort of reasoning is tricky and seems somewhat akin to *post hoc, ergo propter hoc* logic: because MPD responded to treatment, it must have been a disease. Such logic, however, is not entirely without substance; if, for example, a new medication produced relief in Epstein-Barr patients, it would be harder to dispute the reality of that disease. The trick is to show that treatment is more effective than a placebo and the problem is that, to date, the studies on the efficacy of MPD have not been controlled. On the other hand, they have not all been single case studies either,[25] and anecdotal reports suggest that earlier treatments for MPD failed — multiples do not seem merely suggestible patients who respond to *any* form of attention. That certain treatments seem effective does, then, seem to weigh in favor of MPD's existence. And it seems implausible that multiples would simulate recovery, when recovery entails an end to indefinite therapeutic attention, the very attention that is supposed to drive these patients to simulate their illness in the first place.[26]

DOES MPD EXIST? WHO DECIDES, AND OTHER LEGAL QUESTIONS

The skeptical view of MPD seems unpersuasive, at least at present. A skeptic might object to my methodology, however, by pointing out that, by apparent fiat, I have placed the burden of proof on those who do not believe in MPD's existence. This burden, the skeptic might add, would be nearly impossible to carry — how can the *non*existence of a clinical entity be proved? — and I have done nothing more than offer alternative explanations for evidence proffered by the skeptics. I have not given any good reasons to believe that my alternative explanations are true, and test data bearing on alter personalities[27] are only consistent with — hardly dispositive of — the existence of MPD. This objection to my methodology is sound.

The difficulty we face is that, for now, there *is* no evidence that will prove or disprove the existence of MPD. As a scientific matter, there is no pressing need for us to resolve the issue — we can wait until dispositive evidence arrives. Burdens of proof have little place in scientific debates. The law, on the other hand, is intensely pragmatic and needs to act *as if* MPD exists or *as if* it does not. The law must therefore come up with its best — not a perfect, but its *best* — guess as to whether this disorder is real. Who bears the burden of proof takes center stage in the legal debate.

Normally, the question of who bears the burden of proof rests on one or more of several criteria. Often the question is determined by asking who has the best access to information — not much help with MPD, since skeptics and believers have equal access. A second criterion looks to the most serious risk of error — will greater harm come from presuming MPD's existence or from presuming its *non*existence? Again, we don't get a great deal of help, although the balance seems to be in favor of MPD's existence. After all, if MPD does exist, patients will suffer, perhaps quite significantly, if we act as if it does not, much like women who have been violated when told that the violation was actually the fulfillment of an unconscious wish. Moreover, patients who are treated as true multiples appear to improve, whereas patients treated otherwise seem to remain divided. Presumption of MPD's existence may, of course, lead to erroneous exoneration from criminal responsibility, but our entire system of jurisprudence is built around the concept that we would rather free the guilty than convict the innocent; we decided long ago that ties go to the runner.

A third criterion for determining where to place the burden of proof looks to the degree of evidence proffered on one side of the debate. The burden may shift if the evidence appears sufficiently substantial on one side of an issue. As an example, there has been a great deal of debate over whether satanic ritual abuse takes place on a large scale. Those who say yes are adamant in their position yet have not been able to offer evidence to substantiate their claims. When pressed on the lack of evidence — where are the bodies? — they cite numerous explanations such as that the victims of the abuse were bred for this purpose, so there are no birth records; the victims were homeless, and so not missed by anyone; or the victims' bodies were incinerated. While some might find these explanations credible, and so believe that satanic ritual abuse is indeed widespread, the simple fact remains that no corroborating evidence has been produced. For this reason I would place the burden of proof on the believers, at least until they have been able to offer something more. Likewise with individuals claiming to have been abducted and examined by aliens. I would place the burden of proof on believers until they produce corroborating evidence.

As I see it, those who believe in MPD have come up with sufficient evidence to warrant shifting the burden to the skeptics. MPD appears to be an illness, so much so that it has been recognized by the American Psychiatric Association in its official nosology of mental illnesses. MPD's location in the manual indicates that the APA considers MPD a mental disorder, and not malingering. People who present with MPD suffer distress, can be disabled, and are at higher risk of death than the general population. There is a significant degree of consensus over the symptomatology of MPD, and there is a striking degree of agreement in nonobvious symptoms among purported multiples. Empirical studies have indicated psychological, memory, and physiological differences among alters, differences which malingerers, for the most part, have been unable to reproduce.[28] Therapists who approach MPD with a theoretically driven treatment have met with some success, while therapists who conduct treatments on the assumption that MPD does not exist appear to have been less successful. Skepticism about MPD is negatively correlated with knowledge about this disorder—less of one means more of the other. Finally, even vehement critics of MPD admit that it does exist, albeit not as often as proponents think.[29] I would certainly not stake a claim to MPD's existence on any, or even all, of these points. I merely wish to say that, for the purposes of the law, this evidence is sufficient to shift the burden to those who deny that MPD exists.

Having placed the burden of proof on the skeptics, I am quick to add that new evidence could shift the burden in the other direction. If it were found, for example, that mental health professionals regularly screened for MPD and that such professionals were well acquainted with the symptom picture, then the lack of MPD diagnosed by nonexperts would become far more troubling. If better devices were developed to detect malingering, and individuals diagnosed with MPD were found to score the same as malingerers on certain tests, the burden again might shift. If controlled studies indicated that treatments other than those based on a theory of MPD were equally, or more, efficacious, the burden might well revert to the believers. If, yet again, benign neglect experiments, in which MPD symptomatology were ignored, indicated that control subjects continued to display the phenomenology of MPD while experimental subjects did not, the unconscious simulation hypothesis would gain further credence. Finally, if studies showed that subjects skilled in autohypnosis were able to produce physiological differences between "alter personalities," the skeptics' position would be significantly strengthened. The point is that where we place the burden of proof is determined by the best evidence at a given time, and at present the best evidence weighs in favor of placing that burden on those who deny that MPD exists.

For all the reasons set forth here, I believe that the law should act as if MPD is real. Acting as if MPD is real does not, of course, mean that everyone who presents as a multiple genuinely suffers from the disorder. Whether a given defendant suffers from MPD is a factual matter, to be decided at trial, in the same way other questions of fact are decided. Nor does a diagnosis of MPD definitively settle the question of disposition—in later chapters I explore how multiples should be treated under the law. Acting as if MPD is real tells us little, if anything, about what will happen to a particular defendant. For now, I want to ask who should decide whether the law should act as if MPD is real.

Lawmakers or fact finders are the most likely candidates. Lawmakers develop rules through legislative acts, while fact finders work on a case-by-case basis—each trial would raise the question of MPD's existence anew. Put in other words, the choice is between having a predetermined position developed through debate, consensus, and a review of the evidence and arguments both for and against MPD, and having a set of individuals examine the question of MPD each time a new criminal defendant comes to trial.[30]

Three considerations favor having lawmakers develop the rules that will govern how the criminal justice system handles whether MPD exists. First, while juries are quite good at figuring out facts, such as whether a particular event happened at a particular time,[31] they are not nearly as well suited for assessing a complicated body of scientific evidence whose very significance is in question, especially since the rules of trial process restrict the flow of information. Second, the question of MPD's existence is enormously complicated. Legislatures can spend far more time than any jury is allocated to examine these issues, and have carte blanche in terms of the evidence they may consider. Finally, and perhaps most important, standard doctrine does not deal adequately with MPD — special rules are needed. The appropriate body to formulate legal rules is the legislature. For these reasons, legislatures should set forth rules to govern the criminal responsibility of multiples which presuppose a position on whether MPD exists. If, however, we decide to leave the question of MPD's existence to the fact finder, the question of whether to admit expert testimony on the existence of MPD will arise. Expert testimony could, of course, come in two forms — that of the proponents and that of the skeptics.

The cases of *Frye v. United States* (1923) and *Daubert v. Merrell Dow Pharmaceuticals, Inc.* (1993) determine when evidence will be admitted at trial. The *Daubert* standard, considered somewhat more liberal than the *Frye* standard,[32] applies to federal and many state courts, while the remaining state courts rely on *Frye*. The *Frye* case held that evidence is admissible if it is "generally accepted" by the scientific community; *Daubert* rejected *Frye* in favor of admitting evidence that is reliable and relevant.

Proponents' testimony seems clearly admissible under either standard. The American Psychiatric Association has listed MPD in its official manual of mental disorders, and there are units in well-established hospitals designed specifically to treat individuals suffering from MPD. Articles that assume the existence of MPD far outnumber those that contest MPD's existence, and often vehement skeptics reject only prevalence rates, not MPD itself. It seems fairly straightforward to say that MPD is "generally accepted" by the scientific community—it meets the *Frye* test. The *Daubert* case is easier; often considered more liberal than *Frye*, *Daubert* asks only about reliability and relevance. Clearly, evidence about MPD's existence meets the *Daubert* criteria when an alleged multiple is on trial.

Does testimony by the skeptics meet the *Frye* and *Daubert* standards? In terms of the former, it would be exceedingly odd if the scientific community were both to "generally accept" that MPD exists and "generally accept" that MPD does *not* exist. Given that MPD is recognized by the American Psychiatric Association's *Diagnostic and Statistical Manual,* the position of the skeptics would not seem to meet the *Frye* standard. What about *Daubert*? Is testimony of the skeptics reliable and relevant? Putting the first aside, the second of the *Daubert* qualifications—that the testimony be relevant—appears to disqualify the substantial majority of evidence the skeptics are likely to proffer. Recall their first two arguments against the existence of MPD—that MPD is iatrogenic and is unconsciously malingered. Both of these arguments speak to etiology; neither claim, in and of itself, is sufficient to show that MPD does not exist. Quite the contrary: *we would only be concerned about the etiology of an illness if we were sufficiently convinced of its phenomenology.*

That the skeptics are so concerned about the etiology of MPD seems an implicit concession that the phenomenology is real, and it is the phenomenology of the illness with which the law is, and ought to be, concerned. To put the matter another way, a person suffering from an infection suffers no less because the infection has an iatrogenic origin; someone suffering from hysterical paralysis is no more able to move because a scan will fail to indicate a lesion; an individual suffering from psychogenic amnesia will be no more able to recall information — or assist a court, for that matter — simply because the amnesia finds its roots in the unconscious. Real legal consequences turn on a finding of hysterical paralysis or hysterical seizures. People suffering from such disorders can, for example, receive disability benefits and tort damages. They should also be exonerated of wrongdoing. Take the prisoner who suffers a hysterical seizure; surely he should not lose "good time" for some such offense as "causing a commotion." The skeptics' first two claims — that MPD has an iatrogenic origin and that MPD is unconsciously malingered — do not meet the *Daubert* standard because they are irrelevant; neither speaks to the issue at hand, namely, whether MPD is real.

The last of the skeptics' claims — that MPD is consciously malingered — is relevant to a criminal disposition and so does meet the *Daubert* standard. To say that someone is consciously malingering symptoms is to say that the symptoms are unreal both in fact and *to the individual*. It is to say that the production of the symptoms is under voluntary control. Malingerers are perpetrators of fraud, not victims of a mental disease, and are not entitled to any excuse under the criminal law. The problem with this view — and the reason that it will almost never prevail in court — is that virtually no one believes *all* MPD is consciously malingered. Such a view is so wildly implausible — and held by so few — that it is scarcely worth considering.

The skeptics, then, will have little to offer in court. Their claims that MPD is iatrogenic and unconsciously feigned are irrelevant to the trial process, and so fail to meet the *Daubert* standard, because they speak to etiology rather than phenomenology. The skeptics' third claim, that MPD is consciously malingered, is almost entirely unsupported by the extant research. Indeed, even some of the most vehement skeptics concede that MPD does exist — just not to the extent many proponents believe.

A final note: Thomas Szasz (1974) once claimed that *all* mental illness was "a myth." According to Szasz, when people stated their bizarre beliefs it was not because their brain was malfunctioning but because they were liars, engaged in a language game of "false advertising" (Szasz 1969). People rejected Szasz' way of thinking, and today it is widely accepted that mental illness is, indeed, real. Time will tell if the same fate awaits MPD.

The law, then, should recognize MPD, as the American Psychiatric Association has done. Legislatures, as opposed to fact finders, should set forth rules regarding whether the criminal law should accept MPD as a real disorder. The skeptics should not be allowed to proffer expert testimony over the nonexistence of MPD, although testimony that a given defendant is malingering would, of course, be admissible.

How should the criminal law treat multiples? It must first decide upon the status of alter personalities, a question to which we now turn.

4. Alter Personalities

MULTIPLE PERSONALITY DISORDER strikes at the heart of our most fundamental conceptions of self. Violating an unspoken, if not unconscious, presumption that each person has his or her own body, MPD raises questions that, at first glance, seem patently absurd. If, for example, many persons can be found in a single body, should we permit each alter personality to vote? Should we require each separate alter to have his own driver's license? Should separate alter personalities be sworn in before testifying in court? Should alter personalities within the same multiple be permitted to sue one another? Most germane to our present discussion, should we exonerate multiples from criminal responsibility, insofar as within the same multiple there will be innocent, as well as guilty, offending alters?[1]

Mental health experts on MPD generally tend to believe that a multiple is one person with many parts.[2] *DSM-IV*, the official manual of the American Psychiatric Association, has replaced multiple *personality* disorder with dissociative *identity* disorder. Colin Ross (1990b, 349), a prominent MPD researcher, states that "alter personalities are dissociated components of a single personality. . . . The patient's mind is no more host to numerous distinct personalities than his or her body is to different people," while Frank Putnam (1993, 83), whose research on MPD is very well known and respected, notes that in North America most experts "do not believe that the alter personality states represent separate or complete . . . people." Like most MPD experts, Putnam states, rather than explains or justifies, this claim.

Has the apparent consensus among MPD researchers that multiples constitute one, and only one, person foreclosed debate over the nature of alter personalities? By no means. Consider that physicians, who can tell us when a brain is no longer producing waves or when a heart stops beating, are in the best position to provide facts in the debate over when death occurs. Access to physiological facts, however, hardly places physicians in the best position to determine when a person dies, any more than clinical data place mental health professionals in the best position to determine whether a person is legally insane. The question of when death occurs belongs to the realms of law, ethics, philosophy, and spirituality, as well as to science. Likewise, discussions about the nature of personhood cannot be relegated to scientists alone. Each discipline will have something important to contribute.

What do philosophy and theory tell us about the status of alter personalities? I suggested in an earlier work that alters could be conceptualized in one of three ways, as (1) different persons, (2) different personalities, or (3) different parts of one complex, dissociated personality. This tripartite division is not terribly useful for the law because the latter two possibilities focus on the concept of personality, which generally refers to qualities possessed by a person. Alters are not qualities. Like subjects, alters *have* qualities and so are more nominal than adjectival—"Eve White" refers to the subject who is kind and timid, "Eve Black" to the subject who is vivacious and sultry. A more useful categorization, one that frames the inquiry in a manner recognizable to the law, conceptualizes alters as (1) distinct persons, (2) distinct personlike centers of consciousness, or (3) distinct, nonpersonlike parts of one complicated individual.[3] While any one of these conceptualizations may not perfectly describe every alter, the task at hand is to determine which best captures the nature of alter personalities found when a clear diagnosis of MPD is made.

In the following I discuss the ontological status of alter personalities. My discussion is, of necessity, philosophical — there are simply no beings in nature like alters, nor does the law have any good analogies with which to work. I apologize to those of my readers less patient with philosophy; unfortunately, the matter at hand leaves open no other avenue for our discussion.

ALTERS AS PERSONS

At first glance, the idea that alter personalities could be separate people seems, well, crazy. Persons have their own bodies — how could several people inhabit one corpus, and how could one corpus hold several people? Common sense dictates that each person has his or her *own* body. Is our "common sense," though, based upon anything other than experience? And while bodily and psychological continuity go overwhelmingly together in everyday life as we know it, is experience necessarily the best indicator, at least when it comes to determining what makes a person?

Thinking about what it means to be a person involves two distinct, though related, questions. First is the question of personhood or, as Kathleen Wilkes (1988) puts it, the question of identification as a person. Second is the question of personal identity or, as Wilkes has named it, of reidentification as the same person. The question of personhood involves the criteria by which one determines whether an entity is a person. Does someone in a persistent vegetative state, for example, for whom there is no evidence of activity in the frontal lobes, meet the criteria for personhood? Likewise, could an incorporeal Martian be a person? Will alter personalities qualify as persons under the criteria we establish?

The question of personal identity, or reidentification as the same person, asks about identity over time: Is the Julia I meet today the same Julia I knew ten years ago? The Julia of ten years ago had a partner, Mary. She had no children, held liberal beliefs, worked in the Peace Corps, and dyed her hair green. Today's Julia is married to Bob, has two children, considers herself a conservative Republican, and wears her hair in its natural color. What makes these two people the same? Is Eve Black, who appears in Dr. Thigpen's office today, the same person as Eve White, who appeared yesterday? Are Eve White and Eve Black the same person — or different people — when coconscious? To ask these questions another way: What does it mean to be a person? And what does it mean to be the *same* person from day, to day, to day?

/ THE QUESTION OF PERSONHOOD /   Daniel Dennett (1976), a philosopher, has identified six themes that are prominent in philosophical discussions of personhood. According to Dennett, a person (1) is rational; (2) is the subject of Intentional predicates; (3) is the recipient of a certain stance or attitude — a person is a moral *object*; (4) has the capacity to reciprocate when such a stance is taken — a person is a moral *subject* or *agent*; (5) uses language; (6) has a special kind of consciousness, perhaps self-consciousness. Certain cases are straightforward under Dennett's criteria. To whatever extent animals, for example, could be considered moral objects or language users, they could not be considered moral agents. As such, Dennett's criteria would preclude the status of personhood. Other cases are less straightforward. It is imaginable that an intelligent being, perhaps from another planet, could posses all Dennett's criteria, even if it were incorporeal. That such a creature might not have a human body — or even a body at all — hardly seems disqualifying.

Kathleen Wilkes (1988) has asked how alter personalities fit into Dennett's scheme. Alters certainly seem capable of rational thought. Similarly, Intentional predicates are true of alters separately: Eve Black has her own beliefs, intentions, desires, and plans, all distinct from Eve White's. Alters use language to communicate — some alters in the same multiple even speak different languages. Christine Beauchamp, for example, could speak French, while her alter, Sally, spoke only English, and one of Billy Milligan's angry protectors spoke fluent Serbo-Croatian. Alters are both conscious and self-conscious. They experience mental states as their own and distinguish those states from the mental states of their fellow alters — an alter will differentiate his or her own happiness or pain from the happiness or pain felt by another alter.

Whether alters are moral agents and moral objects is a more complicated question. Although alters are sentient beings, it is not easy to determine whether we treat them as separate objects of moral concern, what Dennett calls his "stance criterion." Kathleen Wilkes points out that Morton Prince thought of Miss Beauchamp as one patient who desperately needed to be cured, and no doubt most treaters consider themselves to be working with a single patient. Indeed, treaters make alters disappear when they integrate multiples, yet they do not think of themselves as committing murder. Wilkes goes on to explain, however, that many people apply Dennett's stance criterion in quite another manner. She describes how Prince regarded each member of the Beauchamp trio as worthy of moral attention: "He was worried about the effects on $B1$ of Sally's practical jokes; he sympathized, quite genuinely, with $B4$'s agony when she told him that he was killing her; and, although he deplored Sally's childishness and occasional spitefulness, he was also amused by this 'carefree child of nature'" (Wilkes 1988, 122). Prince's attitude toward alters is common; family and friends often have striking reactions to different alter personalities. They may, for example, like one alter, despise another, and be solicitous to a third, taking care to attend to the separate needs and interests of each. Put another way, people treat each alter personality as a moral entity in and of itself.

The picture is likewise ambiguous with regard to Dennett's reciprocation criterion, which would require that alters be moral agents. While Dr. Thigpen chided Eve Black for denying she was a mother and praised Eve White for taking good care of her child, the public appears to see the matter somewhat differently. The public approved of Juanita/Wanda Maxwell's being sent to prison for robbery, even though Wanda alone committed the crime.[4] Juanita's innocence was presumably beside the point.

On the basis of this discussion one might criticize Dennett by pointing out that his criteria for personhood, insofar as they rely on stance and reciprocation, are circular:[5] a person is anyone or anything we treat like a person. According to this criticism, Dennett's criteria are helpful only if they tell us whom we *ought* to treat as persons — namely, those, in part, who are moral objects and moral agents. But his criteria, in reality, tell us only whom we *do* treat as moral objects and moral agents, not whom we *ought* to so treat. His criteria thus fail to deliver on what they promise; we are no further along in understanding what makes a person a moral object or a moral agent and, as a consequence, we understand no more about the nature of alter personalities. This criticism, however, seems unfounded. Dennett's criteria do refer to whether a person is a moral object or agent, and while Wilkes (and I, following Wilkes) has looked to perceptions as evidence on this issue, perceptions are hardly dispositive, as Dennett himself is no doubt well aware. The questions implicated in these criteria are enormously complicated — indeed, they are the subject of much of this book. For our present discussion, it suffices to say that the criteria for stance and reciprocation notwithstanding, there is a strong case that at least some alters are persons according to Dennett's conception of personhood, a conception considered robust by other philosophers.

Criteria other than Dennett's that likewise support personhood are that individual alters differ from one another characterologically; have distinct senses of self; perceive fellow alters as separate people; have a first-person perspective on the world; possess unique life histories and memories; have the capacity to control their bodies; and evince distinct physiological responses. First, marked characterological differences distinguish alter personalities from one another. Each of the Beauchamp trio, for example, had "entirely distinct, though each internally consistent and coherent . . . , preferences, prejudices, outlooks, moods, ambitions, skills, tastes, and habits" (Wilkes 1988, 123). Eve White was subdued, withdrawn, and depressed, a very conscientious wife and mother, while Eve Black, who denied she was married or had children, was carefree and mischievous. Billy Milligan's alter Arthur was a proper, cerebral, Englishman, while Ragan was a reckless, violent, Serbo-Croatian. As one multiple described her alters: "Karen is much more outgoing and socially comfortable, and Linda can be much more just kind of hurt than I can. Carol is very moral, Joan's very bright. She can be more direct."[6]

Second, alters perceive themselves as distinct people. That is to say, in addition to possessing distinct character traits, alter personalities have distinct senses of self. People often play different roles in their lives, such as student, lover, or worker. Actors manifest different personalities for their audiences. But self as student, self as lover, or self as worker is the *same* self; Mel playing Hamlet thinks of himself as Mel playing Hamlet, not as Hamlet. Mel may try to think, feel, and act as he believes Hamlet would, but unless he is delusional, he does not believe he actually is Hamlet. Alters in the same multiple have such beliefs — beliefs that they are different selves.

Third, as Braude points out, in addition to a sense of their own uniqueness, alters perceive their fellow alters as separate people: "I think of them as other people. I've always thought of them as other people. I still do. But this whole . . . all this stuff that we're doing, is like [the therapist] keeps talking about it being other parts of me, and I know it's only supposed to be one person per body, I know that's the way it's supposed to be, but that's not what it feels like to me."[7] Like ordinary people, alters have direct access to their own thoughts and feelings yet can often only make inferences about the thoughts and feelings of their counterparts. Thus, alters experience other alters as other people.

Fourth, alters have a first-person perspective. In discussing how each alter has its own point of view, Wilkes draws upon Nagel's well-known inquiry into what being a unique agentic force in the world is like. According to Nagel, an agentic force — a bat in his example — has its own way of looking at the world, part of which is the experience of "me-ness." Wilkes demonstrates how alters have this very same experience. "There was," she points out, "something that it was like to be Sally, something that it was like to be B1, something that it was like to be B4," so that each alter could make "the fundamental and heartfelt claim 'That's not *me*.'" In contrast to this experience, Wilkes explains, there was "*nothing* that it was like to be 'Miss Beauchamp' during the time that she was split up into three dominant personalities" (1988, 127).

Fifth, alter personalities have unique histories and memories. Like people, alters have a continuity of consciousness reaching into their pasts, in virtue of which they develop rich and detailed life histories. Like people — and unlike actors — alters have their own unique memories that, because alters are self-conscious, can be reflected upon and appreciated *as their very own.*

Sixth, as Wilkes (1988, 124) points out, alters can often manage "for long periods in sole charge of the body." Each of the Beauchamp alters, for instance, "came across as a relatively normal individual, however dissimilar they were from each other in character and temperament." Someone in contact by telephone alone could easily have believed Miss Beauchamp was an entire family. If each alter is a person when in control of the body, it seems undeniable that each is also a person when *not* in control of the body; we would otherwise be committed to the untenable position that persons appear, lapse into nonexistence, and then reappear.

Finally, research suggests that alters within the same multiple have unique physiological processes.[8] Striking examples of differences have been noted; one alter, for example, had an allergic reaction when eating an orange, while another alter in the same multiple did not. Responses to medication have differed, and brain wave patterns have been seen to vary between alters in significant ways. While this research remains in the preliminary stages, and so can lead only to provisional conclusions, the findings are impressive and consistent with conceptualizing alters as separate persons.

Do these and other arguments, including those based on Dennett's criteria, really convince us that alter personalities are people? Dennett's criteria, it can be argued, constitute a conventional catalogue of human attributes — he merely forgot to include a body in his list. That alter personalities meet other criteria for personhood, even robust criteria, does not strike us as dispositive on this issue; in our everyday experience, psychological and bodily continuity go together. At the heart of personhood, at least human personhood, we find a human body. Or do we? To answer this question, we turn to the issue of personal identity.

/ THE QUESTION OF PERSONAL IDENTITY: WHAT'S A BODY GOT TO DO WITH IT? / Sameness of personal identity — reidentification, in the words of Kathleen Wilkes — provides another avenue for thinking about the status of alter personalities. Does a person remain the same person over time by virtue of possessing a particular body, or does having a particular history and way of looking at the world explain this sameness? Those who choose the former hold a bodily theory of personal identity, while those who choose the latter hold a psychological theory of personal identity. Which theory of personal identity we choose will tell a great deal about how we conceive of personhood and, as a consequence, whether we believe alter personalities are persons.

From a bodily theory of personal identity comes the following reasoning: if one must have the same body to be the same person, then to be a person one must have a body. Because each alter does not have its own body, alter personalities cannot be persons. A bodily theory of personhood is the necessary corollary to a bodily theory of personal identity, as can easily be shown: if, to be a person, one did not need to have a body, then Dennett's criteria would strongly argue in favor of the personhood of alter personalities. The law of noncontradiction would demand that alters who have different characteristics would be *different* persons, insofar as the same person could not both identify himself as John and, at the same time, not identify himself as John. The indiscernibility of identicals — the proposition which holds that identical entities have identical qualities — demands that alters having different qualities be different persons. Yet if one holds a bodily theory of personal identity, then alters would necessarily be the *same* person since they have the same body. Adopting a bodily theory of personal identity therefore forecloses the debate — alters could not be separate persons. Note that the reverse is not true — adopting a psychological theory of personal identity will not be dispositive on the question of whether alters are persons.[9] While a psychological theory of personal identity would certainly be consistent with the personhood of alters, it will not allow us definitively to conclude that alters are persons.

We have at present two questions on the table: first, what makes me a person; and second, what makes me the same person over time? In attempting to answer the former we turn to the latter and ask whether it is my body in virtue of which I am the same "me" as the years pass (in which case alters cannot be persons) or whether I remain "me" because of my psychological traits (in which case alters may or may not be persons). Philosophers have come up with thought experiments as a way of thinking about the problem of personal identity, virtually all of which are variations on Locke's famous puzzle case.

In thinking about whether psychological or bodily characteristics explain the sameness of personhood over time, John Locke (1960) asked what would happen if a Cobbler and a Prince were to exchange psychological characteristics. The question, in Locke's view, was whether we would identify the Prince with the Prince-bodied person or with the Cobbler-bodied person. He points out that the person in the Prince's body would look, feel, sound, and even smell like the Prince. Upon questioning this person, however, we would encounter the Cobbler's memories, hopes, wishes, dreams, and fears. To Locke it was obvious that people are identified by their psychological character-istics—the Prince would be the person in the Cobbler's body.

Bernard Williams (1973, 46) poses the following puzzle, which, like Locke's, supports a psychological theory of personal identity. Williams asks us to imagine implanting the brain traces of person A into person B's brain, and then implanting B's traces into A's brain. The following day one of the bodies will be tortured, while the other will receive one hundred thousand dollars. If A is allowed to choose which body will be tortured and which will receive the money, what will she decide? Williams says that A's choice will almost certainly be that the B-bodied person will get the money and the A-bodied person will be tortured — like the Cobbler and the Prince, A and B have merely switched bodies. Most people, Williams argues, will be led by their intuitions to the same conclusion. Put another way, most people intuitively hold a psychological theory of personal identity.

Williams then presents a second story, which, he believes, will lead people in a very different direction, toward a bodily theory of personal identity. Williams now asks us to imagine that we will be tortured tomorrow but that, before the torture actually begins, all of our memories, intentions, dispositions, and ambitions — in short, all of our psychological traits — will be removed and replaced with those belonging to another person. Williams suggests that it would be natural for us to be terrified by the prospect of the impending torture, the switches notwithstanding. As Williams sees it, our terror shows that our intuitions can accommodate the idea of a person remaining the same, despite the absence of psychological connectedness or continuity. Intuitively, he now concludes, we hold a bodily theory of personal identity.

This second story is problematic for reasons that detract from Williams's claim that it supports a bodily theory of personal identity. Williams's version — I am told that it is *I* who will be tortured tomorrow — implicitly asks me to imagine that I will continue to exist. It is not, as some have argued, that the story begs the question — Williams does not assume his listener's continued existence. Williams does, however, urge the listener to imagine that she continues to exist in the only way available to her, through her body. Moreover, in Williams's first story A's psychological characteristics reappear in B, while in the second story they do not. Torture in the second story may elicit fear, not because people intuitively hold a bodily theory of personal identity but because the body in that story is the only candidate for their continued existence. To put the matter another way, the second story asks the listener to choose not between a bodily or a psychological theory of personal identity but between torture and ceasing to exist altogether. Given the choice between *being one's body* or *ceasing to exist,* most people will choose the former. Given the quite different choice presented in Williams's first story — the choice between *me* being *my body* or *my mind* — people choose to identify themselves with their minds. In short, when asked what makes and keeps them who they are, people look to psychological, rather than corporeal, characteristics.

William Carter's (1990) thought experiment about Felix the cat is another argument for the bodily theory of personal identity:

> We start with two felines, Felix and Jefferson say, who are treated by the same veterinarian. A bizarre surgical blunder occurs and Felix's brain winds up in Jefferson's head. The resulting cat, call him Felixson, *looks* for all the world like Jefferson, but *behaves* exactly like Felix (and not at all like Jefferson). The situation is complicated by the fact that Felix's debrained body is provided with enough transplanted brain tissue so that it continues to live and function in feline-like ways. (Let's call this cat Felixless.) We are confronted here by certain questions of feline iden-

tity. To my way of thinking, these questions have rather obvious answers. It is true that Felixless is (=) Felix. Accordingly, it is false that Fe-
lixson is (=) Felix. My guess is that this assessment of the matter will
encounter little, if any, serious resistance. (Carter 1990, 71)

As Carter sees it, whether such a switch occurs in a cat or a person is
irrelevant — the outcome is the same. Personal identity follows the
body.

Cats are known, at least to cat lovers like myself, for their unique
personalities. To my way of thinking, Felix is the cat with the likes,
dislikes, and habits of Felix — traits that vary widely from cat to cat.
Certainly if my cat, Fizzy, underwent such a mix-up, and her brain/
personality were to land in Jefferson's body, I would want the Jefferson-
bodied cat curled up in my lap each night and would not much care
what happened to the old Fizzy-bodied cat. Conversely, the more
impoverished the personality, the more we look to corporeal aspects
for identity; while amoebae may vary in terms of their stimulus-re-
sponse histories, they cannot be said in any meaningful way to have
personalities. If two amoebae were to undergo the equivalent of Carter's brain transplant, I think Carter's conclusion would make perfect
sense — we would identify the amoeba by, and only by, its body. Put
another way, the richer the personality — whether belonging to a person, a cat, or an amoeba — the more we identify the psyche as the
repository of the entity's essence.

Parfit (1984), a philosopher whose work in the area of personhood
and personal identity is arguably the most important of this century,
offers a quite different way of thinking about personal identity by
suggesting that the answers to some of these questions may be
"empty." For Parfit, a question is "empty" when we have available to
us all the relevant data yet are nevertheless left empty-handed. As he
sees it, the principle of "reductionism" best explains the problem of
personal identity. Reductionism claims that personal identity consists
in our bodies and brains functioning together in certain ways, and
stands in contrast to nonreductionism, the position that personal identity resides in some further, as yet unknown, fact, such as a separately
existing soul. According to Parfit there *is* no unknown fact that, as if a
deus ex machina, will provide an answer.

Parfit is not concerned with what constitutes personal identity, does
not think it much matters anyway, and urges us not to occupy ourselves
with talk of different and same people. What does matter to Parfit

are psychological continuity and connectedness, what he calls the "R-relation," a concept that can be applied to alters. If, as Parfit argues, what matters is whether Eve White is psychologically connected to and continuous with Eve Black — whether Eve White and Eve Black are "R-related" — then we need not become caught up in a debate over whether Eve White and Eve Black are different persons. What is important is whether each, over time, evinces a sameness of memory, intention, wish, dream, and fear. Since they do not, Eve White and Eve Black are not "R-related." For those to whom personal identity does matter, Parfit proposes a psychological criterion, hardly surprising given his emphasis on psychological continuity: If personal identity is based on psychological criteria, Eve White and Eve Black are different persons.

Our review weighs in favor of a psychological criterion of personal identity or, if not of personal identity, of what matters in determining why a person remains the same person over time. There may nevertheless be arguments that support adopting a bodily criterion. While Williams and Carter are not convincing in this regard, other philosophical claims, such as the problem of duplication of psychological characteristics, albeit not without their counterarguments, are more persuasive. Philosophy aside, the administration of the legal system provides a powerful incentive for adopting a bodily criterion of personal identity. Administratively, it may simply be too inconvenient to identify persons by other than bodily means. Moreover, common intuitions assume that bodily and psychological continuity go together — naming purely psychological entities like Eve White and Eve Black different people might expose the law to public scorn. Unfortunately for alter personalities, the public has very little taste for the philosophical.

To sum up, while administrative convenience provides a powerful argument for adopting a bodily theory of personal identity, we have nevertheless found no easy answer to the question of whether alter personalities are persons. Alters meet at least four of Dennett's criteria, and may well meet all six. Empirical observations that support personhood are that alters differ characterologically, have distinct senses of self, perceive fellow alters to be separate people, see the world from a first-person perspective, possess unique life histories and memories, take control of their bodies, and evince unique physiological responses. Arguments to the contrary notwithstanding, that alters are persons is provocative yet philosophically plausible.

We have found philosophical arguments and empirical data that support the personhood of alter personalities. True, alters lack a body, and that will make us less likely to think them persons, but we have seen how the status of a body in this regard is unclear. If alters are not persons, then they are certainly *like* persons.

Precisely which qualities make alters most like persons? And can we distinguish alter personalities from ordinary parts of you and me — the contemplative, rageful, or kind parts? It is to these questions we now turn.

ALTERS AS PERSONLIKE CENTERS OF CONSCIOUSNESS

If alters are not persons, are they person*like?* The answer should be fairly clear. If the only reason we deny that alters are persons is that they lack a body, then alters must have all the other qualities of personhood: they are as personlike as one can be without actually being a person. Indeed, we had our doubts about whether having a body was even a qualification of personhood, let alone a crucial one. All of the arguments of the last section, then, that alters were persons, are also arguments that they are person*like.*

What qualities of alter personalities are especially important to their being personlike? And how are alter personalities different than ordinary parts of people? Stephen Braude (1991), a philosopher, has developed the concept of an "apperceptive center" to describe the nature of alter personalities. Braude uses several technical terms to capture what he means by this concept, two of which are "autobiographical" and "indexical" states. States of mind are autobiographical if a person experiences them as her own; they are indexical if she believes them to be her own. Autobiographical states, consisting of sensations, emotions, wishes, memories, and the like, are phenomenological, while indexical states, consisting of beliefs about such experiences, are epistemic.

Normally, although not always, states of mind are both autobiographical and indexical. In our usual waking lives, experience and belief go together; my experience of going to the farmers' market goes hand in hand with the belief that my last half hour was spent in front of a fruit stand. Autobiographical and indexical states may, however, diverge in a variety of ways. In terror, for example, characterized by epistemic poverty, experiences may be autobiographical but not indexical—I am too terrified to actually form beliefs, so I do not acknowledge the experience as my own. Other states are the reverse — indexical but not autobiographical. When depersonalized, for example, a person believes a state to be her own but does not experience it as such.

An apperceptive center, by definition, is a subject of autobiographical states, most of which are indexical as well — the majority of the time what I feel, think, say, and do seem like my feelings, thoughts, words, and deeds, and I believe them to be so as well. Subjects are *distinct* apperceptive centers if their respective autobiographical and indexical states are largely nonautobiographical and nonindexical for the other. Eve White took excellent care of her daughter, while Eve Black disowned and rejected the child. For Eve Black, Eve White's care and acceptance were nonautobiographical and nonindexical; for Eve White, Eve Black's rejection was nonautobiographical and nonindexical. If most of their experiences are of this sort, Eve White and Eve Black are distinct apperceptive centers. Now consider a man who is both a father and a teacher. If, while teaching, he becomes angry at his students, the father is also angry at the students. The father experiences the anger as — and believes it to be — his own, even when he leaves the classroom and walks home for lunch. Put in Braude's terms, experiences that are autobiographical and indexical for the teacher are both for the father as well. Unless this is usually *not* the case, the father and the teacher are the same apperceptive center. While Braude's distinction between autobiographical and indexical states may be sharper than the way things actually happen in the world, it goes a long way in explaining the phenomenology of MPD, a condition in which one body simultaneously houses distinct apperceptive centers as Braude conceptualizes them. It may well be the only such condition, ordinary dividedness and other dissociative disorders, even in their extreme forms, notwithstanding.

The "hidden observer," a phenomenon arising when a hypnotized subject is instructed not to feel pain, provides an example of how even dissociated individuals may not house distinct apperceptive centers. Despite the instruction, a certain percentage of people in trance do appear to experience pain; their hidden observer — the part of them that responds in trance — indicates as much when asked to give a signal by the hypnotist. While the experience of pain is nonautobiographical for the hypnotized individual — she experiences no pain — it is indexical for her, insofar as she would believe that the pain was her own if shown a videotape of the session. By contrast, the pain is both autobiographical and indexical for the hidden observer, since it is she who reports the experience. Such asymmetries between autobiographical and indexical states do not in and of themselves, however, make the subject and hidden observer distinct apperceptive centers. Despite such asymmetries, the pain remains indexical for the hypnotized individual.

Nor do other dissociative disorders involve distinct apperceptive centers of the kind that characterize MPD. Depersonalization and psychogenic amnesia, for example, involve a *single* apperceptive center. Psychogenic fugue is a form of dissociation in which there may be different apperceptive centers — yet these apperceptive centers are neither simultaneous nor recurrent. MPD is different, insofar as its *defining* characteristic is to have more than one apperceptive center that recurs and can be simultaneous.

At this point one might raise five objections to Braude's way of thinking. One may object, first, that alters are not apperceptive centers at all; second, that even should they be apperceptive centers, alters are not distinct apperceptive centers; third, that according to Braude's reasoning ordinary parts of people are also distinct apperceptive centers, so applying the term to alters doesn't really mean much; fourth, that being an apperceptive center tells us very little about what we really want to know, namely, whether an alter is personlike; and fifth, that the defining characteristics of an apperceptive center look solely to subjective experience that can be mistaken, delusional, or both — flimsy bases on which to form a rule about criminal responsibility.

The first objection, that alters are not apperceptive centers at all, is not overly persuasive. Certainly some alters may not be; take as examples alters who are fragmentary and ephemeral, or an alter whose sole function is to sleep. These examples notwithstanding, the arguments based on criminal responsibility are valid as long as at least some alters are apperceptive centers, and I believe this can easily be shown. Consider that, for the objection to be correct, *no* alter could be an apperceptive center. Given that Braude came up with the concept of an apperceptive center as a way of explaining the distinct nature of alter personalities, and that the concept has been criticized for merely restating in philosophical language the familiar features of alterhood, it would be exceedingly unlikely that no alter could be characterized in this way.

A more substantive response to the first objection looks to alters' autobiographical and indexical states. If no alter is an apperceptive center, then, by definition, alters could not be the subjects of autobiographical states when most of those states are indexical as well. Put more directly, for the objection to stand alters could not have experiences that, in most cases, they believed to be their very own experiences. Yet, because alters *do* describe having their own experiences, alters would have to be always mistaken in this regard. People can perhaps be mistaken about their experiences in different sorts of ways — but can one be mistaken about whether one is having an experience at all? The first objection rests on the premise that no alter is ever correct in reporting an experience as her own, a premise that is simply not credible.

Equally implausible is the second objection that alters, albeit apperceptive centers, are not distinct apperceptive centers, insofar as their experiences are not sufficiently dissimilar. Clinical data support quite the opposite conclusion — Eve White was an excellent mother, no doubt in virtue of strong maternal tendencies, which Eve Black repudiated. A variation of the second objection concedes that Eve White and Eve Black had very different experiences of motherhood yet points out that, for Braude, states must be *largely* nonautobiographical and nonindexical for apperceptive centers to be distinct. Perhaps, the objection would go, many seemingly different apperceptive centers are actually the same because they share more experiences than we realize. This form of the objection likewise fails in light of empirical data; while alters do speak of "leaking" experiences and of shared memories, such experiences are rare, at least relative to the more predominantly described streams of experience.

Yet another variation turns the objection on its head. The claim now is not that *we* are mistaken about the degree to which alters share experiences but that *alters* are mistaken when they own and disavow experiences as their own — there are no truly discrepant experiences among alters. The argument, in Braude's terms, is that *all* experiences are autobiographical and indexical for *all* alters in a multiple, even though certain experiences appear discrepant to particular alters. Consider a teacher alter and a father alter having discrepant autobiographical and indexical experiences. The teacher alter feels pain and believes it to be his own, while the father alter feels joy and believes it to be his own. The teacher disavows the joy, and the father disavows the pain.

This variation of the second objection claims that all alters are the same apperceptive center; to be correct the father and teacher alters must be mistaken in their beliefs — each experiences both pain and joy. The problem is that even were an alter to be mistaken about its experience on a particular occasion — say, for some intrapsychic, perhaps defense-related, reason — it could hardly be mistaken about its experience on every occasion. For this objection to be correct, every alter would have to be mistaken in every instance both about what it feels and about what it does not feel; if the teacher alter and the father alter accurately report different affective experiences, this version of the second objection falls and no longer stands in the way of our concluding that alters are distinct apperceptive centers. Empirical data are fatal to the second objection in either version.

The second objection nevertheless suggests a problem with Braude's conceptualization of alter personalities as distinct apperceptive centers, a problem that, if answered, would remedy the second objection and its variation. As Braude sees it, different apperceptive centers may share experiences, and the same apperceptive center may include experiences that are extrareferential, that is, experiences that are nonautobiographical, nonindexical, and assigned to a different center of consciousness. I call the latter experiences "discrepant"; such are experiences which the subject assigns to another apperceptive center. On Braude's view apperceptive centers who share experiences are distinct only if they have other, "largely" different, experiences. Note what happens if Braude is incorrect, as I believe he is, that distinct apperceptive centers share experiences; when, under this new way of thinking, we find discrepant experiences, we will necessarily find distinct apperceptive centers. As a consequence, we need not worry about shared experiences; our focus, rather, will be on discrepant experiences, the presence of which will lead us to conclude we have distinct centers. I believe this, rather than Braude's position, to be the right one.

Consider reasons for rejecting the idea that two alters might share an experience. All of our experiences are, in some sense, metaphenomenal — we have an experience, and we experience ourselves having the experience. Even if one center of consciousness were to "read" another center's mind, there would still be important and dramatic differences between the experience as *experienced* and the experience as *read*. Going to the circus is a joyous event in the life of a six-year-old — popcorn, candy, horsies, and the like. Assume that somehow her twin sister had access to the six-year-old's joyous experience as she steps inside the big tent and sees the elephants, lions, and tigers, all in a big circle. Each twin's experience will nevertheless differ; while the two centers of consciousness will have similar experiences — each will experience the elephants, lions, and tigers — at the very least, *they will not be the same experience of that experience.* Braude's claim that two centers largely sharing experiences are really one and the same center is therefore off base. Different apperceptive centers share *no* experiences, and the same apperceptive centers share *all* experiences — there is no sharing *some* experiences. One experience disavowed by an alter and acknowledged by another renders false the claim that alters are really the same apperceptive center — all of the "sharing" in the world will not collapse alters into a single center. Because clinical data show that alters frequently disavow thoughts, feelings, and memories that other alters claim as their own, Braude's position — that alters share experiences — must be modified. The modification, more consistent with clinical data, is that alters which have discrepant experiences are distinct.

The third objection, that alters are no different than ordinary parts of people, fares no better than the first two. Automatic writing would seem to provide a perfect example of a nonmultiple whose states qualify as distinct apperceptive centers. A person who engages in automatic writing experiences the handwriting as, and believes it to be, her own — it is both autobiographical and indexical — yet she does not experience as her own either the will to write or the thoughts transcribed. Automatic writing, however, fails to support the third objection for the same reason amnesia fails in this regard — although the subject disavows experiences as her own, she nevertheless fails to ascribe those experiences to another subject, who, in turn, accepts the experiences as autobiographical, indexical, or both. Put another way, the subject does not assign the experience to another apperceptive center, and there is no other apperceptive center that says "This experience belongs to me."

Unusual experiences like automatic writing, however, are not the only potential problem in this regard. Consider Katherine, an investment banker, who is sometimes angry at her superiors, greedy about all the money she will make, and kind toward homeless people she encounters on the street. Why are all these different parts of Katherine not distinct apperceptive centers? When Katherine says, "The angry part of me wants to get even with my boss," what she is really saying is

"I want to get even with my boss when I feel angry." When, in turn, she remarks, "The greedy part of me wants to take over that deal," her thought is actually, "When I'm feeling greedy I want to take business away from that person." And when she murmurs, "The kind part of me wants to feed that hungry person dinner," what she means is "I am feeling kind and I want to buy that person something to eat." The subject of each utterance is Katherine, not Katherine's angry, greedy, or kind part. Katherine will avow the anger, greed, and kindness — each is hers, and hers alone.

One might ask whether angry, greedy, and kind *people* are apperceptive centers, even though angry, greedy, and kind *parts of people* are not. My thinking is that they could be — if the angry, greedy, and kind Katherine were all apperceptive centers, they would all be the *same* apperceptive center. In the alternative, we might say that neither the angry, the greedy, nor the kind Katherine are apperceptive centers at all — *Katherine* is the apperceptive center. Central to our discussion is the notion that we have only one apperceptive center. To put the matter a bit differently, we would not say "Angry Katherine wanted to get back at her boss" but rather, "When Katherine was angry, she wanted to get back at her boss." Katherine, for her part, will not regard this anger as "angry Katherine's experience," but as Katherine's experience of being angry.

Katherine's willingness to rewrite the description in the first person sets her apart from alters in a striking and empirically verifiable way. Ragan would not, for example, be willing to concede that his anger actually belonged to Billy Milligan, any more than Adalana would ascribe to Billy her lust. Billy would presumably own neither the anger nor the lust as his. Ragan and Adalana would object, perhaps vehemently, if we rewrote the script to read, "When Billy was angry he . . ." or, "When Billy was lustful he . . ." Subjects who are distinct apperceptive centers, such as alters, talk about themselves in ways markedly different than single apperceptive centers who, like Katherine, are experiencing distinct affective states.

The fourth objection assumes that alters, unlike ordinary parts of people, are indeed apperceptive centers. The objection is that an entity can be a distinct apperceptive center without meeting Dennett's, or anyone else's, criteria for personhood. As a consequence, knowing that an alter is an apperceptive center tells us very little about what really interests us, which is whether the alter is personlike. Take as an example an alter who emerges twice for some trivial purpose, say to have a headache. Suppose, as we easily could, that this alter is an apperceptive center; it experiences the pain as, and believes the pain to be, its own — in Braude's language, the pain is both autobiographical and indexical. Do we want to say that this alter, whose entire "life" consisted of two headaches, is a person, or is even personlike? I think not. While the alter may be self-conscious, it is only very minimally, if at all, the subject of Intentional predicates, a user of language, a rational being, a moral agent, or a moral object. As this case illustrates, apperceptive centeredness does not necessarily entail personlike-hood.

The objection is correct to make a distinction between being personlike and being an apperceptive center — the two are not synonymous. Neither, however, is an alter personality synonymous with an apperceptive center. Some alters may be apperceptive centers; some apperceptive centers may be personlike; and — what the empirical data strongly support — some alters may be *both* apperceptive centers *and* personlike. That certain alters are too fragmentary or ephemeral to qualify as either does not detract from the arguments for criminal nonresponsibility. As long as alters can be both apperceptive centers and personlike, exoneration on the basis of MPD remains a viable disposition.

The fifth objection looks to how Braude's definition of autobiographical and indexical states is based entirely on subjective experience. According to this objection, an entity could render itself a personlike apperceptive center merely by virtue of thinking certain things about itself, regardless of how delusional the thinking might be. Put another way, if to *think* I am a personlike apperceptive center, however delusionally, is enough to *make* me a personlike apperceptive center, then calling me — or anything else — a personlike apperceptive center doesn't really mean much. The implications for our analysis are troubling — if this objection is correct, legal consequences that turn on the status of alters may hang on no more than a fantasy.

As an initial matter, say that persons can be mistaken about their experiences. This case is easy because our response is that delusional persons are just that — delusional. Psychotic individuals may believe they house distinct apperceptive centers but may be mistaken in this regard — and then their discrepant autobiographical and indexical experiences are no more than figments of their imagination. Now take the more challenging case, in which we say that people cannot be mistaken in this way—people are accurate reporters of autobiographical and indexical experiences. Even were this to be the case, the characteristics of being a person, or of being personlike, are far more complex and correspondingly difficult to create through thought alone. That one thinks his or her self holds distinct apperceptive centers is a far cry from having apperceptive centers that meet our criteria for personlike-hood. Thinking that distinct apperceptive centers are present is not at all the same as having centers that are rational, self-conscious, and treated as unique objects of moral concern; use language; differ from one another in character and physiology; possess unique life histories, memories, and perspectives on the world; and are able to control the body. These characteristics are robust, rich, and complex; what's more, they can be empirically examined. Indeed, the sort of integrated, tex-tured, cohesive whole of a personlike apperceptive center will stand in stark contrast to a delusional system that, even if named, will have little else to support its status as a person or personlike entity.

Apperceptive centers, while perhaps less than persons, are more than fantasies. Alters, as distinct apperceptive centers, may sometimes be persons or personlike. Their relevance to the criminal law rests on our showing that certain alters achieve person or personlike status, and empirical data do precisely this. What, though, of those who maintain that whatever alters may be, they are decidedly *not* like persons? To this stance we now turn.

ALTERS AS PARTS OF COMPLEX, NONINTEGRATED INDIVIDUALS

Thus far we have concentrated on what qualities alters possess and what status we should accord them. An observer might point out that while alters are distinct from mere parts of persons, distinctions can likewise be drawn between alters and whole persons, distinctions we have overlooked for our own advantage. Should we choose to examine these differences, the thinking goes, we might conclude that alter personalities are more partlike than personlike. Alters appear to resem-ble parts more than whole persons because they lack bodies, have immediate access to one another's mental states, share memories, and are capable of being integrated into one person.

Alters seem more like parts than whole persons because, first, lacking a body, they cannot easily be differentiated from one another, are often disabled from acting in the world, and are "out" only in intermittent phases. When neither out nor coconscious, it is as if alters are nonexistent, much like the angry or greedy parts of Katherine that, at any given time, lie dormant. Second, alters appear to have access to one another's mental states in a way that people do not, although parts of the same person may. As an example, Katherine's greedy and kind parts may be present to and accessible by one another; different people, almost by definition, are not privy in this sort of way to what others are thinking and feeling. Third, alters, unlike people, may share memories. Psychological theories of personal identity see continuity of memory playing a central role in psychological continuity and connectedness. While alters, and perhaps parts of people, may have shared memories, people do not. Finally, alter personalities can be integrated into one person, something unthinkable for two people. While parts of people blend and redifferentiate all the time, people remain separate. For all these reasons, alter personalities appear to resemble parts more than they resemble whole people.

Are these arguments persuasive? To a certain extent yes, but they take us only so far. First, it is true that alters are intermittent in a way that people are not — people come into and depart from existence only once in a lifetime. That aspect of personhood, though, is due largely to the continued life of a body. More to the point, there are frequent breaks in the continuity of consciousness; people experience dreamless sleep each night and dissociate in the midst of everyday experiences such as driving a car or knitting a sweater. Some alters, as it turns out, are present all the time, even if not in control of the body; their consciousness seems as continuous as that of any person. Alters are intermittent in a way that is not foreign to personlike-hood.

Access to the mental states of other alters is likewise not the pronounced distinction between alters and persons it may initially appear. The access is significantly attenuated — one alter reads another's experiences as the experiences of another alter, not as its own. While the phenomenon is more immediate than what happens between people, who infer thoughts and feelings from observing behavior, there nevertheless remains an "as if" quality that is not found in relation to one's own mental states. Alters, moreover, seem no more like parts of persons than like persons in this regard; we don't say, for example, that Katherine's angry part has access to what her greedy part is feeling but that Katherine feels both angry and greedy. Parts are not subjects of experience in the way alter personalities are — it doesn't make sense to speak of Katherine's angry part having access to her greedy part, while it both makes intuitive sense and is consistent with clinical experience to say that Eve White had access to Eve Black's intentions.

We get no further by saying that alters share one another's memories in a way that people do not. Certainly alters can have the same memories, if by this we mean they remember the same things. Perhaps if they could share the *same* experience of remembering we would have to renounce the view that they are personlike. What would it even mean for *people* to be so merged in this way? Yet, as we have seen, distinct apperceptive centers will have distinct experiences. One experience will be the remembering, the other will be the experience of that alter remembering — something like the Vulcan mind-meld whereby Spock, by placing his hands on someone's head, could literally experience what that person had experienced. Regardless of how closely an alter can "read" another alter's experience, there will be two, rather than one, "rememberings," and the memories will continue to belong to one, and only one, alter.

Finally, what shall we make of the fact that alters can be integrated through talk therapy? We are presented here with an impossible case — aside from science fiction, we simply cannot imagine putting two people together. Alters are quite unlike people in this regard — but note how they are quite different from parts of people in this way as well. While parts of people are merged and blended in a talk therapy — intense affects are modified, conflicting thoughts integrated, traumatic experiences placed in the context of other, more benign, happenings — parts of people do not have the capacity to reflect on the experience of integration or merger. Alters do. Sally Beauchamp, for example, claimed that she was being murdered by Dr. Thigpen — she could feel her self-consciousness fading away. Once again, alters seem no more like parts than they do whole persons.

An incorporeal nature, access to mental states and memories, and the capacity to be integrated into a single, unified whole set alter personalities apart not only from persons but from parts of persons as well. For every way in which alters are personlike (they are, for example, apperceptive centers), there seems to be a way in which they resemble parts of persons as well (they can be merged and integrated). For every way in which alters are not like persons (they lack a body), there seems to be a way in which they are not like parts of persons either (they can reflect upon their own memories and experiences). Perhaps the most obvious conclusion is that alter personalities are a category unto themselves. Alters are not quite like anyone, or anything, else.

Braude, who has probably spent more time than any other philosopher thinking about these matters, believes that a deep unity underlies alter personalities. The implications of his claim are not clear; Braude stresses that the unity does not detract from the status of alter personalities as apperceptive centers, and his discussion of personhood shows that, according to certain definitions, alters would indeed be persons. Perhaps there is nothing inconsistent between finding a deep unity and according alters the status of personhood, or at least the status of being like persons. Braude's way of thinking is nevertheless interesting and merits some discussion.

Braude finds evidence for an underlying unity in the defensive nature of dissociation and in the repertoire of abilities that alters share. As he sees it, "The personal conflicts and coping strategies at issue in the case of MPD seem to make sense only relative to a deeper synthetic psychological unity" (1991, 186), while "a single individual's repertoire of abilities and dispositions undergirds the functional distinctness of alternate personalities" (188). In making his first observation, Braude is especially concerned with refuting what he calls the "colonial view," according to which all of us originally consist of a colony of selves. As Braude sees it, this view of the self is inconsistent with the role of trauma and dissociation in MPD; trauma and splitting happen to what was originally *one* person.

Braude's points are well taken but need elaboration. First, while the concept of splitting does imply a preexisting unity, perhaps the split occurs in one of several unities — there seems no compelling reason to assume a single original unity. Or, perhaps the trauma destroys the original unity, and then personlike entities emerge. Second, it does not seem necessary that an underlying unity maintain the split. What needs explaining, after all, is how the parts come together, not how they stay apart, and a therapist is our answer here. Staying separate is easily explained — many alters are all too happy to remain distinct from their brethren. Third, the difference between ordinary hypnotic dissociation, in which, as Braude points out, we posit a single subject, and MPD, in which we posit multiple subjects, is accounted for by Braude's own concepts. Alters are, and ordinary hypnotic subjects are not, distinct apperceptive centers, and so we more readily see lack of unity. The adaptive nature of dissociation, while consistent with an underlying unity, is by no means definitive in this regard, and certainly does not rule out the possibility of a deep disunity after the split-inducing trauma has occurred.[10]

Braude next looks to shared abilities as evidence of a single, unifying ego. In pointing out that most alters in a multiple can read and speak the same language, and often share other talents such as the ability to drive a car, Braude convincingly argues that the distinctiveness of individual alters does not derive from the distinctiveness of their abilities. He then argues for shared, rather than numerically distinct, capacities, capacities that find their origin in a unified ego underlying separate alters. This claim for an underlying unity seems less compelling than Braude's previous claim. First, Braude never makes clear precisely what "numerically distinct" abilities are and whether there is any way to examine them. Second, Braude is not clear about what he means when he says that a "unifying ego" explains common abilities. All sorts of unifying principles explain common traits and abilities. Members of the same family, for example, may share many abilities and will virtually always speak and read the same language. An enormously robust unity — a common gene pool and upbringing — underlies all the members; is this the sort of thing Braude has in mind? Siamese twins joined at the hip may share the ability to walk; is this what Braude is talking about? Third, although Braude quite strenuously objects to the concept of numerically distinct abilities within the same individual, he is quite open to single individuals having numerically distinct senses of self, what seems to be a much more powerful claim. That alters have abilities in common does suggest some unity — after all, alters share the same brain — but Braude explains neither what this unity consists of nor what it tells us about the nature of alter personalities. The concept of an underlying unity speaks to our intuitions — alters certainly share something — but it does not get us terribly far. Thus, Braude's concept of a unity underlying alters does not mean that alters are mere parts of persons. Before we decide on the nature of alter personalities, more robust empirical data will be needed — but are certain to be a long time coming.

IS INTEGRATION THE EQUIVALENT OF MURDER?

Kathleen Wilkes (1981), a philosopher, has made the interesting observation that if alter personalities were persons, treaters who work toward integration would be guilty of murder. I have encountered no treater who would seriously equate integration with murder, and the suggestion itself belongs decidedly to the realm of philosophy. Wilkes's point is nevertheless intriguing and presses for clarity in how we conceptualize alters. How can we believe that doctors treating multiples through integration are working toward something good and, at the same time, believe that alters are persons[11] who will no longer be when the integration is complete?

Four responses to the claim that integration is the equivalent of murder seem plausible: first, that multiples must consent to integration, which makes integration suicide at worst; second, that the term "homicide" refers only to the act of depriving a human body of life, and so does not apply to integration; third, that through integration alters are not really killed but only transformed into different, yet nevertheless recognizable, parts of a person; and fourth, that unlike death, integration can be reversed — alters can reemerge under various conditions. Regarding the first, consent is an enormously complex matter with individuals suffering from MPD and merits a much fuller discussion than I will provide here. For the present, it suffices to say that integration can take place only when all alters consent — and that is surely enough for competent consent on anyone's theory. Consent in and of itself, however, does not solve the problem Wilkes raises. A patient may consent to an injection that will cause death; if the doctor's direct involvement is sufficient, he or she may be guilty of homicide, the patient's consent notwithstanding.[12] Moreover, even were the act deemed assisted suicide, the charge is still quite serious.[13] Wilkes's point remains — our willingness to exonerate doctors of any wrongdoing does not square with conceptualizing alters as persons. Our first response fails.

The second response, that integration does not turn a live body into a corpse, has some force. Homicide, in our legal system, is corporeal in nature, for good reason — bodily continuity is generally a good proxy for psychological continuity and connectedness. Nevertheless, a person who puts another into an altered state of consciousness — say a persistent vegetative state — is guilty of a serious crime, even if not of murder. And were we to adopt a psychological criterion of personal identity, such an act might well constitute murder. Wilkes's point still stands — we simply do not believe that doctors are doing anything wrong when they treat multiples through integration, a belief that cannot be reconciled with conceptualizing alter personalities as persons.

The third response to Wilkes is that alters are actually preserved, rather than destroyed, through integration. Put another way, doctors do not eliminate alters through integration — they combine them with other alters. Like its two predecessors, however, this argument is ultimately unpersuasive. Alters undergo drastic changes when integrated. A very aggressive alter and a very peaceable alter, for example, may combine to become a moderately aggressive person.[14] Consider the analogy of baking a cake: if we value eggs in their unadulterated state, mixing in sugar and butter would leave us quite dissatisfied. We care about the continued existence of alters because they are unique loci of consciousness, and it is the loss of that *uniqueness* that Wilkes underscores. Her point remains.

The fourth and final response is that integration is reversible: after integration, alters can nevertheless reemerge in their original form given certain conditions. The problem with this fourth response is that often patients' wants are transformed so that integration, rather than dividedness, is their preferred state. The patient learns new methods of coping and, even under stress, does not revert to a condition of dividedness — she relies on defenses other than dissociation. That some alters can potentially return from their state of merger does not deprive Wilkes's point of its force — doctors intend that the alters never return, and are thus guilty of *attempted* murder, should we hold to our premise that alters are persons.

If alters are indeed persons, integration does seem the equivalent of murder — or some other serious crime. Can it be justified?

Certain homicides are obviously justified. In self-defense, the self-defender has the right to kill: where the choice is between the death of an innocent and the death of a wrongdoer, we protect the innocent. And even where the victim is not a wrongdoer, he must sometimes die to serve a greater good: in the situation of necessity it is acceptable to kill one person so that more may live.[15] A doctor can justifiably kill one Siamese twin if the alternative is that both will die.[16]

The problem with these analogies is that a doctor working toward integration can raise no such claim — integration is hardly required for another to continue living. Consider, however, the following. If a doctor kills one of a pair of Siamese twins, first, the other will be able to lead a normal life, while if she does not kill one twin both will lead very difficult lives; second, the twin to be eliminated and the surviving twin *both* consent to the elimination; third, the elimination can occur only with the cooperation and assistance of *both* twins; fourth, the twin's elimination will not be entire, since his personality characteristics will be "mixed in" with the other's; fifth, the twin has not been irrevocably eliminated, since he can return, at least potentially; and sixth, there is a high degree of consensus among experts in the field that the end result is good. If all of these conditions are met — as they must if integration is to be successful — then the "killing" might well be justified.

None of these circumstances in isolation would justify the doctor's act, if indeed alters are persons. Consent, for example, would not by itself suffice — it would be murder to kill two paralyzed persons so that a third could move, even should they consent to such an act. Similarly, we cannot justify killing, despite consent and a modicum of psychological survival, unless the being that results is likely to be considerably better off than his "ancestors." Finally, the reversibility of the procedure is not alone enough to interrupt the force of Wilkes's argument if the doctor's act is not independently justified. When, however, the outcome seems justified, the reversibility adds to our comfort level: should the patient come to disagree about its justifiability, she may restore herself to the status quo ante by bringing her alters back to life, as it were. When a set of conditions is met — consent, cooperation, a considerably better life, consent among experts in the goodness of the outcome, psychological survival, and reversibility — integration, even if labeled homicide, may well be justified, our concession that alters are persons notwithstanding.

I do not wish to insist that alters are persons, personlike, or fragmentary parts of persons. Quite to the contrary, I view this work, in large part, as an exploration into the status of alter personalities and an exploration of the legal consequences that flow from various possibilities. My purpose in this section is only to answer Wilkes: our intuition that integration is acceptable is not inconsistent with claiming that integration is homicide and that alter personalities are persons. These claims can live comfortably side by side.

Alters are enigmas, and Wilkes's argument does not settle the controversy about their ontological status. I therefore analyze the criminal responsibility of alter personalities under three conceptualizations — that alters are persons, that alters are personlike, and that alters are fragmentary parts of a complex and deeply divided person.

5. One Crime, One Body, Many Personalities

Billy Milligan, accused of a series of rapes and robberies that had plagued Ohio State University, had twenty-three different personalities (ten known at the time of the trial), including a helper personality with an English accent who read and wrote fluent Arabic, a sixteen-year-old escape artist, and an eight-year-old who absorbed all the hurt and suffering of the other personalities. Ragan, "keeper of the hate," was the protector personality who planned the robberies because the "young ones must have clothes for coming vinter [sic] and food to eat." During the robberies, a lesbian personality, Adalana, "stole time," and had sex with the three rape victims. To one she said, "Do you know what it's like to be lonely? . . . Not to be held by anyone for a long time? . . . Not to know the meaning of love?" Following an agreement between the defense and the prosecution, Judge Jay C. Flowers acquitted Milligan by reason of insanity.

Juanita Maxwell was a timid, soft-spoken, kind, and anguished woman in Florida who worked as a maid at a local hotel. One day she loaned her pen to one of the guests, a 73–year-old woman. When Ms. Maxwell went to retrieve the pen, the woman denied borrowing it and slammed the door. Enraged, Wanda emerged, bludgeoned the woman with a lamp, and strangled her to death. When discovered as the perpetrator, Juanita had no memory of the crime. Her attorney put the quiet, timid Juanita on the stand and, after a time, elicited the boisterous, raging Wanda. Judge Hugh Starnes acquitted Maxwell of the crime.

RE MULTIPLES responsible for their crimes?[1] Milligan and Maxwell were exonerated on the basis of their multiple personality disorder. Others have been, and still others are likely to be as well. This chapter will analyze the criminal responsibility of individuals suffering from MPD in light of the three conceptualizations presented in the last chapter: that alters are different people; that alters are different person*like* centers of consciousness; and that alters are *non*personlike parts of one complex person.

CRIMINAL RESPONSIBILITY IF ALTERS ARE PEOPLE

The criminal responsibility of multiples seems straightforward if alter personalities are different people. The alter who committed the crime, if not meeting the legal definition of insanity, is responsible. The other alters, unless complicit in the act, are not.[2] Because we cannot punish the guilty alter without punishing the other, innocent alters, we should find the multiple as a whole nonresponsible.

Holding the multiple nonresponsible raises an important problem: the guilty alter goes unpunished. The dilemma is whether punishing innocent people is worse than not punishing guilty people. Of course, not punishing guilty people does not mean allowing dangerous, violent criminals to roam the streets. We can meet the incapacitative goals of the criminal justice system by means other than punishment, for example, by civilly confining the patient in a psychiatric hospital. While not strictly punishment, confinement in a mental institution may be aversive enough that it serves as a deterrent to criminal behavior, as tort liability serves as a deterrent to tortious behavior.

The question is whether it is permissible to sacrifice retribution in order to spare innocent people. Thoroughgoing retributivists would argue that it is wrong not to punish someone who deserves punishment. Their claim would be either that punishing the offender rights an imbalance, an imbalance that society has a duty to right, or that punishing an offender recognizes his personhood, as if to say "You have chosen to do wrong, and now you must suffer the consequences." Whatever the merits of these arguments, the critical question is whether the guilty person's right to be punished, or society's duty or right to punish the guilty person, is absolute. If these rights and duties are not absolute, then they may yield to other, more compelling rights, such as the right of an innocent person not to be punished.

As a society, we have made a judgment that, in the words of Blackstone, "it is better to let ten guilty persons escape, than that one innocent suffer."[3] The elaborate procedural protections surrounding criminal prosecution depend on this very supposition. The Supreme Court has gone as far as to suggest that "even one day in prison would be a cruel and unusual punishment for the 'crime' of having a common cold."[4] Unless guilty of criminal conduct, one cannot be punished.

Imagine a pair of Siamese twins, one of whom impulsively commits a murder in which the other was in no way complicit. Would we put the twins in prison for the rest of their lives? I think not. If the homicidal twin remained dangerous, we would no doubt confine them in a nonretributive institution to protect the public. But we would not require the innocent twin to spend the rest of his life in jail solely so that we could punish the guilty twin. We would rather the innocent twin be spared prison than the guilty twin be imprisoned.

Blackstone's maxim, as this example illustrates, raises two questions. First, why is it so wrong to punish an innocent person? And second, what happens when we must choose between punishing a guilty person and allowing an innocent person to go free? In regard to the first question, *that* punishing an innocent person is contrary to the law and common sense does not tell us *why* it is so wrong. To understand why it is wrong to punish an innocent person, consider that punishment involves condemnation and stigma, assaults on dignity and liberty, and a wide variety of other deprivations. It therefore inevitably involves suffering. Indeed, punishment can be thought of as the deliberate infliction of suffering on another human being. As such, it requires justification. A necessary, albeit not sufficient, justification for punishment so defined is merit — the person must deserve it. The innocent person has done nothing to merit punishment, and that is why punishing the innocent person provokes outrage in us. At bottom, then, we are left with the values we as a society have chosen, two of which are that only the guilty merit punishment and that it is wrong to punish someone who does not merit punishment.

That punishing an innocent person is wrong is insufficient to answer our second question: What happens when we must choose between punishing an innocent person and allowing a guilty person to go free? How we think about this question depends, once again, upon our values. Behind Blackstone's maxim is the value upon which our entire system of criminal jurisprudence is based — we are more concerned with protecting the innocent than punishing the guilty. Such a statement, predicated upon our core values, cannot be analyzed further.

Another way of thinking about the second question is to put the matter in terms of rights or duties. The guilty person has a right to be punished — a right that protects his dignity as a human person capable of freely choosing between alternatives. The innocent person has a right not to be punished. What happens when these rights clash? My own intuition is that it is more important to spare innocent people pain and stigma than to provide an offender with recognition of his personhood by visiting upon him the consequences of his freely chosen actions. Put another way, we are more concerned with protecting the rights of someone who has freely chosen to obey the rules of society than we are with protecting the rights of someone who has freely chosen *not* to obey the rules of society. If we speak of a duty to right an imbalance in the moral order created by an unjust act, we must consider that by punishing an innocent we create yet another imbalance.

But what about the rights of the victims — or society as a whole — to vent their anger against the wrongdoers? They are as innocent as the innocent alters. Yet even if we accept frank vengeance as a legitimate goal of the criminal justice system, do we think that most people would want to punish a guilty person if that meant punishing an innocent one? How would most people feel about expressing their anger in such a way that it would harm an innocent bystander? Imagine you had to imprison your perpetrator's sister in order to satisfy your anger at him. Most people, I think, would sacrifice the satisfaction of vengeance to shield innocent people from punishment — provided the public were protected.

What would happen if we could never punish guilty people without at the same time punishing innocent ones? Suppose all the world were Siamese twins, in which case we would have to sacrifice all punishment to protect the innocent. Not punishing the guilty in this scenario would mean depriving the guilty of their personhood. Consider, though, the alternative. Every act of punishment would involve punishing an innocent person. Our choice, then, would be between a world of no punishment and a world of massive punishment of innocents. Hard though it may be to imagine such a world, my intuition leads in the direction of sparing the innocents. Note that the goals of the criminal law other than punishment could be visited upon the guilty parties. We might, for example, place dangerous offenders in settings that minimize their capacity to inflict harm upon innocents. This would spare innocents of punishment as well as protect other innocents from harm.

Blackstone was right — it is better to let ten guilty people go free than to punish one who is innocent — but might other theories of criminal responsibility apply? Consider alter personalities under a theory of group liability, which assigns liability simultaneously to more than one individual. Perhaps under such a theory all of the alter personalities could be held criminally responsible for the deeds of one.

The difficulty in applying a theory of group liability to alter personalities is that current theories invariably make reference to some individual culpability by the group members. For instance, in crimes of complicity the aider and abettor must intentionally encourage or aid in the commission of the crime. In conspiracy, there is an intentional agreement to commit a crime, together with acts in furtherance of the agreement. Even in corporate criminal responsibility, where some individual members of the corporation may have no knowledge of what is going on, there is fault either in the form of negligence (the party should have known what was going on) or in the form of having delegated responsibility to the wrongdoers and/or reaping the benefits of their acts. It is precisely such forms of culpability, however, that may be lacking in the case of a multiple — some alters may not even know that other alters exist. If they are aware of other alters, they may have no means of controlling them, and may not benefit from their acts. The psychic structure of individuals suffering from MPD, then, prohibits us from applying a theory of group liability. When alters do act in concert, or are so organized that a group liability theory does make sense, criminal responsibility may be assigned; I discuss these possibilities below.

What about theories of group liability that do not require individual culpability? Older concepts allowed punishment without fault merely on the basis of group membership. The Old Testament is filled with accounts of individuals suffering punishment for the wrongdoing of others: the sins of the fathers shall be visited upon their sons.[5] Notions of collective liability not requiring individual fault persisted in Europe into the nineteenth century. Non-Western cultures provided an even more conducive environment for collective responsibility. Chinese law, for example, historically imposed sanctions on families for individual wrongs, though it varied the severity of sanctions depending upon the proximity of the relationship (Kim 1981). Such theories have generally been abandoned, and their willingness to punish innocent people argues against their being revived.

Consider the matter from another point of view: What if we could find a way of punishing guilty alters that would not involve punishing innocent alters? One could imagine, for example, confining the multiple in a nonretributive institution, while depriving the offending alter of an object or activity especially important to it. Billy Milligan had an alter personality who loved to paint; perhaps we could deny that alter the opportunity to practice its art. We do not know enough about the psychic structure of multiples, however, to be able to punish the guilty alter alone. First, we cannot reliably tell when the guilty alter is "out." Second, we have no means of making the guilty alter stay out to receive its punishment. Indeed, the inadequacy of this solution becomes clear when we realize that, were it workable, we would have a much more just solution at hand: continue to punish via imprisonment but impose imprisonment only when the offending alter is out. That would protect the public without subjecting innocent alters even to confinement-that-is-not-imprisonment. But again, there is no predicting when the offending alter will come or, once out, guaranteeing that he will stay.

What if we could find a way to bring the guilty alter out for the duration of his sentence? Imagine, for example, a pill that tolled the existence of the other alters until the offender had served his term. Would this be a good thing? On the one hand, certainly, yes; we could punish the guilty alter without punishing the innocent ones. On the other hand, no. Administering such a pill would be tantamount to banishing the innocent alters for the term of the sentence — which could, after all, be life. The slightest consideration illustrates that administering such a pill would make no sense as a policy matter. If we could toll the existence of the innocent alters, why would we not much rather toll the existence of the guilty ones? We would then be left with the best the multiple had to offer.

Given that there is no way to bring the guilty alter out solely for the purpose of punishment, perhaps we should consider integrating multiples for the purpose of imprisonment. While healing a multiple for the sake of punishing him may seem like a silly idea, remember that the Supreme Court of the United States has upheld the constitutionality of curing a death row inmate solely for the purpose of killing him. The problem with this analysis, though, is that it equates the integrated person with the guilty one. The integrated person would be as much a different person from the guilty alter as the guilty alter is from the innocent alters. Thus the culpable person would no longer exist, and the new person would not be culpable. To test this intuition, imagine an operation that combined all of your psychological characteristics and memories with those of another. If that other person had committed a murder, would it be just to imprison this new person for the rest of "your" life? I suggest that most would say no.

Putting the possibility of confinement aside for the moment, might there be other ways at our disposal for punishing guilty alters alone? We might, for example, impose a criminal record and/or a fine. Each of these possibilities, however, is problematic. Both criminal stigmatization and imposition of a fine inevitably burden the innocent alters. Often, though, the law permits innocent people to be burdened in order to punish a guilty party. A husband, for example, suffers when his wife is fined. According to the law his suffering is not punishment. Though regrettable, it is legally permissible. Of course, some stigma may attach to the husband when his wife is fined. But it is not the stigma of his punishment.

In the case of MPD, it would be impossible to preserve the distinction between *being punished* and *being burdened* by a punishment.

Indeed, the very nature of the psychopathology undermines maintaining a distinction between the party who is guilty and innocent, yet affiliated, parties. To the outside observer, it can be difficult, if it is even possible, to determine who is who. Stigma attaches to the whole.

As this analysis demonstrates, MPD challenges our usual way of parceling out punishment and stigma. While there does not seem to be an easy or, as I see it, even intuitive resolution to whether fines or convictions would be workable ways of punishing multiples, we can say that they are relevant to very few offenders. Indeed, most offenders who raise a plea of nonresponsibility do so because they face imprisonment or death.

Fines and convictions, thus considered, do not seem to be the answer in our search for ways to punish guilty alters while sparing innocent ones — might we reconsider the possibility of confinement? If we can imprison multiples without punishing their innocent alters, we need not occupy ourselves with devising and evaluating special ways of punishing multiples. Perhaps there is something special about imprisonment — as separate from fines and convictions — that will allow us to preserve the distinction between being punished and being burdened by a punishment. The Supreme Court itself has held that to incarcerate a person, even in a prison, is not necessarily to punish him.[6] And when we imprison a multiple, our punitive intent is directed at the guilty alter, not the innocent ones.

A moment's consideration shows that imprisonment is more, rather than less, likely than fines or conviction to serve as punishment. Indeed, whatever our final theory of punishment, imprisoning an innocent alter to punish a guilty one would constitute punishment. Even the Supreme Court concedes that mere absence of punitive intent will not, solely of itself, vitiate punishment.[7] Thus, if a person (1) is imprisoned following conviction of a crime for the length of time deemed appropriate for the crime; (2) suffers the same detriments that imprisoned convicts suffer; (3) feels punished; and (4) is seen by society as being punished, then it hardly seems deniable that she is indeed being punished.

Perhaps most defining of imprisonment as punishment in this context are society's perception of imprisonment as punishment and a person's experience of being punished. In terms of society's perception, consider the case of a convict who sleeps through his entire imprisonment; call him Rip Van Convict. Society would still see punishment, and so would not countenance imprisoning Rip as a criminal were he innocent, even if we could be assured that he would sleep through his entire term. Equally important is a person's experience of being punished; this experience is what we aim for in the case of the guilty and abhor in the case of the innocent.

When imprisoned, innocent alters are likely to be seen by society as being punished and are likely to feel punished. As with fines and convictions, society will have a hard time keeping innocent and guilty alters separate; all but the most intimate with the multiple, seeing one body in jail, are likely to see one guilty party. Moreover, the vast majority of people imprisoned are being punished, while the vast majority of people suffering financial limitations are not. Thus, society is likelier to see punishment, and the innocent alter is likelier to feel punished; all the accoutrements of punishment surround his confinement.

The Supreme Court's jurisprudence would probably not permit imprisoning innocent alters. The Court has held that, if there is an intent to punish, punishment is found. Absent an intent to punish, the court must consider a multitude of factors:

> Whether the sanction involves an affirmative disability of restraint, whether it has historically been regarded as a punishment, whether it comes into play only on a finding of *scienter*, whether its operation will promote the traditional aims of punishment — retribution and deterrence — whether the behavior to which it applies is already a crime, whether an alternative purpose to which it may rationally be connected is assignable for it, and whether it appears excessive in relation to [that] purpose. (*Kennedy v. Mendoza-Martinez* 1963, 168–69)

Imprisonment of innocent alters counts as punishment by all but the last two of these factors, hands down.

Unfortunately for alters, courts have made the last two factors — whether there is an alternative purpose and whether the punishment appears excessive — the most prominent of the considerations. The first of these requires that there be a purpose other than punishment that is rationally connected to the action taken. There are two reasons for confining an innocent alter: to permit us to punish the guilty alter and to protect the public from the guilty alter. If "rational" is understood in a weak sense, then these reasons are rational. In a stronger sense of "rational," however, they are not: it seems unjustified — and therefore irrational — to so severely burden an innocent person in order to punish a guilty one. It also seems irrational to sentence someone to a term if protecting society is one's concern, insofar as the danger may abate sooner. Thus, whether there is a rational connection depends on how robust we require our concept of rationality to be.

The second consideration asks whether the restriction appears excessive in relation to the purpose invoked. First, in the literal sense, it is excessive to incarcerate one person in order to punish another — an "excess" person here is subjected to "excess" harm. (One might say it is necessary to punish the innocent person to punish the guilty, and so it is not excessive. But one might also say it is not necessary to punish the guilty person, so it is excessive to punish an innocent person.) Second, if the term of a sentence reflects retributive ends, as well as incapacitative concerns, sentences will be "excessive" in relation to the sole purpose of protecting society from danger. Indeed, it is possible to protect society from danger by confining the multiple in a hospital, thereby eschewing punishment altogether. Finally, even if the Supreme Court rejected all of these arguments, that would show only that incarcerating innocent alters would be constitutional, not that it would be right as a matter of morality or policy.

Imprisoning Siamese twins or alters, even if not punishment, is still too injurious for us to countenance. Collateral harms — such as foster care for children — are not avoidable as consequences of another person's imprisonment. (Presumably it would be administratively unworkable to confine all but infants with their parents. If it is workable, the reason we do not confine children with their parents must be that we judge foster care to be the lesser harm.) While "splitting" of this sort in the case of a multiple is obviously impossible — one could not place alters in different, separate settings — it is possible *both* to avoid imprisoning a multiple *and* to protect society. Such is one purpose of mental hospitals. My point is that certain injuries are too severe to inflict on innocent people.

While imprisonment is the typical sanction, most jurisdictions have the death penalty. Those readers who can tolerate the idea of imprisoning innocent alters to punish guilty ones should ask themselves whether they are willing to put innocent alters to death to execute guilty ones. I myself could not.

At this point the reader may balk at the idea that we are punishing an innocent *person* (in the form of an alter) when we imprison or execute a multiple. Or, even if the reader is willing to abide by the assumption behind this section — that alter personalities are persons — she may claim that it matters that these persons do not have bodies. While conceding that we would not imprison or execute an innocent Siamese twin or an innocent person solely in order to imprison or execute another person, such a reader will counter that innocent twins or other people have their own bodies, while alters do not.

Such an objection is not really an argument. It fails to explain why having a body is relevant to whether punishing innocent people is permissible. While such a reader may point out that there are more bodies suffering when Siamese twins (as opposed to alters) are punished, the fact is that bodies do not suffer; their inhabitants (their minds) do. And in the case of alters, there are at least as many, if not more, minds at issue than in the other cases. Nor could it be claimed that alters suffer seriatim while Siamese twins or separate people suffer simultaneously; alters, some of which are coconscious, can suffer all at the same time as well.

Such a reader, if persistent, may object yet again by pointing to the public's perception. The public, she might say, sees double punishment when Siamese twins are incarcerated. We are more likely to consider this to be punishment, she will point out, because the punishment of both people is visibly in front of us. It may be countered, however, that her point gets things exactly backward. If one of the twins is innocent, the public is likely to be sympathetic toward that twin. The public is likely to see punishment of the whole when the multiple is imprisoned. Because the innocent alters are likely hidden from the public's eye, they are even more likely to suffer punishment.

To close this discussion of multiples' criminal responsibility if alters are persons, I wish to return briefly to the issue of the last chapter, where we struggled with defining personal identity. While not adopting any standard, we found the psychological criterion compelling. Our discussion was perhaps somewhat incomplete, insofar as we failed to ask "a person *for what purpose?*" Phrasing the question in this manner invites us to adopt a functional approach to personhood. Such an approach defines a person, at least in part, in relation to a given end. What constitutes a person for the criminal law, for example, may be different than what constitutes a person in certain civil contexts. This makes sense; as the criminal law and civil law serve different ends, so different constituents of personhood may be entirely, or not at all, relevant in a given context.

Consider an example of the functional approach to personhood. One goal of polygamy laws, which prohibit people (usually men) from marrying more than one person, may be population control. We would not count alters as separate people in light of this purpose because, no matter how many alters constituted a given multiple, the multiple would have only one body, and so could procreate no more than any nonmultiple could. Put in other words, saying that alters are not separate people would leave our efforts to control the population unfettered. Another purpose of polygamy laws, however, may be to foster commitments between two people and to nurture the well-being that such commitments bring. Because alters can be quite jealous of, and even destructive toward, one another, this purpose *is* thwarted if we do not count alters as separate people. That is to say, allowing multiples to marry might well defeat this purpose of polygamy laws, since it would promote the very strife which the laws were intended to discourage. We can see, then, that how we define personhood may depend upon the purpose which our definition serves.

If, in our attempt to define "personhood," we were to adopt a functional approach, the psychological criterion of personal identity would make the most sense in the context of the criminal law. To determine criminality, we look to a person's mental state. That is to say, the criminal law cares about persons as psychological beings, not as bodies. Persons as psychological beings entertain criminal purposes, intend criminal acts, and choose to respond or not to respond to the threat of sanctions. Bodies are not irrelevant — we need bodies to enact criminal purposes. But imagine a person who could communicate through some nonembodied means. If he commanded someone else to commit a murder, we would not be disposed to find him innocent simply because he lacked a body.

Do psychological continuity and connectedness — deemed central to personal identity in our earlier discussion — play an important role for the criminal law? Clearly. Continuity of personality traits — what we call "character" — is important because it is in virtue of character that a person is who she is. It is this person — the person with this character — who is dangerous and bad. It is the person of this character whom we fear. Continuity of memory is important because it helps constitute character. Memory shapes both the actor's self-concept and her nature: who Jane is, in large part, is what Jane remembers of her life and times. Memory also connects the criminal to her past act. She can truly own the act as *her* act only if she has memory for it. And she can truly experience some past person as herself only if she feels connected to that person in her memory.

Memory and personality play a central role for the criminal law not only because they are integral to our concept of personhood; they are integral to our moral intuitions as well. Consider a person who is utterly discontinuous psychologically from the person who committed some harm. In such a case, retribution seems wholly inapposite. Some may persist in wanting to punish such a person but only because there is no other candidate; recall our analysis of Williams's two stories. When there is another candidate — when there is a choice — we will, I think, want to punish the person who is psychologically, not physically, continuous with the offender. Consider again Locke's puzzle of the Cobbler and the Prince. If the Cobbler had murdered someone, would we want to punish the Prince-bodied person or the Cobbler-bodied person? The public would no doubt raise an outcry if the Prince-bodied person were to be hanged, but that is because this was their dear Prince's body. We normally identify people with their bodies because bodily continuity is a good — usually our best — proxy for psychological continuity and connectedness. Yet once the public saw the Cobbler-bodied person act in a princely manner and heard him recount experiences that only the Prince could have had, and once they saw in the Prince-bodied person a coarse, vicious man with no regard for human life, I suggest they would want to see the Prince-bodied person, if anyone, hanged.

This thought experiment does more than show that our intuitions favor a psychological criterion of personal identity. It also shows that our intuitions favor blaming the psychological being — the being with the thoughts, intentions, and malice of the murderer. Common sense clings to the idea that the body is the best marker of these — only, though, until shown otherwise. When we see that the Prince-bodied person has the objectionable thoughts, intentions, and malice, it is he whom we want to punish. In short, persons are psychological beings for purposes of the criminal law. Mens rea is just that — a guilty *mind*. Criminal law can rationally take no other position.

As Parfit sees it, psychological continuity and connectedness (R-relatedness), rather than personal identity, are what matters. Psychological continuity and connectedness are also, as we have just seen, what matters for blame and punishment. Alters, however, are not psychologically continuous or connected with each other. Thus, if we so choose, we could dispense with talk of different persons and make the very same argument for the nonresponsibility of multiples based upon the weak R-relatedness of the alter personalities.

This section has discussed the responsibility of multiples under the assumption that alter personalities are persons. We have concluded that, given this assumption, multiples should be held nonresponsible for their crimes. We have held to this assumption even though separate alter personalities do not have separate bodies. As we discussed earlier, however, there are two reasons that the law might prefer a bodily concept of personhood: first, identifying persons psychologically might be too administratively inconvenient; second, a psychological concept of personhood might be too hard to square with common intuitions. The first problem remains for the criminal law: if it is too hard to identify persons on psychological grounds generally, it is too hard to do in the criminal law context. The second problem may not remain. Even if it found the notion of a person without a body incredible, the public may nevertheless accept the proposition that bodies are not particularly important to the concerns of the criminal law. Thus, for the purposes of the criminal law, we could adopt a psychological concept of personhood.

Fortunately, we need not make a definitive choice between a psychological or a bodily concept of personhood. Nor need we definitively choose between a theory which states that a single concept of personhood must apply to each and every legal circumstance or a theory which holds that our definition of personhood might depend, at least in part, on the particular legal context. The salient point at present is that, for the criminal law, it is psychological characteristics that are important, even if we insist that persons must have bodies.

What if we decide that alter personalities are not actual persons but have important characteristics of personhood? That is to say, are multiples criminally responsible if their alters are different person*like* centers of consciousness? It is to this question we now turn.

CRIMINAL RESPONSIBILITY IF ALTERS ARE PERSONLIKE CENTERS OF CONSCIOUSNESS

One way of thinking says that, if alters are personlike centers of consciousness, multiples are not responsible for their crimes; if alters are like persons, they should be treated like persons. The same arguments of the last section would apply; we do not punish an innocent person for the crimes of a guilty person. Since it is not possible to punish a guilty alter without punishing innocent alters as well, multiples should be held nonresponsible for their crimes.

Some will object that if the alter who committed the crime is not judged insane, he is responsible. It follows, they conclude, that the multiple is responsible. In fact, carefully thinking through the protasis of this clause leads to exactly the opposite conclusion. If the offending alter is considered a responsible agent, it follows that there may very well be nonoffending — innocent — agents in the multiple. Thus, by arguing that the offending alter ought to be considered an agent, and ought to be judged sane or insane, as well as guilty or not guilty, people holding this view must also be open to the presence of alters who are likewise agents and who are both sane and innocent. Because innocent agents should not be punished, the multiple should be held nonresponsible. Thus the assumption upon which this argument is based leads to precisely the opposite of the conclusion often reached.

Our first argument, then, is short, sweet, and to the point: if it walks like a duck (or a person) and talks like a duck (or a person), treat it like a duck (or a person). While compelling, this way of thinking about alter personalities begs an important question: What precisely is it that alters share with people so that, in the eyes of the criminal law, they should be treated like people?

Perhaps we should start by turning the question on its head: What is it about a person that matters to the criminal law? In a phrase, what matters in the eyes of the criminal law is whether a person — or a personlike entity — is a fit subject for punishment. What do we mean by this? Fitness for punishment means that, in the eyes of the criminal law, an entity, under certain circumstances set forth by the law, is subject to criminal sanctions. An entity that is an appropriate object of punishment may, however, deserve not to be punished — when it is innocent. Thus the criminal law concerns itself with guilt and innocence.

What characterizes fitness for punishment? Certainly, fitness for punishment can only be found where there is the capacity to commit a crime — the capacity for guilt or innocence; it makes no sense to punish an entity that cannot be guilty or innocent. Fitness for punishment also implies the capacity to be punished — the capacity to understand, or appreciate, the punishment. That is to say, if one lacks the capacity to understand why one is being punished, or that one is being punished, fitness for punishment is absent. Fitness for punishment therefore implies an array of conditions and capacities.

How do we determine whether an entity possesses fitness for punishment? Our whole criminal law rests on the premise that persons generally possess such fitness. What, though, about entities that may not be people? How are we to assess their fitness for punishment? As a starting point, let us consider whether Dennett's six criteria help: (1) persons are rational; (2) they are subjects of Intentional predicates; (3) a certain stance or attitude must be taken toward them — they are moral objects; (4) they can reciprocate when such a stance is taken — they are moral agents; (5) they are language users; and (6) they have a special kind of consciousness, perhaps self-consciousness.

Does an entity that can be considered a person or personlike under Dennett's criteria possess the capacities implied by fitness for punishment: the capacity to be guilty or innocent of a crime, and the capacity to appreciate one's punishment? Let us start with the capacity to be guilty or innocent: which of Dennett's six criteria help us here? First, only rational agents can commit crimes; that is the lesson of the insanity test. Second, only a subject of Intentional predicates has the capacity to commit a crime; that is, the being must be able to intend, to wish, to plan, and so forth — no Intentional predicates means, by definition, no mens rea. Dennett's third condition, that persons are moral objects, is more relevant to the capacity to be punished than the capacity to commit a crime. His fourth, moral agency, strikes at the heart of the capacity to commit a crime. Fifth, being a language user seems not terribly relevant, except insofar as it is necessary for rationality or one's being subject to Intentional predicates. Dennett's sixth criterion, self-consciousness, is unarguably a sine qua non of the capacity to commit a crime. Indeed, if one lacks the capacity to identify one's acts as precisely that — one's own acts — one is thoroughly disabled from taking a critical stance toward one's choices, nor can one accept responsibility for taking a given course of action.

Now let us turn to an entity's capacity to be punished. What do Dennett's six criteria say in this regard? First, only a rational entity could perceive the connection between its crime and the punishment; thus rationality seems a prerequisite for this capacity. Second, only a subject of Intentional predicates could be attributed an aversive state; put in other words, to receive punishment there must be a subject that can feel, perceive, or experience that punishment as its own. Third, punishment implies an object of a particular sort — a *moral* object — because to punish is to impose suffering on the basis of moral blame, and only moral objects can suffer punishment so defined. Indeed, it is because the object of punishment is a moral object that we must always be concerned that punishment is justified. Fourth, entity as moral agent seems a complement to entity as moral object; only when an entity is a moral agent would we think to punish it. Fifth, the use of language seems not directly relevant, except to the extent that language is necessary for rationality or being the subject of Intentional predicates. Finally, self-consciousness once again proves the most basic characteristic. Only a self-conscious entity appreciates that *it* is being punished, and no one or nothing else. Conversely, a self-conscious entity suffers when wrongly punished, for it carries the sense that an unjust punishment is being imposed upon *it*.

Dennett's criteria thus speak directly to the two capacities embedded in our notion of fitness for punishment — the capacity for guilt or innocence, and the capacity to receive punishment. Indeed, we found that fitness for punishment requires most, if not all, of Dennett's criteria. In fact, a moment's reflection shows that these six criteria — as they serve as six criteria that establish personhood or a state like personhood — can also serve as criteria for determining fitness for punishment. To say more, while it is not clear that all six are required for fitness for punishment, if all six are present, as they generally are in a person, fitness for punishment is clearly present as well.

Do alter personalities have this characteristic that we have termed "fitness for punishment"? Our analysis seems clear: if alters fit Dennett's six criteria, then they do possess this fitness. We concluded in our earlier discussion that alters meet at least four of the six: they are rational; they are the subject of Intentional predicates; they are language users; and they are self-conscious. Can they be thought of as moral objects and moral agents? In one way, that is precisely the question this book is attempting to answer.

Where do we go from here? Four considerations lead us to a tentative conclusion that alters, like persons, possess fitness for punishment. First, we know of no other rational, self-conscious language user who is the subject of Intentional predicates who is *not* a moral object and a moral agent. That is not to say, of course, that none may exist; it is simply to say that experience leads us strongly to believe that where the former four qualities are found, the latter two will be found as well.

Second, our discussion in the last chapter provided a number of reasons for thinking that alters are both moral objects and moral agents. Third, being a moral agent really tells us the least of any criterion about fitness for punishment. Why? A moral agent, by definition, has the capacity for guilt and innocence; one who has the capacity for guilt and innocence is, by definition, a moral agent. The four criteria which we know alters possess are the real pay dirt; to say that an entity is a moral agent is simply to say, in other terms, that it has the capacity for guilt and innocence. Fourth, and finally, there are criteria for personhood other than Dennett's six which alters possess and which seem to speak directly to fitness for punishment. Continuity of memory, for instance, seems a characteristic of persons and personlike entities, and is also an important constituent of punishment. It is difficult to imagine, for example, punishing an entity that would have no memory of the deeds for which it was being punished, or indeed any recollection of the punishment as soon as it ceased. Punishment may fail to be significant — it may fail even to be punishment — if one forgets it even as it is occurring. To sum up, every argument is in favor of considering alters fit for punishment.

What implications does our conclusion that alters possess fitness for punishment have for the criminal law? At first glance, the answer seems clear: alters have the same status as persons. If guilty, they should pay the consequences for their actions; if deemed not guilty, they should be treated as any other innocent person. Put simply, it is as wrong to punish an innocent entity that possesses fitness for punishment as it is to punish an innocent person.

This argument can be developed further: entities that are fit for punishment have a greater claim than all other entities not to be punished if innocent. There are at least two reasons for this. First, entities that lack capacity for criminality are not truly *innocent* of crime — they are capable of neither guilt nor innocence; if they have not committed a criminal act, their "innocence," so to speak, is a matter of accident. An entity that is fit for punishment, by contrast, is innocent by choice; she has chosen to avoid doing wrong. As such, punishing her — implying that she has done wrong — is a greater insult. Her righteous indignation at her punishment is more understandable, inasmuch as she merits praise for her intentional choice to do right (unlike the accidentally virtuous) — and what she gets is punishment.

Second, it is worse to punish alters than other "innocent" entities because alters have the capacity to be punished. When someone has capacity to be punished, punishing him unjustly causes him more suffering than punishing unjustly an entity that does not have capacity to be punished. To take the extreme case, a nonsentient being — like a rock — does not suffer from punishment. Less extremely, a being that lacks self-consciousness does not appreciate that *he* is being harmed when he is punished; even though he may feel aversive sensations, he does not connect them to himself conceptually.

Still further up the scale, an irrational being may be unable to grasp the concept of punishment, and so may not realize that he is being harmed as a result of people's anger at him for his wrongdoing. Without a concept of punishment, a being who is unjustly punished may not suffer from punishment and the pain of punishment. Now in a sense it is worse to feel unjustly punished than simply harmed. When an infliction of harm is understood to be punishment — and not just simple harm — the person being punished suffers shame and humiliation as well as pain. In addition, he suffers from knowing that the one inflicting the punishment feels justified — even righteous — in his infliction of suffering. Punishing an innocent entity that possesses fitness for punishment is therefore as severe a harm as one can suffer from unjust punishment. Moreover, other "innocent" entities do not suffer as much from unjust punishment (if that is what their aversive treatment should be called) — although they may suffer some, so that action against them may still require justification.

Consider the following objection: is it not wrong to punish innocent parts of people — innocent hands, feet, torsos — just as it is wrong to punish innocent alters? The answer is clear: such parts of people do not meet any, much less all, of Dennett's criteria. They are not, for example, rational, nor are they self-conscious, nor do they use language, nor can they be said to be the subject of Intentional predicates. As such, they do not possess fitness for punishment. And because they are not truly capable of innocence, and do not suffer from punishment in the peculiar way that entities capable of being punished do, punishing them is not a serious wrong.

What about a harder case, which may seem much closer to that of an alter: can we judge the guilt or innocence of psychological aspects of people, such as a generous part, a kind part, and so forth? The same analysis appropriate to physical parts of people applies. Such psychological parts, because they meet none of Dennett's six criteria, lack fitness for punishment. If we are tempted to attribute rationality and self-consciousness to the generous part of a person, we must be as clear as we can be about what we mean. There is no "part" that is generous or greedy, but simply a person acting in a generous or a greedy *manner.* Because the generous *person* — if she commits a crime — is *not* innocent, it is perfectly just to punish her; our problem dissolves. That is, to the extent that we are talking about a part, punishment is permissible, because a part lacks all fitness for punishment and so cannot be "punished." To the extent that we are talking about a *person,* it is just to punish her, because she is not innocent. Alters, as entities that possess fitness for punishment, ought not to be punished when innocent.

While we are not inclined to punish the Cobbler-bodied person for the Cobbler's past acts when the Cobbler's body houses the *Prince,* suppose we were dealing not with totally different persons who have exchanged bodies but with a different personlike entity overtaking a person's body and committing a crime. If that personlike entity departed, would we then punish the person whose body was implicated in the act? Pete, a wonderful person — conscientious, kind, funny, sensitive, warm, empathic — would never harm a flea. Everyone who knows him is crazy about him. One day an evil scientist slips a drug into Pete's diet cola, and Pete is transformed into someone mean and vicious for an hour — call this character Paul. Paul is crossed by someone and, consistent with his character, kills the person. The drug wears off and Pete returns, only to find himself in jail charged with murder.

Do we want to punish Pete for Paul's crime, even if we assume that Paul is not a different person from Pete but is just Pete transformed? We might insist that Paul *is* a different person from Pete, and so, while Paul is guilty of murder, Pete is not. But we might feel that, since Paul shares a body with Pete, he is not a different person, and was too short-lived to be a person anyway. That is the theory of this section; different people have different bodies, but the same body may house different person*like* entities.

Even given the assumption of this section — that Paul is not a different person from Pete — I nevertheless suggest that Pete ought not to be punished for Paul's crime. One might immediately object: who other than Pete would we punish for this murder? Certainly, our objector may concede, Pete's transformation into Paul is a sort of illness. But illness as a cause of crime is a defense in a single jurisdiction. Nor is it shown how this illness caused some impairment that had an impact on the commission of the crime. Continuing, the objector may likewise concede that giving someone a different character may make it harder for him not to offend. But come on — many individuals who commit crimes have upbringings that produce a character making it nearly impossible for them not to offend, but no one would take that as an excuse. Our objector, savvy fellow that he is, would make yet a third concession — that if the character compelled the act, there would be a defense. He would point out, though, that conceding the presence of a compulsion is an easy case, which answers nothing — Paul committed the murder of his own free will, under no such compulsion. Thus, our friendly objector concludes, Pete should be held guilty of the murder.

While our objector's points are indeed persuasive, our intuitions will leave us troubled — do we really think that Pete should be held guilty of murder under these circumstances? Even though perhaps difficult to put into words, something about our sense of justice says no. Elsewhere I have attempted to explain such intuitions by invoking the character-based theory of the excuses: to be guilty of a crime, an act must reflect on one's character. Paul's act does not reflect on Pete's character; Paul's act is exactly what Pete would not have done. The character-based theory, however, has been significantly challenged and has not come to be widely accepted.

Nor does it seem necessary to invoke this theory in order to explain our intuition, which is perhaps best understood by saying simply that one should not be punished for the acts of another person*like* entity any more than one should be punished for the acts of another person. This leads us directly to the case of MPD. Indeed, the only important difference between alter personalities as personlike entities and truly different people is that people have their own bodies, while alter personalities do not. Pete is clearly capable of guilt and innocence, and was wholly innocent of the murder committed by Paul. A self-conscious being, Pete will also suffer gravely from the punishment the law imposes; he will be aware, for instance, that he is suffering harm for what society perceives as *his* wrongdoing. Our intuition leads us to directly the opposite conclusion than that of the objector: Pete should not suffer for Paul's act any more than the Prince for the Cobbler's. Person*like*-hood — even in the absence of a body — is an adequate repository for guilt and innocence, as much so as if Paul were a different person from Pete. The criminal law should act accordingly.

The theory presented — that personlike entities ought to be judged guilty or innocent in the same way as persons are — will raise at least three objections. The first is that only a person can be held guilty or innocent, and that the criminal law should not concern itself with personlike entities. The second objection is that alter personalities are held together by an underlying unity, in virtue of which unity the whole — all of the alters — should be held guilty or innocent. The third objection, which takes the second objection one step further, is that even if alters should be conceptualized as personlike entities, multiples are nevertheless one *person*. It is that one person, according to this objection, who should be held responsible, regardless of how deeply divided he or she may be.

The first objection ignores the thrust of this section: that it is unfair to blame and punish one personlike entity for the acts of another. One may counter that only entities possessing bodies ought properly to be judged guilty or not guilty of a crime or, alternatively, that for administrative convenience we should draw the line at the acts of a different person, not just a different personlike entity. That bodies should be *the* touchstone for criminal guilt or innocence, however, seems rather trite. Consider the accessory before the fact who commands a brutal murder; his act could be so minimal as to utter a few words, give a nod, or wink an eye. If we imagined an accessory before the fact who could communicate his wishes without any bodily movement, we could have unadulterated guilt without a body. Of course, alters can communicate to each other without talking out loud, and so can be complicit in crime without being in control of any body. About the only reason a body might be important is that it makes counting people easier; but then the first argument reduces to the second: we should talk about people, and not person*like* entities, for administrative convenience. This too seems rather weak. Alters are fairly easy to distinguish from each other when they so desire. It is also fairly easy to distinguish personlike entities from fragments. More importantly, there are, relatively speaking, so few multiples in the world, let alone criminal multiples, that the administrative burdens of using a standard referring to personlike entities would be small indeed.

The second objection is that the unity underlying the alters justifies finding the whole responsible. Earlier I discussed the suggestion that we punish the innocent foot for the act of the hand, or the innocent generous part for the act of the mean part. Now the claim is that, because there is a unity connecting the foot to the hand, and the generous to the mean part, the foot and the generous part are derivatively guilty. It is then permissible to punish ordinary parts — not despite their innocence but because of their guilt.

The unity of the body, however, seems a flimsy basis on which to punish parts of the body — if it even makes sense to speak of doing so. It is the unity of the person that permits us to punish parts of the person. Moreover, the unity that underlies different alter personalities does not seem robust; it is not like the unity of a person. Indeed, what characterizes MPD as a psychopathology is precisely the *fragmentation* of the different personalities. Alter personalities are distinct enough that one alter may not be aware that another alter even exists, much less be aware of its specific plans and deeds. For a personlike agent to be guilty of the misdeeds of another simply because they are united by a body would be like saying everyone who works in a particular building is guilty of one worker's crimes just because they are working under the same roof. The second argument, like the first, is not compelling.

The third objection is that, even if multiples house different personlike entities, they are also one person, and we can hold that person guilty of the criminal act, regardless of the other personlike entities within. This argument, however, seems foreclosed by earlier arguments. If one accepts that it is not permissible to punish one person or personlike entity for the crimes of another, it would seem not to matter much whether the "guilty person" is an alter or the multiple as a whole. In both cases there is an entity that is guilty and deserves punishment. In both cases there is also an entity that is innocent. Because of this innocence, it is unjust to punish that entity — an injustice exacerbated by the fact that the entity, as self-conscious, would suffer from punishment as fully as any person would.

Perhaps, though, there is a difference when the guilty person is constituted by the innocent personlike agencies, as opposed to when he simply coexists with them. Imagine a house whose walls were constituted by tiny little houses. We could still judge the house as a whole as, say, handsome, without thereby passing judgment on the constituent houses; maybe each is dreadfully ugly. Could we, in the same way, judge the multiple as a whole guilty — and punish her — without thereby passing judgment on her constituent parts, namely, her alters? The problem with this way of treating multiples is that it is *not* possible to punish the multiple as a whole without punishing her alters; the analogy with the house fails at this crucial point. Moreover, while we may be able to see the house as a whole without seeing the constituent houses, we cannot see the multiple as a whole without seeing her alters. It is only because one of her alters acted wrongly that the multiple is guilty — she cannot act apart from them. And whether we speak of the guilty alter or the guilty multiple as a whole, there remain innocent alters who will have to suffer punishment if the whole is punished.

Implicit in this discussion is a question whether we should see the multiple as one person. I will consider this issue more closely in the next section. It is especially problematic to consider multiples as one whole person on the view that their alters are persons or person*like*. At the very least, a multiple is a special kind of person made up of personlike entities. Unlike the house, there seems no one whole whose contours can be sketched, but simply a being who is now one of its parts, now another. This one person is so divided that we cannot predict her states or behavior; she does not seem a *single* Intentional system. Thus, the premise of this third and final objection — that multiples as a whole are one person who can be held guilty — fails.

There seems no compelling counterargument against the view that if multiples consist of personlike centers of consciousness, they should be found nonresponsible for their crimes. Some alter personalities will be innocent, and it is not permissible to punish an innocent personlike entity for the crimes of its brethren. Punishing an alter is worse than punishing ordinary parts of people precisely *because* alters are personlike: they are capable of guilt and innocence and capable of fully experiencing their punishment as such. We saw in the last section that being embodied does not seem important for personhood for purposes of criminal responsibility. If administrative convenience or some other reason counsels us to say it is, we come to see that personhood itself is not important for purposes of criminal responsibility; person*like*-hood is. Multiples, then, are generally nonresponsible on the view that their alters are personlike. In the next section we consider what follows if alters are *non*personlike parts of one deeply divided person.

CRIMINAL RESPONSIBILITY IF ALTERS ARE NONPERSONLIKE PARTS OF ONE DEEPLY DIVIDED PERSON

Thus far we have discussed the impermissibility of punishing innocent persons or personlike parts of multiples. Our position is that while an alter could be both sane and guilty, it is impossible to punish that alter without punishing innocent alters as well. Because it is wrong to punish innocent alters, whether they be persons or personlike, multiples should be considered nonresponsible for their criminal acts.

How do we assess the criminal responsibility of multiples if alters are neither persons nor personlike — if, that is, they are *non*personlike entities?[8] As an initial approach to this problem, consider reflexes, sleepwalking, hypnosis, and posthypnotic suggestion, phenomena sometimes grouped together — although incidentally so for our purposes — under the rubric of involuntariness.[9] What do these phenomena have in common that recommends grouping them together as a basis for a finding of nonresponsibility?

Commentators have searched for a principle to explain the underlying unity of these phenomena,[10] yet none of their suggestions has been entirely satisfactory. Some commentators look to the absence of consciousness, and cite sleepwalking as an example. Because a person under posthypnotic suggestion, or exhibiting reflex movements, however, is not unconscious, this suggestion must be modified to include "absence of consciousness or conscious control," and so seems somewhat ad hoc. Other commentators suggest that these phenomena all involve a lack of will or volition, so that acts performed in such states are not voluntary acts. As others have pointed out, however, it is impossible to determine when an act is an "act of will." We could not know, for example, whether an act performed under posthypnotic suggestion is accompanied by volition. That volition accompanies an act is simply a conclusion we assert when we wish to say that an act is voluntary — as if to say "voluntary acts are volitional, and volitional acts are voluntary."

Other commentators eschew talk of volition altogether and speak instead of ordinary effort or determination accompanying an act. Thus the Model Penal Code has a catchall category of involuntariness, under which an act lacking effort or determination is involuntary. While "effort" seems somewhat more accessible than "volition," whether and when we shall find "effort" accompanying an act seems equally problematic. Acts in response to posthypnotic suggestion, for example, involve effort, yet most commentators call these acts involuntary. If we simply deny that such acts involve effort, we again make the words mean whatever we want: "Involuntary acts are not the result of effort, and acts not the result of effort are involuntary." Still other commentators have proposed that involuntary actions, such as kicking one's foot in response to a tap on the knee, are actions over which the agent lacks control. Such a position, however, is likewise problematic, for a number of reasons. How do we know that control is lacking in all the cases classically cited as involuntary? When sleepwalking Mrs. Cogdon struck two swift blows with an ax to the head of her daughter, her acts seemed quite well controlled. They may not have been controlled by her ordinary conscious state, but they were certainly controlled — to deny that is again to draw conclusions to suit our theories.

While yet other commentators have attempted to organize "involuntary" phenomena under one principle or another, I want to point out one striking feature shared by these and other phenomena deemed involuntary by the law: all involve dissociation. Sleepwalking, hypnosis, and posthypnotic suggestion are classic cases of dissociative phenomena, in which there is a "disruption in the usually integrated functions of consciousness, memory, identity, or perception of the environment" (APA 1994, 477). In sleepwalking and hypnosis, there is an altered state of consciousness that maintains control over motor behavior; ordinary waking consciousness is "dissociated" or divorced from the behavior. In posthypnotic suggestion, a split-off bit of consciousness (or unconsciousness) is responsible for the behavior; there is another center of control. Reflex actions are not often cited as cases of dissociative phenomena, yet they seem to fall in that category as well. The person is in a state of ordinary waking consciousness, but his behavior is not integrated with his conscious state — there is a center of control outside his consciousness. The kicking of the foot is not the *person's* act. Other instances of involuntary behavior, such as temporal lobe epilepsy — or even a swarm of bees' making one's limbs go wild — are also dissociative in this way.

What is it about dissociative phenomena that should lead to a finding of involuntariness and consequent exoneration? In dissociative phenomena there is no single center of consciousness overseeing and controlling behavior. How would this understanding apply to multiples? If the dissociative phenomena discussed here — sleepwalking, reflexes, hypnosis, and posthypnotic suggestion — are counted as involuntary, then the behavior of a multiple must be involuntary as well. Why? Because when a multiple acts, there are entire centers of consciousness that do not participate — are not even aware that "she" is acting. While the multiple, unlike the sleepwalker, is conscious when she acts, the person acting under posthypnotic suggestion and the person performing reflex movements are conscious when they act. Like the person acting under posthypnotic suggestion or in the midst of a reflexive reaction, the alters who are not "out" are not performing the behavior; another center of consciousness is.

As an example of one's ordinary, waking consciousness not being in control of behavior, consider the person who, under posthypnotic suggestion, twirls around three times on her desk when she hears the word "umbrella." If asked, she will come up with an explanation for her behavior. Here we have someone who is aware of what she is doing and believes she knows why she is doing what she is doing — whom we nevertheless deem to be acting involuntarily and whom we would hold nonresponsible for her behavior. All the more reason for holding nonresponsible someone who has aspects of herself that are unaware of her actions and do not know why she is behaving in a particular manner — to wit, the multiple.

Having concluded that multiples should be held nonresponsible if other individuals, acting in "involuntary" ways, are held nonresponsible, we are left with a question: Why *should* dissociated consciousness vitiate responsibility? At least three theories support a finding of nonresponsibility on the basis of dissociated consciousness. The first holds that there is a center of consciousness that did not do wrong and hence does not deserve to suffer. Take the case of the sleepwalker. While the normal, waking self is submerged when the sleepwalker acts, the "sleeping self" acts with knowledge and intent; the acts of the latter are too complicated to be simple reflexes and too goal-directed to be simple motions. Our reason for excusing the sleepwalker is not that no "mind" governs his action but that his ordinary, waking self does not. Traditional sleepwalking doctrine aims to protect the normal waking self from the acts of the sleeping self — as one court put it, Mrs. Cogdon's act while sleepwalking was not "her" act. This first theory for a finding of nonresponsibility on the basis of dissociated consciousness is most robust when the "self" to be protected is a self with a modicum of integrity, such as the normal, waking self in the case of the sleepwalker. A person, or personlike agency — as alters were defined in the previous two sections — would also constitute such a self.

The second theory that supports a finding of nonresponsibility on the basis of dissociated consciousness holds that, when consciousness is dissociated, there are significant parts of the self that cannot be brought to bear on the act. If a person lacks unity and continuity of mind, significant parts of herself cannot participate in the decision to act or not act. Consider again the sleepwalking cases. The person as a whole, if she suffers distinct gaps in knowledge, cannot be said to "know" what she is doing sufficiently so that she should be held responsible for her act — large parts of herself are not involved in the decision to act. The blackout cases provide another example — because of distinct, and discrete, gaps in knowledge, the person cannot bring enough of herself to bear on an act for that act to be considered responsible. The same theory is also operative in hypnotic and posthypnotic suggestion: dissociated parts of the person acted, while the rest of person was not at all involved.

Robert Schopp (1991) has formalized this second theory in his recent book on insanity and automatism. Incorporating his language, we can say that, in cases of dissociation, acts are not a product of the actor's wants and beliefs, or are not produced by his comprehensive set of wants and beliefs in the manner characteristic of ordinary human action. Such an actor has reasons for his acts, but they are not available to play their appropriate causal role *as* reasons. Hence we do not appropriately attribute the act to the actor in his capacity as a practical reasoner.

Several reasons argue for deeming nonresponsible acts in which significant parts of the personality do not participate. Parts of the person that were disabled from participating may have been precisely the parts that were best equipped to pass judgment on and control the act. Moreover, as I suggested in an earlier work, if significant parts of the person are not involved in the act, perhaps the person *as a whole* cannot be said to know what he is doing — and if one does not know what one is doing, one cannot be faulted for doing it. Finally, if significant parts of the actor's personality do not participate in his act, a small and nonrepresentative portion of his wants and beliefs cause the act, so that we cannot attribute the act to *him*. Once again, we return to the court's claim in the case of Mrs. Cogdon: the murder was not "her" act.

The third theory that supports a finding of nonresponsibility on the basis of dissociated consciousness holds that criminal responsibility requires the acting self to be integrated. Because there is no "executive" standing back and choosing the course of action when consciousness is dissociated, actors in such cases should be held nonresponsible. Note that, while this third theory is closely related to the second, it is distinct: the second theory holds that individuals with dissociated consciousness cannot bring all of themselves to bear on deciding whether to act; the third theory holds that such individuals lack an integrated, cohesive self that determines whether or not to act. Consider the case of posthypnotic suggestion or sleepwalking under the third theory: the executive that does exist does not have access to the variables motivating the action. There is no unified self. In the case of the multiple, there is no executive to act — just a series of split-off centers of consciousness, each performing its own acts, based on its own wishes and beliefs, divorced from the concerns and issues of the others. That is the sense in which there is no unified self in the case of the multiple; there is no overarching executive. The reason an executive is important is so that a true choice can be made based on the person's competing wishes and beliefs.

The need for a unified self to hear and decide among competing wishes and beliefs is related to Frankfurt's (1971) notion that an entity must have second-order beliefs and desires about its first-order beliefs and desires in order to be considered a responsible agent. The idea behind Frankfurt's claim is that only from second-order beliefs and desires can an agent evaluate and choose among its first-order beliefs and desires. I would add to Frankfurt that there must be a unified agent that has access to the relevant wishes and desires; if the agent is not unified, it cannot compare the different sets of conflicting wishes and desires with each other.

I do not want to suggest that the executive has to be single — just unified. There can be group leadership, as long as there is *some* leadership. Imagine a business group that has become chaotic in its organization: there are no senior decision makers, no lines of authority, no delegation of tasks, no role assignments. The individual members of the group may still act individually, but can we in any meaningful sense attribute those acts to the group as a whole? If one of the members commits a crime, do we punish the whole? Without some central decision-making authority — even if the only decision is to delegate decision making — this group lacks cohesion as *a group,* and it would be unfair to punish it as a group. Indeed, in some sense it has ceased to be a group at all.

Our second and third theories for finding nonresponsibility on the basis of dissociated consciousness, while closely related, thus focus on different aspects of the dissociation. The problem with dissociated consciousness at the heart of the second theory is that these wishes and beliefs are not aired — do not receive a hearing. The problem with dissociated consciousness at the heart of the third theory is that there is no integrated, unified self to "hear" and decide among the wishes and beliefs. Without some kind of executive to hear and decide, the choice is, as it were, random; it is not the choice of a unified self that has considered the issues and taken its stand. As such, the choice cannot be attributed to the person as a whole.

Given these understandings of why dissociated consciousness leads to nonresponsibility, multiples have an excuse for their crimes *even if their alters are not personlike centers of consciousness.* The second two theories in support of holding individuals nonresponsible for acts committed in periods of dissociated consciousness apply to multiples, regardless of whether we consider alters persons, personlike entities, or nonpersonlike parts of people. The second — that significant parts of individuals suffering from MPD, dissociated from the acting alter, are nonparticipants in the act — applies no matter how we conceptualize alter personalities. If the angry personality acts, and the generous, prudent, and moral personalities are all behind amnesia barriers, it is not surprising that the act should be aggressive: the generous, prudent, and moral parts were not brought to bear on this act. This act does not represent the person as a whole. The third is that criminal responsibility requires an integrated self acting, while individuals suffering from MPD, by very definition, lack an integrated self. In the ordinary case of dissociation, there are split-off centers of control, but an executive remains. In the case of the multiple, there *is* no executive — just a series of split-off centers. Because there is no executive, there is no agency with responsibility to adjudicate among conflicting wants and desires, and no agency to make a choice that represents the whole.

I am suggesting that multiples might be sufficiently unlike persons that we should not hold them criminally responsible. Perhaps this is best put by saying that an individual suffering from MPD is not a *unified* person. I do not wish to make the formalistic claim that only persons can commit crimes — my claim is more explanatory, and is that a person must be unified to commit a crime. And the important question is not whether some agent is or is not unified but whether he was sufficiently unified at the time of the crime.

Having discussed why dissociated consciousness should vitiate responsibility, I want now to return to the concept of "involuntary," a concept used by the law to explain why an individual should, or should not, be considered criminally responsible. Consider once again reflexes, hypnosis, posthypnotic suggestion, and sleepwalking — phenomena the law calls "involuntary" and psychiatry calls "dissociative." In each, a dissociative aspect of the person is acting — ordinary, waking consciousness is neither in control of, nor responsible for, what is happening. Contrast this state of affairs with MPD, in which an ordinary, waking state of consciousness is quite firmly in control of — and so responsible for — what is going on. What is striking about MPD is that, at the very same time as this ordinary, waking consciousness is in charge, there are other, ordinary, waking consciousnesses that are, in effect, dormant; they are neither in control of, nor partners in the decision making for, how the individual is behaving.

Our problem is therefore how to define "involuntary." Should we characterize as involuntary acts where an ordinary, waking consciousness is not controlling the act, or rather acts where, in addition to the ordinary, waking consciousness that is acting, there is present in the individual an ordinary, waking consciousness that is *not* acting as well? Put differently, is the problem with involuntary acts that there is no waking consciousness controlling the act — as in the case of reflexes, sleepingwalking, hypnosis, and posthypnotic suggestion — or is the problem rather that, regardless of the quality of the consciousness controlling the act, there is a waking consciousness that is *not* controlling the act? To put the matter yet a third way, should our focus for assessing involuntariness be the quality of the consciousness that is acting at a particular time, or the quality of the consciousness that is dissociated at that time?

If, in coming to a definition, we look to the phenomena the law characterizes as involuntary, either definition or way of looking at things would apply. With regard to sleepwalking, for example, it is both that there is no waking consciousness controlling the act and that, present in the individual, there is an ordinary, waking consciousness that is not in control of the act. We might well adopt the more modest definition — more modest in that it applies to fewer phenomena — and call those acts involuntary when no waking consciousness is in control.

I am going to argue that the second definition of "involuntary" — an ordinary, waking consciousness is present that is not in control of the act — is the more plausible and captures more what we really mean when we deem an act involuntary. When we try to understand why a person should be nonresponsible if no waking consciousness controls his act, the reasons apply equally to the cases when there are waking consciousnesses *not* controlling the act. The real problem, as I shall attempt to illustrate, is not lack of conscious control — as the first definition would have us believe — but lack of *unity,* which results from the presence of ordinary, waking conciousnesses dissociated from the acting consciousness. This is the state of affairs which our second definition captures.

We have already discussed three reasons for holding nonresponsible an individual in whom there is an ordinary, waking consciousness not controlling the act: first, it is unfair to punish blameless aspects of an individual that meet a certain threshold of integrity; second, significant parts of the individual do not have any decision-making role (the Schopp theory); and third, an individual lacks an executive authority when there are multiple waking consciousnesses not participating in the act. When we go on to ask why an act should be considered nonresponsible when no waking consciousness is in control, two things become apparent: first, the reasons we give for considering such acts nonresponsible *are the very same reasons* we gave for considering acts nonresponsible when there was an ordinary, waking consciousness *not* in control of the act; and second, our way of answering this question shows that our concern lies not with the nature of consciousness in control of the individual at a particular time but rather with how integrated the individual's different states of consciousness are with one another.

To begin our discussion of why a person should be held nonresponsible when no waking consciousness is in control of an act, consider one theory which holds that an individual needs consciousness in order to act. A moment's reflection shows this way of thinking cannot be right — that we have an involuntariness problem is proof itself that consciousness is not a prerequisite for acting. The sleepwalker, for example, while not conscious, acts in a perfectly coherent fashion. Another reason for a finding of nonresponsibility when no waking consciousness is in control might be that conscious control is necessary for behavior to be a responsible act. Several reasons support this position. Take as an example someone in a dissociated state whose unconscious rage causes her to act in a certain way. Aspects of this person other than her rage do not get any input into her behavior. About such a case one could say that the act is not representative, either because her waking consciousness was disabled from participating in the decision to act, or because waking consciousness, dissociated from this behavior, was not able to survey all the person's conflicting needs and wants. Either way, the decision is not a responsible decision. It will be clear to the reader, however, that these are two of our theories for why involuntary acts lead to nonresponsibility — that significant aspects of the individual are not able to participate in the decision-making process, and that an executive decision maker is lacking.

The sine qua non of a responsible act is not that *a* consciousness chooses to act but that a *unified* consciousness chooses to act. Unity is necessary so that all one's parts can play a role in the decision — are at least *available* for playing a role. Only when all of a multiple's parts are available in this way can a unified agent stand back, survey, and choose among the conflicting agendas. Integration is the gold standard for responsibility. While necessary, a consciousness choosing to act is not a sufficient condition for responsibility; as in the case of the multiple, consciousness can be fractured, and from a fractured consciousness arise all the problems associated with involuntariness.

Still another theory claiming that waking, conscious control is necessary for acts to be responsible is that conscious control is necessary for there to be control at all. Put another way, no waking consciousness means no control, which, in turn, entails nonresponsibility. Consider the person acting under posthypnotic suggestion who thinks he knows why he is acting — he tells himself a story — but in fact does not know why he acts as he does. His behavior is impelled by a powerful unconscious force. Despite his experience to the contrary, he has no control over his act. A reflex movement likewise is not under the control of the person whose limb is moving; a force impels the movements. In both these instances, however, the problem is not lack of control but lack of control *by consciousness*. In the case of the person under posthypnotic suggestion, there is ample control — control, however, belonging to the unconscious. Reflex motions seem uncontrolled but in fact are not; they are controlled by the physiology — the part of the person that makes one's limbs move in response to a particular stimulus. As these cases illustrate, the absence of an ordinary, waking consciousness does not necessarily imply the absence of control — just the absence of conscious control, which really says very little.

Still other theories for finding acts nonresponsible because they are not the product of a waking consciousness merit our consideration.

Perhaps only consciousness is "smart" enough to make decisions. Unconscious impulses, however, such as those planted in posthypnotic suggestion, lead individuals to act. While posthypnotic suggestion does require an outside intelligence, in the form of the hypnotist, to provide a suggestion, other acts deemed involuntary, such as those that take place while sleepwalking or during psychomotor epilepsy, require no such outside intelligence.

One could finesse this position a bit by saying that only decisions under the control of waking consciousness are "smart" enough in the sense of being representative — and hence only those could be responsible decisions. A waking consciousness in control of the act, however, while necessary, is not sufficient; there must also *not* be other waking consciousnesses that are dissociated from the act. If there are, the act will fail to be representative. Similarly, one could say only decisions under the control of waking consciousness are "smart" enough in the sense of being *considered* decisions. But part of a decision's being considered is the (executive) decision maker's having access to all the considerations — requiring the absence of other waking consciousnesses dissociated from the act. Once again, it is *integration* — not consciousness — that is decisive.

Is lack of conscious control alone sufficient for nonresponsibility? Yes — not, however, because *consciousness* or *control* is lacking but because *integration* is lacking. When integration is lacking, three reasons — familiar to us by now — compel a finding of nonresponsibility: (1) unintegrated parts may be innocent of wrongdoing, hence blameless; (2) significant aspects of the person are not brought to bear on the decision to act; and (3) a unified, integrated executive agency is lacking, so that we cannot say *this individual* has made a choice. Absence of conscious control, then, while sufficient for nonresponsibility, is not necessary. The reasons it is sufficient — the three just given — apply equally to cases where integration is lacking.

In sum, acts can plainly occur without conscious control. The reason conscious control may be significant is not that consciousness is necessary for control. It may be significant, on the other hand, because conscious control is necessary for an act's "smartness" — its sufficient representativeness or consideredness; but then so is absence of other dissociated consciousnesses. Behind our concept of involuntariness, it is plain, lies something deeper than absence of conscious control. That deeper something is lack of integration.

Thus, even though the classically cited cases can be understood as saying that a lack of conscious control is the cornerstone of involuntariness, lack of conscious control should *not* be understood as the unifying principle. Involuntariness arises when there is a consciousness that is not participating in the act — when the self is unintegrated in a significant way. And a lack of integration is the defining characteristic of MPD. Involuntariness ought therefore to include MPD, as well as the other classically cited dissociative phenomena. MPD is the most severe of the dissociative phenomena; it would be surprising if other dissociative phenomena gave rise to exoneration and MPD did not.

Our conclusion in this section is that multiples should be nonresponsible even if alters are nonpersonlike parts of a person. What, though, of the objection that this position threatens to undermine the criminal law, because it would encompass a wide range of phenomena and would be applicable to virtually every single one of us? An objector might well point out that both of our reasons for holding multiples nonresponsible on the basis of dissociated consciousness — assuming that alters are nonpersonlike entities — are problematic.

The first reason for a finding of nonresponsibility on the theory that alters are mere parts was that, if an act is to be considered responsible, the decision maker should have access to all significant parts of herself bearing on the decision. Yet, as our objector will point out, what of an individual who does not have access to her generous side because she is under the sway of strong feelings of greed — our reasoning would appear to excuse her for acting greedily. And does our reasoning mean that anyone who acts out of character — whose characteristic responses were not brought to bear on a particular occasion — should be held nonresponsible as well? What about the wide variety of occasions under which people act on unconscious impulses? The conscious part does not get to express its wishes and beliefs, nor does it have access to the unconscious forces responsible for the act. Is anyone with an unconscious to be held nonresponsible for his or her acts?

The second rationale for a finding of nonresponsibility was that, for a decision to be responsible, a unified executive must decide. But, as our objector would continue, who is completely unified? Does not everyone suffer from conflicts, ambivalences, and tensions among different sides of the self? Indeed, is not everyone a collection of different parts taking control of the body in turn? The idea of a unified executive in ordinary people may be a complete myth. Does that mean that no one should ever be held responsible for what they do?

These objections should not be surprising. The premise of this section is that alters are not special — they are not different persons or personlike centers of consciousness. Rather, they are ordinary, nonpersonlike parts of complicated people. But if that is so, then it would seem either that nothing special follows (multiples are as responsible as the rest of us) or that something very special follows (we are all nonresponsible).

How do we respond? Take our objector's point that often people do not have access to significant parts of themselves when they act; their generosity may be weakened by strong feelings of greed, their normal character may not exert itself when they act, or they may act under an unconscious impulse, their conscious wishes and desires having little effect. The first thing to be said in response is that it cannot be right that all parts of oneself must have maximal effect on all acts — otherwise, given intrapsychic conflicts, no one would ever make *any* choices. Choices do not have to be the perfect compromise among a person's competing wants and desires to be representative. Some parts of a person will obviously be less active in certain decisions — that much I am willing to concede. What is necessary is that significant parts of oneself are *available* to the decision-making executive, and that the choice represents the chooser's adjudication among such parts.

Take this way of thinking and apply it to the person experiencing strong feelings of greed. In such a case we should ask whether the greed totally submerged the person's generosity, or simply outweighed it. If the person lacked any access to her generosity, that is a different matter than if she contemplated her generosity but rejected it as a reason for acting on this occasion. Since there is no way to tell — or even reason to believe — that the generosity was disabled from exerting any influence on her decision, she should not be allowed to avail herself of this defense — namely, that parts of herself were not, could not be, brought to bear on the act. Unlike MPD, sleepwalking, and hypnosis, this behavior does not involve sufficient dissociation.[11]

The same analysis can be applied to out-of-character acts. The issue would be whether the person's normal characteristics were submerged behind barriers that prevented their having any effect, or whether such characteristics did have an effect but were outweighed by other factors. Did the person simply choose on this occasion to do something uncharacteristic, having considered all the issues? Again, we must remain agnostic — there is simply no way to peer inside a person's head to see what goes into a decision. Because there is both no way of telling and no reason for believing that the person's normal character was disabled from having its normal effect, the person should not have the defense that parts of herself were not available, and so could not be brought to bear on the act. There is insufficient dissociation to allow an involuntariness defense.

What about unconscious wishes? Unconscious wishes bring about acts without the person's conscious wishes and desires having any effect. The person choosing does not even know about the unconscious wish, and so cannot consider and reject it as a basis for her choice. Again we have to remain agnostic. We cannot know, that is, whether conscious wishes and desires had no effect or whether they just lost out in the battle of wishes. While the person's conscious self did not know about the wish, that does not mean that the effective decision maker did not — we simply don't know very much about how decisions get made. Posthypnotic suggestion involves an unconscious desire giving rise to an act, but there we have vivid evidence that the desire *is* separated from the rest of the self — it is behind amnesia barriers, not simply unconscious — and we know that it exerts compulsive force. We have evidence of neither in the case of ordinary unconscious wishes — indeed, we can only guess when they are even operative — and so it makes sense to deny an unconscious chooser a defense based on parts of herself not being available to the executive who must decide whether or not to act.

These arguments are based largely on our ignorance: we have little evidence, in nondissociative cases, that the disabling condition is actually happening. We are, however, likelier to err if we allow people the option of raising a defense which there is no way of definitively establishing. Moreover, given that anyone can allege one of these scenarios, allowing the defense might indeed threaten to swallow up the criminal law. If evidence in the future should show that these cases differ little from true dissociation in the relevant respects, we shall have to reconsider this position and face all the thorny issues raised by the possibility of widespread exoneration. At present, there seems no reason to expect such a turn.

For now there is good reason to say that only people experiencing dissociation at the time of the relevant acts should be entitled to the defense that significant parts of themselves were not available to the process of decision making.[12] Indeed, the very term "dissociation" means that there is a rift in consciousness, that there are barriers preventing access of one part to another. Sleepwalkers, those acting under hypnotic and posthypnotic suggestion, those responding to reflexes, and multiples all suffer from this disability. Drawing the line at dissociative disorders does not threaten to unravel the fabric of the criminal law — few are affected.

Let us examine, in turn, the objection to the second rationale for holding multiples nonresponsible if alters are nonpersonlike entities. The second rationale was that, for a decision to be responsible, a unified executive must decide; the objection was that no one is completely unified — indeed, everyone may be a collection of selves. While it is certain that everyone suffers from some disunity, it is just as clear that mild conflicts, ambivalences, and tensions are not remotely like significant dissociation. A conflicted person can still be *one* person — and that person can decide among competing wishes, fears, and desires. When one aspect of a person does not even know what the other is doing — as happens in dissociation — we have good reason to speak of a breach of unity. The same is true when one aspect of a person identifies itself as a wholly separate agent from another.

The objection that none of us has an executive self — that we are all a series of selves — is more of a challenge. That position — that we are all multiple selves — may or may not be true; we just do not know. Even if it is true, however, the different "selves" of the multiple — even should we deem them nonpersonlike — are still very different from the "selves" of the ordinary person. The differences between the selves of the multiple are profound: they often have amnesia boundaries, and each has its own sense of self, as well as its own sense of agency. Nonmultiples, on the other hand, do not experience themselves in this way.

Do, or should, these differences between multiples and nonmultiples matter? The implication is that whoever is "out" in the case of a multiple is not an executive fit to decide for the whole, while whoever is "out" in the case of the nonmultiple is. This position makes sense. The alter "out" in the case of a multiple is very different from the other selves; she is not a good representative, for at least two reasons: first, she lacks access to the other selves who are behind amnesia barriers; second, she distinguishes herself from the other alters — their concerns are not her concerns. To put the matter in legal terms, we might say that no alter would be fit to serve as the named plaintiff in a class action brought on behalf of the alters. None of these disabling conditions is true in the case of the nonmultiple. The only conceivable similarity is that the "self" who is out now may be very different from the "self" who animated the body at some time very many years ago. But these differences are much more attenuated — there is psychological continuity and connectedness, in Parfit's sense, between phases in a person's life.

Multiples suffer a unique form of nonrepresentativeness. The "executive" in the case of a multiple is not fit to speak for the person as a whole *at any time*. A nonmultiple, by contrast, identifies herself as one person who persists over time and undergoes certain changes, taking it as her obligation to consider the interests and wishes of at least closely past and future "selves," which she perceives as parts of herself. She is a single person who will suffer these things in the future, so she had better decide wisely. While the multiple feels as if she has different selves, and these different "selves" feel no such allegiance to each other, the "selves" of the nonmultiple are very different. Though nonmultiples may have no "executive" who stands over and above this succession of "selves," each "self" is generally fit to speak for the whole. This is decidedly not the case in MPD.

The concern that the theory put forth in this section will lead to wholesale exoneration in the criminal law is unfounded. The reasons for exoneration apply to individuals suffering from MPD and some other dissociative phenomena. The reasons do not apply to people not suffering from dissociative disorders, however conflicted they might sometimes be. Multiples should thus generally be held nonresponsible even if their alters are ordinary, nonpersonlike parts of a complicated person. MPD is on a spectrum with other dissociative phenomena for which the law now provides an excuse — indeed, MPD is the most extreme phenomenon on the spectrum. And the rationale that explains why these phenomena should lead to exoneration applies fully — most fully — to MPD.

Are multiples always nonresponsible, or are there exceptions to their general nonresponsibility? And what exactly should a rule governing the nonresponsibility of multiples look like? What do the courts say about these cases? And what do therapists add to what the courts have said? We turn to these questions now.

6. A Rule for Nonresponsibility

A PROPOSED RULE: CRIMINAL RESPONSIBILITY AND NONRESPONSIBILITY

In Chapter 4 we asked whether alter personalities are best conceptualized as different people, different personlike centers of consciousness, or nonpersonlike parts of very complicated people. We concluded in Chapter 5 that multiples should be held nonresponsible for their crimes regardless of which conceptualization we chose. We reasoned that if alters are different persons, punishing a guilty alter would inevitably entail punishing innocent people; if alters are different personlike centers of consciousness, punishing a guilty alter would entail punishing, and hence causing to suffer, blameless centers of consciousness; and if alters are nonpersonlike parts of complicated people, the individual suffering from MPD is not sufficiently integrated to execute criminally responsible acts. Within the same multiple, certain alters may be persons, others personlike, and still others ordinary, nonpersonlike parts. Our rule, however, remains the same: multiples are generally nonresponsible for their crimes.

I suggested in an earlier work that a presumption of nonresponsibility should follow when a defendant is shown to suffer from MPD (Saks 1992). In that work I cited circumstances that would rebut that presumption, and hence possibly result in a finding of guilt. A presumption seemed warranted because I judged the rebutting circumstances to be extraordinarily rare; given the unlikelihood of finding a defendant guilty, we should presume a person nonresponsible on finding he was a multiple. We would risk fewer mistakes that way since the vast majority of multiples would indeed be nonresponsible.

I would now like to modify and elaborate my position somewhat. First, I am less certain about the frequency with which the rebutting circumstances will be present. While I still believe they are quite rare, I no longer believe they are virtually nonexistent.[1] Second, given my change in thinking about the rarity of rebutting circumstances, I see the question of who should bear the burden differently. I had previously favored placing the burden on the prosecution. I would now favor placing the burden on whichever party ordinarily bears the burden of proof in insanity cases in the particular jurisdiction; I do not think the facts of the MPD case are so unique in this regard as to compel a special procedure.

Given these shifts, I no longer believe that a mere finding of MPD should presumptively lead to nonresponsibility. In insanity doctrine a diagnosis alone never results in a finding of nonresponsibility, and to say that a mere diagnosis would result in a finding of nonresponsibility would be to vest enormous power in psychiatrists — the diagnostic authorities. We should, of course, be willing to accept these consequences if the conditions of MPD speak to nonresponsibility. But they ought not to be taken lightly.

In this section I explore circumstances in which individuals suffering from MPD should be held responsible for their crimes. We begin with the following scenario: imagine an alter (call him Rob) of a fairly simple multiple who conceives of a plan to rob a bank. He is the intellectual alter who makes all the calculations necessary to commit the robbery. He consults his two fellow alters, and both are eager to join in his plan. One, Richard, happens to be a safecracker, and the other, Rex, an ace getaway driver. There are no other alters in this multiple. Each of the alters then performs his assigned role, and they abscond with one million dollars. If caught, this bank robber should be found guilty and punished regardless of how we conceptualize alters. If Rob, Richard, and Rex are all people, they are all guilty people, and guilty people should be punished; if personlike centers of consciousness, they are still guilty and deserving of punishment; if parts of one complex person, that person nevertheless has enough integration that he should be found guilty — all of his parts agreed on his actions, so that none were prevented from making their influence felt.

Our first two ways of conceptualizing alters, as different people and different personlike centers of consciousness, lead to guilt on ordinary principles of group liability or complicity in a crime. We sometimes hold people liable who do not themselves commit the criminal act; they are complicit in the crime, either by commanding or encouraging the crime or by facilitating the perpetrator's escape from detection. Indeed, we may be especially concerned to discourage group criminality because groups of people, by virtue of their encouragement of each other — as well as their combined talents — may be more dangerous than single individuals. The alters in a multiple can all be accessories to a crime, in which case the multiple should be guilty.[2]

Ms. Marie Moore, a multiple with two personalities, Ms. Moore and Billy Joel, provides an example of complicity (*State v. Moore* 1988). Billy Joel held hostage and terrorized a group of children, eventually participating as one of the children was beaten to death. But Ms. Moore was no stranger to the crime. Speaking on the phone, she would tell the children that Billy Joel was calling with instructions for their daily routine and discipline. She skillfully deflected the police when under suspicion. Marie Moore may have been a very disturbed woman who had a defense based on her mental illness, but she did not deserve to be exonerated by virtue of her MPD. There were no innocent alters within her.

We glean our rule about MPD and criminal responsibility from our bank robber and Ms. Moore: a finding of guilt requires both *knowledge* and *acquiescence*. First, alters must know about the crime. As in other areas of the law, willful blindness should count as much as knowledge. If an alter has a sense that something is amiss, and absents herself precisely so as to avoid responsibility for what occurs, she should be deemed to know about the crime. Consider one of the court's concerns in *Rutherford v. Rutherford* (1990), where the question was fault in a dissolution case involving adultery. The trial court had found that the personality that committed the adultery was not the appellant's wife, Carol, but another alter, Rose. This court's concern was "whether Carol has the ability to consciously engage the Rose personality. If it is determined that she has that adeptness, then our concern is that she may have conveniently utilized her psychological disorder to engage in adultery with Tedder which, as Carol, she knew was wrong" (1990, 181–82). In other words, one alter cannot know an act is wrong but use another alter to commit her crime — and then, in turn, claim innocence.

Second, a finding of guilt requires acquiescence. Acquiescence should be found if the alter participates in the crime in any way — as by performing, or encouraging, any of its constituent acts. Anything that would render an ordinary person an accomplice is sufficient to find that an alter acquiesced in a crime. I would hold alters to an even higher standard and require that, under appropriate circumstances, they intervene in order to prevent the crimes of other alter personalities.

Acquiescence has special meaning for multiples because of their unique psychic structure, and so merits further discussion. Applying the concept of acquiescence to multiples implicates three issues. We must explain, first, how we justify departing from legal principles that ordinarily decline to impose affirmative duties; second, the circumstances under which the duty to intervene arises; and third, how this way of thinking about acquiescence plays out in practical terms. I discuss these issues in turn.

First, acquiescence entails an affirmative duty long eschewed by our system of jurisprudence, the duty to intervene. How do we justify creating such a duty for multiples? Traditional ways of thinking about affirmative duties have several underpinnings: we are (wisely) reluctant to impose a duty to act, when acting may actually increase the danger both to the victim and to the rescuer; we do not wish to burden an individual with remedying a wrong he did not cause; we do not wish to create the possibility of blameworthiness solely because another party has chosen to do wrong; and we have great difficulty determining responsibility in cases where many people could possibly intervene (e.g., the Kitty Genovese case). All of these reasons support the principle that individuals do not have a duty to prevent the crimes of another; are there reasons for modifying this principle in the case of individuals suffering from MPD?

While some of these considerations do apply to multiples (alters may well not know, for example, that a crime is occurring, any more than an individual who, on a hot summer night, hears a sound in the distance that might possibly be a cry for help), others apply not at all, or to a much lesser degree. The danger of intervening, for example, is much less for alters: there will be no scuffle, no fight, no clash of bodies. While there may be some danger, of emotional trauma or of physical harm to the alters' common body, the danger is less. A more significant departure from the preceding considerations is that alters might simply feel under a greater obligation to intervene when the offender is another alter who shares his body — *his* body is being used to perpetrate the offense.[3] The alter may feel that he is implicated in the act and feel a moral obligation to rectify that for which he is partly to blame. If, for example, someone used another's body to harm a third person, the second person might feel more responsible for rescuing the third than if he were a complete stranger to the act. Even though the act occurred without his consent, he was nevertheless somehow involved. The case of the multiple is the same.

There is a principle in the ordinary context that has some force here: in certain jurisdictions, those who put another in danger must then intervene to ameliorate the danger. In a sense, the alter has put the victim in danger insofar as his fellow alter used their common body. There is another circumstance in which the law imposes a duty in the ordinary context: once one has started a rescue, and thereby discouraged others from initiating a rescue, the attempt must be completed. This case provides a close analogy to the case of the alter: since the alter is somewhat involved in the act already — even though not of his own doing — he should try to see that a decent outcome is reached. Even if only unwittingly complicit, he is inextricably involved nonetheless, and this imposes on him a duty to help make things right. For those who reject the idea that the innocent alter himself is somehow involved, we might use the analogy of the family. It is true that only certain members of a family are in any way legally responsible for the acts of other members — namely, parents for their children. Where there is a relation of dependence, affirmative duties may be imposed. While most alters do not stand in that relationship to other alters, all family members probably feel more responsible for the acts — and well-being — of their relations than for those of strangers. On this basis, too, alters might rightly feel more of an obligation to intervene than do people in the usual case. A duty to intervene should be imposed on alters because considerations behind the traditional rule of nonintervention (primarily the potential danger involved) are much less salient, while reasons that have supported affirmative duties (putting another in danger, having begun a rescue, and having a special relationship with an individual who commits a crime) are especially relevant to multiples.

The second issue implicated by our concept of acquiescence addresses the circumstances under which the duty to intervene arises. Commentators in the "duty to rescue" context have generally recommended only "easy" rescues. If intervention is required in difficult situations, there is a risk of actually increasing danger to people. The obvious example is the person who, attempting to rescue a drowning person, ends up drowning himself along with that person. Imposing a duty to intervene in difficult situations therefore imposes an onerous burden on others, exposing them not only to the risk of increased danger but also to the risk of psychological conflict over meeting (or failing to meet) the demands of such a heavy obligation.

What analogous dangers might there be for alters that would warrant an "easy control" rule? Two kinds of harm are possible: first, a danger of serious emotional trauma; and second, a danger of serious physical harm in the form of one alter physically injuring the body when another alter is out. In terms of the latter, some alters may be so vindictive that they are willing to suffer themselves in order to impose suffering on their fellow alters. Moreover, perhaps indifferent to the body when not out, such alters may believe that *they* will not suffer if they commit all but the most final acts of destruction.[4] In regard to emotional harm, one alter may likewise suffer at the hands of another. Unlike people, who can get away from each other, alters cannot leave the field. A crossed alter can emotionally abuse another nonstop, with no escape available to the victim. As a consequence, the duty to intervene arises only when an alter can exercise "easy control" over another alter.

The duty to intervene should not be overly burdensome or expose alters to increased danger of emotional and physical abuse. Thus, we should not require alters to intervene if they actually and reasonably apprehend significant physical or emotional harm, or if intervention requires more than reasonable effort. Moreover, we should not take failure to intervene (or intervene appropriately) as a sign of acquiescence unless the alter is aware of what reasonable steps can be taken; misjudgment about what is reasonable should result at most in a crime of negligent failure to act. To expect people to be anything more than reasonable is too burdensome an obligation.

The third issue addresses how our concept of acquiescence plays out in practical terms. What happens, for example, when an alter knows a fellow alter is committing a crime? If the alter can prevent the crime in progress simply by taking control of the body or by talking to the acting alter — asking him not to do it, arguing with him, commanding him — without undue chance of harm, he has a duty to intervene. Likewise, if an alter *knows* that a crime will be committed at some unknown future time, and so taking over the body is a much less sure solution, he nevertheless has this duty. Taking himself to a psychiatric hospital would be one manner of intervening, and might be appropriate for especially serious crimes such as murder.

Fragmentary personalities create special exceptions to the requirement that all alters must know about and acquiesce in a crime before a multiple can be held criminally responsible. Fragmentary personalities are unidimensional and ephemeral. Often serving a single function, they virtually never have personal histories, nor can they be compared to people as more well-rounded alters can.

Two of the theories under which I have argued for criminal nonresponsibility are problematic when the alters who did not know about or acquiesce in the crime are highly fragmentary. First, such fragmentary alters are clearly not persons, so in punishing the multiple we would not be punishing innocent people. Nor are such alters personlike apperceptive centers, so that in punishing the multiple we would not be punishing innocent entities that possess "fitness for punishment." Now recall our third theory of nonresponsibility, which applies to alters conceptualized as nonpersonlike parts of complicated people. This rationale — relevant to fragmentary personalities — is that the individual is not sufficiently integrated to make a criminally responsible decision and, therefore, his acts are not representative, insofar as significant aspects of his person played no role in the decision to act or not to act. If the only aspect of a person not to participate in an act is a fragmentary personality, then even these reasons do not apply — that is, despite the absence of the fragmentary personality from the decision-making process, enough of the person is present for us to say that his acts are representative. Punishing this multiple will cause only a trivial harm if the fragmentary alter's appearance is extremely limited. We therefore need to qualify the earlier claim that, in order to find a multiple criminally responsible, all of the alters must know about and acquiesce in the crime. Our modified rule states that for a multiple to be held criminally responsible, all the alters must know about and acquiesce in the crime, unless the alters who failed to acquiesce were fragmentary.

The multiple nevertheless remains criminally nonresponsible if there are enough fragmentary alters. Consider a multiple who has two very personlike alters, both of which planned and participated in a crime. The multiple also has fifty fragmentary alters, none of which knew about or acquiesced in the crime. Moreover, these are the alters who are in control of the multiple most of the time. Though his personlike parts participated in the crime, his fragmentary alters — which constitute the largest part of him — did not. This multiple should be not guilty, either because he was not sufficiently integrated or because significant parts of himself were not brought to bear on his act. Where there are a significant number of fragmentary personalities who did not know about or acquiesce in the crime, the reasoning behind our third theory of nonresponsibility applies.

The evaluation for responsibility will be straightforward in the majority of cases. Most multiples will have at least one personlike alter who did not know about the crime, and therefore cannot be said to have acquiesced in it. Even for those few multiples who have no alters amnestic for the crime, the majority will have at least one personlike alter who did not acquiesce. The point is that most multiples have personality systems with pockets of amnesia much of the time. And most multiples have personality systems at odds with themselves; they do not act in unison with all of their parts — that is almost definitional of a multiple.[5]

We have concluded that we should depart from our general rule of criminal nonresponsibility when all alters know about and acquiesce in a crime, unless the only alters who did not are fragmentary and few relative to the number of alters constituting the multiple. I believe — although somewhat tentatively — that another situation calls for a finding of responsibility. This situation arises when, even though some alters may not know about the crime, the multiple as a whole is sufficiently organized that an inference of guilt seems warranted. Imagine a scenario in which all of the alters in a quite organized multiple have a specific function within the system, which each performs smoothly — like clockwork. There are alters who perform specific tasks on her job, alters who take care of her children, alters who socialize, and so forth. All of the alters are in general agreement about who does what, and there are rarely, if ever, disputes about how things will work.

In the case of important decisions the alters consult each other to reach an agreement that will best accommodate the interests of all. There may even be some form of executive body or community council that runs the whole show. If, in this arrangement, one of the alters commits a crime, we should perhaps hold the multiple criminally responsible. We would do so on a theory of corporate liability, the ordinary principles of which I sketch out in the following.

Ordinarily, a corporation is liable for the acts of its agents if they are within the scope of their employment and are taken on behalf of the corporation — that is, with an "intent to benefit the corporation." To say that the act must be within the scope of employment means that the act must be "directly related to the performance of the type of duties the employee has general authority to perform."[6] To say that the agent must be acting "on behalf of" the corporation is to say that the agent must be "acting with the purpose of forwarding corporate business" (Brickey 1990, 26).

The reasons for these two requirements are clear. Acts not within the scope of the agent's employment are maverick acts for which it is not fair to burden the corporation; such acts could not have been foreseen or controlled. Acts taken on behalf of the corporation can be fairly attributed to the corporation itself. In that case the agent is acting ("speaking") for the corporation, and the acts are meant to benefit the corporation, which suggests the corporation would have wanted them could it act itself, or at least reaps some benefit from the acts.

Authorities are split over a third feature of corporate responsibility: at what level within the corporate structure an employee must be before a corporation can be charged with a crime. The Model Penal Code and some states require that the commission of the offense be "authorized, requested, commanded, performed or recklessly tolerated by the board of directors or by a high managerial agent acting in behalf of the corporation within the scope of his office or employment" (ALI 1985, sec. 2.07 (1)(c)). Federal law and some state law, by contrast, permit imposition of corporate liability for criminal acts performed by officers or agents in the course of their employment without regard to their status in the corporate hierarchy. Even the acts of menial employees have resulted in liability under this rule.

The rationale behind the Model Penal Code rule is plain on the face of its definition of a "high managerial agent": an officer or other agent of the corporation "having duties of such responsibility that his conduct may fairly be assumed to represent the policy of the corporation" (ALI 1985, sec. 2.07 (4)(c)). The MPC provision basically recognizes the unfairness of holding a corporation liable for the acts of each and every one its agents. The respondeat superior rule of the federal courts and some state courts recognizes a basic flaw of the MPC approach: that it too easily permits corporations to insulate themselves from liability. A rule of respondeat superior permits less opportunity for corporations to insulate themselves from liability.

A fourth feature of corporate liability is that, no matter what the crime, we cannot imprison a corporation. The most customary penalty for a corporate crime is a fine, although sometimes corporations are sentenced to community service and probation as well. Some may see corporate criminality as nothing more than overzealous business and punishment of corporations as closer to a fee to conduct business than to a criminal sanction. However viewed, the opprobrium of a criminal sanction is not as great for a corporation as for an individual.

Can we draw a feasible analogy between corporations and organized multiples? Between punishing corporations and punishing organized multiples? There seem to be four dimensions along which multiples can be compared to corporations for the purpose of assessing criminal responsibility: first, their structure; second, the manner in which parts experience the whole; third, how the organization is managed or directed; and fourth, how sanctions are implemented. First, consider that a corporation's organization is generally clear: there will be a board of directors, managers, high-level employees, low-level employees. This structure makes the whole an organization, so that blaming the whole for the malfunctioning of one of its parts is just. The structure both tells us when the part is acting its assigned role and gives meaning to the phrase "scope of employment."

The organization of a multiple, by contrast — even a highly structured multiple — will be much looser and much more ad hoc. Sometimes there will be a leader ("president"), often not. Sometimes there will be something akin to high-level management, often not. Sometimes the alters will have different jobs in the system in the literal sense: one will take care of the children and one will fill out the taxes. More often they will have different "jobs" in the sense of different roles in the psychic economy: one will express anger, another, tenderness.

While corporations will generally follow standard forms of organization that lead to an inference of guilt for the whole, it may not be so clear that the whole multiple is culpable when an alter acts. In the same way, it will be much less clear when an alter is within the scope of her authority, as it were, and when not. We will have less of a sense when an alter's act is an unforeseeable, maverick act for which we should not hold the whole in any way responsible, and when the part is performing its role, albeit in a way we disapprove of.

We shall therefore have to be careful in evaluating multiples for liability on a corporate theory. We will need to examine whether the multiple is indeed organized, and if the organization is such as to permit an inference of culpability when the part acts. Similarly, it will be much less clear when an alter is acting within the scope of her authority (or what this even means in a given multiple's system), and evaluators will have to ascertain whether this condition has been met in a way that makes it fair to hold the whole culpable.

One consideration will be how much control there is over each alter. Corporations hire their employees and can fire them as well. Multiples of course do not; no multiple has control over which alters develop. Unless the system can keep troublesome or otherwise unwanted alters from taking control — even if not from developing — the analogy with the corporation will be too attenuated to work. In such a case it is clearly unfair to blame the whole for the acts of this concededly unwanted part. Well-organized multiples can sometimes exert this kind of control — Billy Milligan's Arthur and Ragan tried to "banish" unwanted alters from "the spot." These "managerial" alters were not entirely successful; managers in other multiples may be.

In terms of the second dimension along which corporations and multiples may be compared, consider that the members of a corporation see themselves as such — there is a whole for which they work — while alters in an organized multiple may not. Alters may be organized as a way of furthering the individual interests of each, but each may see itself as a separate individual, not as a part of a whole. While organized multiples *may* see their alters as parts of a whole, it is more likely that each part will see itself as an individual. As a consequence, when the alter acts, we cannot see the act as the act of the whole. Here is where the "intent to benefit" provision is important. Only when alters have an intent to benefit the whole — only if they are acting *for* the benefit of the whole — can we rightly impute the intent of the agent to her principal. Only then can we rightly say that the multiple, and not just the alter, intended to commit the crime.

In terms of the third dimension along which multiples and corporations may be compared, the vast majority of multiples do not have alters that are equivalent to the board of directors and managers of a corporation. This means, of course, that if we adopt the Model Penal Code version of corporate criminal liability — which depends on the act's being authorized, commanded, performed, or recklessly tolerated by the board of directors or a high-level managerial employee — virtually no multiples will be liable. According to the federal rule, on the other hand, organized multiples may be liable on the traditional respondeat superior theory if *any* of their alters commits a crime while acting within the scope of its authority and with an intent to benefit the whole. While this seems a plausible move, the MPC may be right to view the corporation as "the embodiment of the acts and intent of only its 'high managerial agent[s]' " (Bucy 1992, 202). In that case, the federal rule for multiples threatens to be somewhat unfair.

The unfairness may be more pronounced given what we have identified as the fourth dimension along which multiples and corporations may be compared: corporate criminality is not all that stigmatizing, while criminality of persons is. Even though, on this theory, the multiple will be being punished as a kind of corporation, society will see a person being punished. The alter or alters in control during the punishment will feel a stigma directed against him or her. It will be as if you or I were being punished, not Exxon. Also, corporations are not put in prison, however serious their crimes, while people are.

In considering whether to have a corporate liability vehicle for punishing multiples, we must decide whether to follow the rule on punishing corporations. One argument is that we ought to punish corporations by imprisonment for serious crimes but we just can't. Where is the corporation? Whom would we jail? The board and high-level employees? All the employees? The shareholders as well or instead?

Of course, we can just *decide* "who" the corporation is. Suppose we decide the corporation is constituted by the board of directors, officers, and employees. If one corporate employee commits a serious crime, is it fair to imprison all these people? All have some responsibility. Some, for example, will have explicitly delegated the job to this employee, and all depend on him to do the job — have implicitly delegated it to him. Some will or should know what he is doing. All may stand to benefit in some way from his wrongdoing. In reality, however, the responsibility of many — probably most — of the employee's colleagues will be extremely attenuated. They will not have delegated the job to him in any real sense, will not know or suspect what he is doing, are not responsible for the organization of the corporation, and may not care a whit about the added benefit to the corporation. Many will be law-abiding citizens who abhor the idea of the crime, and some will have taken active efforts to prevent such behavior in the corporation. Is it fair to put all of these people in jail? The answer, I think, is no, and that is the principal reason we do not "imprison corporations." Indeed, the only reason we may tolerate corporate punishment at all is that any stigma associated with the punishment does not attach to the individual members of the corporation who were innocent of the wrongdoing.

There is therefore a real question about whether we should ever hold multiples liable on a corporate criminal liability theory. Both the multiple as a whole and individual alters will feel the stigma of any punishment acutely, especially when imprisonment is at stake. I would therefore propose that, if we are to hold multiples liable on a theory of corporate liability, imprisonment should not be an available punishment: fines, community service, reparation, yes; imprisonment, no. This proposal is in line, I think, with the culpability of individual alters when a multiple is organized. Many of the individual alters will be at worst somewhat negligent in not attending adequately to what their co-alter was doing. But the minimum mental state for serious crimes is *criminal* negligence. Most of the alters, even of an organized multiple, will not have that mental state. While perhaps guilty of some lesser crime like "negligent supervision," organized multiples should not be imprisoned if one of their alters commits a crime, because other alters will not be sufficiently culpable to merit that degree of punishment.

Some punishment may nevertheless be warranted. There are important similarities between organized multiples and corporations. Group liability for organized multiples may seem reasonable for the same reasons it is reasonable for ordinary corporations: first, the multiple has put society at risk; second, the multiple has, in a sense, delegated authority to his alters to act — has hired his alters, in a manner of speaking; finally, we want to encourage alters to exercise control by keeping other alters within the bounds of the law. When a multiple is sufficiently organized for this kind of liability to hold may be a difficult question. In certain cases, however, it is clear that the multiple will not be criminally responsible on this theory: if he had unknown alters at the time of the crime; significant amnesia; insufficient ability to control alters who are out; significant disorganization, with alters taking over from each other at will; significant fighting among alters; or ignorance of his MPD. In each of these cases — and there are no doubt others — the multiple is not well organized. There is not sufficient knowledge, harmony, and accord — coordination — among the alters that it would be fair to hold the multiple liable.

In short, the criminal liability proposed for organized multiples is a kind of mitigated liability. They are responsible only for a crime of negligence — not the underlying offense of the guilty alter — and they cannot be imprisoned on this basis. They are not wholly nonresponsible, but they are not wholly responsible either.

Although multiples will be nonresponsible for their crimes in the majority of cases, the mere claim of MPD, of course, will not inevitably lead to exoneration. A defendant has to prove that he is a multiple, something that may be quite difficult. I would require that a defendant meet the *DSM-IV* criteria, which include significant amnesia, important to our theories of nonresponsibility for two reasons: first, amnesia helps make the case that alters are persons or personlike; second, it suggests that the multiple is sufficiently unintegrated to be considered nonresponsible, either because there is no integrated executive or because considerable parts of the multiple were not brought to bear on the act. Nor is it easy to malinger MPD over long periods of time — one needs to be able to act several parts at once, keeping clear the differences among them — and the subtle symptoms of MPD, which regularly characterize the disorder, are not a matter of common knowledge. Further still, there will generally need to be evidence of dividedness in one's past — indeed, in one's early childhood. For example, multiples are often accused of doing things they deny having done. If there is no evidence of such occurrences in a multiple's past — or other evidence of amnesia — the diagnosis becomes less believable. Given both the general skepticism about the disorder and the famous cases of defendants attempting to malinger MPD — such as the "Hillside Strangler" — it is unlikely that a defendant's claim of MPD will be accepted without hard scrutiny. The defendant will have a high hurdle to overcome.

Because multiples are liable under certain conditions, my proposed rule is not a license to commit crimes with impunity. If all multiples were nonresponsible, anyone knowing he was a multiple, and knowing this rule, would lack criminal law incentives not to offend; he would know he would be found not guilty. Under my proposed rule multiples are not in this position: there are situations in which they will be found guilty. Indeed, any alter who knows of the crime has an obligation to stop it if he can, and any alter who tries to absent himself precisely so as to avoid this obligation remains subject to its dictates for that very reason.

An evil alter who knows of innocent amnesiac alters does know that he can commit a crime and not be punished for it. Thus, we have the offensive situation of someone knowing that he will get away with doing wrong. On the other hand, "getting away with" the crime is something of an overstatement, because the person will lose his liberty — he will be committed to a mental hospital until he is no longer ill or dangerous. That is not a trivial sanction. While he will not be punished, I nevertheless suggest that this loss of deterrence is something we have to live with in order to do justice.

In this section we have carved out two exceptions to our rule of general nonresponsibility. We now turn to what the courts have done in assessing the criminal responsibility of individuals suffering from MPD.

THE CASES

The nonresponsibility of multiples is a subtle question, which becomes even more challenging when forced into the standard language of insanity and involuntariness. Instead of looking at the question of MPD afresh, courts often try to speak the language of traditional rules that were not formulated with MPD in mind and, what is worse, often leave experts to derive their own theories of how the standard rules of insanity and involuntariness apply. How to assess the criminal nonresponsibility of individuals suffering from MPD is a question for law, not psychiatry. Experts should not be left to their own devices — and their own prejudices. They must be given guidance.

Traditional concepts of criminal responsibility and competency are based on relatively common mental illnesses, such as schizophrenia and manic-depressive disorder. Looking to these disorders, the law has formulated tests that focus on an agent's cognitive or volitional impairments at the time of her act. Thus, the traditional insanity test, with minor variations, says that a person is not guilty by reason of insanity

(NGRI) if she lacked substantial capacity either to appreciate the nature or wrongfulness of her actions or to conform her conduct to the requirements of the law. The first part of the test is called the "cognitive" part, while the second — which some jurisdictions are now rejecting — is referred to as the "volitional" part.

Multiples, unlike many other people with mental illnesses, are both cognitively and volitionally intact at any given time. The traditional insanity test, because it focuses on cognitive and volitional deficits, is therefore a poor fit with MPD. Central to MPD is a dividedness that may be inconsistent with viewing multiples as single agents. When assessing responsibility, impairments in the realm of cognition and volition are beside the point — our analyses must hinge on this radical dividedness.

The traditional view of involuntariness looks to an agent's conscious control of her acts. That formulation, as we discussed in the previous chapter, does not make complete sense of the grab bag of phenomena called "involuntary" — sleepwalking, hypnotic and posthypnotic suggestion, and reflexes. Adding MPD to the mix does not clarify the picture. The principle that unites these phenomena — and lies at the heart of MPD — is a lack of integration.

In this section I first present and critique how courts have assessed the criminal responsibility of individuals suffering from MPD. I then go on to compare these rules with the special rule I have proposed for MPD and to address how the language of the traditional insanity defense, if we choose not to adopt wholly new language, could be applied to multiples in light of my proposal. I begin by calling attention to the propensity of courts to rely unduly on expert opinion. There is a tendency for experts simply to conclude that a multiple could know or not know the nature or wrongfulness of her act, and for courts then to repeat these conclusions in rote fashion. In *Tanner v. State* (1970), *State ex rel. Lowery v. Abrahamson* (1988), *Ex rel. R.H.L. v. State* (1990), and *State v. Jolley* (1993), for example, we are told of expert conclusions that track the language of the relevant tests, but we are not told how the experts — or the courts — understand the language of these tests to apply to multiples.

Consider a likely issue before the court in an insanity case: whether a defendant knew the nature of his act. When do we find that a multiple lacked this capacity? Did the multiple lack this capacity when the alter in control did not know the nature of his act? When any of the alters lacked this capacity? When most did? When the multiple "as a whole" did? We do not know what it means when an expert asserts that a multiple knew or did not know the nature of his act. The simple assertion, without explanation, is less than helpful.

The difficulty in relying on experts to apply the traditional test is brought out clearly in the testimony in *State v. Jackman* (1986, 31), a case that concerned a lesser dissociative disorder, depersonalization. In this murder appeal, the court-appointed expert found that the defendant's depersonalization disorder "caus[ed] him to have a split personality." Originally arguing that the defendant would not have registered that his act was wrong, the expert later indicated that "it becomes impossible to deliniate *[sic]* what part of himself was seeing it as wrong and what part wasn't. Part of him was and part of him wasn't, and I think the jury is in a very difficult situation of trying to assess how that comes out, what percent was which. I think both were there." Here we can hear — if not feel — the expert grappling with how to define insanity. Should the right-wrong, or volitional, test be applied to the part of the defendant that was acting? To other parts? To the defendant as a whole? Because the law has given virtually no guidance on how the insanity test applies to multiples, leaving the matter to experts makes little sense.

The error is compounded when the experts are permitted, as we saw above, to make conclusions that track a test's language yet are not required to explain clearly how they are applying the test. This is not the familiar problem of experts testifying in conclusory language without elaborating on the facts; here the matter is worse because the experts are testifying in conclusory language without explaining what they take the test to mean — without elaborating on their theory of the insanity defense as it applies to defendants suffering from MPD and other dissociative disorders. Indeed, a theory of insanity should come from the law, not from an expert, and it is the law's job to provide experts with this theory.

Not all experts have been so enigmatic about their theories; some have taken care to explain how they apply the insanity test to the case of multiples. In *Parker v. State* (1980, 587), for example, the argument was that "it was Pam Lease, not Pat Parker, who conducted the check 'kiting' scheme and Pat Parker had no control, knowledge or responsibility for what Pam Lease did. However, Pat Parker would serve the sentence, not Pam Lease." Similarly, another defendant attempted to demonstrate through his expert that " 'Othello,' not Melvin, assaulted and killed Joyce." Since Melvin was suffering from a dissociative disorder, the defendant argued, "he was insane and could not have entertained the requisite intent to kill and torture Joyce. Thus, the principal question for the jury . . . was whether 'Othello' existed as a separate personality and whether he, rather than Melvin, killed Joyce" (*People v. Wade* 1988, 802–3). In yet another case the expert testified that "one of defendant's other personalities, over whom defendant had no control, committed the criminal acts" (*State v. Shickles* 1988, 302).

Despite speaking of knowledge, control, and intent, these experts, happily, did not adhere strictly to the language of the relevant insanity test. Moreover, left to their own devices, these experts were careful to explain how they defined insanity. Other experts have looked to the concrete language of traditional rules, yet have managed to avoid relying solely upon conclusory statements. Thus the expert in one case testified that "the conscious personality would have no control over or memory of what happened during a period when he was taken over by the other 'evil' personality. The defendant thus . . . could not have distinguished right from wrong during the killing because he was virtually unconscious of what was happening" (*State v. Bancroft* 1993, 484). Experts also rely on traditional tests to explain why defendants are responsible. One expert, for example, testified that

> multiple personality in itself is not an exonerating condition. It is not a psychosis, and, although alternate personalities may show behavior often diametrically opposed to the usual behavior of the principle *[sic]* personality, it may still be contended that alternates were once part of the original personality but became dissociated as alternates. Although the principle *[sic]* personality may not have any recollection of the behavior of an alternate, it is somewhat comparable to the behavior of a man who has no recollection of doing something while under the influence of drugs or alcohol but is still held responsible for such behavior. (*State v. Beverlin* 1993)

None of the foregoing cases in which an expert fit MPD into traditional involuntariness or insanity defenses contains language indicating that the court either approved or disapproved of the theories presented. Thus, none of the cases has precedential value in this regard. Experts, and the ultimate fact finders, have been given little, if any, assistance as to how the insanity defense applies to multiples. Experts and fact finders should not be left to fend for themselves. The law must provide direction.

Courts that have taken this task upon themselves are not always clear in their reasoning or their language. Nevertheless, they seem to have developed three theories[7] on how the insanity defense applies to multiples:[8] a multiple is insane, first, if the alter who committed the crime meets the insanity test; second, if any of her alters meets the insanity test; and third, if the host personality was unaware of and did not participate in the crime. Here I review the language from court opinions suggesting these three theories and then go on to discuss the merits of each.

The first theory — the earliest of the three — holds that for the multiple to be nonresponsible the alter who committed the crime must meet the test for insanity or involuntariness. *State v. Grimsley* (1982) provides a clear statement of this theory. In *Grimsley,* a defendant who was accused of drunk driving argued that she was not acting consciously or voluntarily. She claimed that at the time of the offense she was dissociated from her primary personality (Robin) and in the state of consciousness of a secondary personality (Jennifer): "Robin was not conscious of what was happening and lacked voluntary control over Jennifer's actions" (1982, 1075). The court, disagreeing with defendant's theory, found that the evidence failed to establish that Jennifer, Robin Grimsley's secondary personality, "was either unconscious or acting involuntarily. There was only one person driving the car and only one person accused of drunken driving. It is immaterial whether she was in one state of consciousness or another, *so long as in the personality then controlling her behavior,* she was conscious and her actions were a product of her own volition" (1982, 1075–76, emphasis added). *Grimsley*'s treatment of involuntariness provides an excellent example of the first theory applied: what is significant is the consciousness or voluntariness of the alter acting at the time of the crime.

Subsequent cases have treated insanity in the same manner as *Grimsley* treated involuntariness. In *Kirkland v. State* (1983, 564), for example, the court reasoned: "The law adjudges criminal liability of the person according *to the person's state of mind at the time of the act;* we will not begin to parcel criminal accountability out among the various inhabitants of the mind" (emphasis added). Because the alter who committed the crimes (bank robberies) did so with "rational, purposeful criminal intent and with knowledge that it was wrong" (1983, 565), the appeals court sustained the lower court's finding of Guilty But Mentally Ill (GBMI).[9] In *Commonwealth v. Roman* (1993), the defendant argued that the lower court's instruction to focus on the defendant's mental state at the time of the act was erroneous. While defendant wanted the instruction to focus on the issue of whether " 'Norma,' the 'core personality,' lacked 'substantial capacity to control "Vicky" and thereby to conform her conduct to the requirements of law,' " the court cited the precedent supporting the lower court's understanding and noted that defendant cited no authority to the contrary: "Our law requires jurors to determine criminal responsibility of the person at the time of the commission of the crime. The judge so instructed the jury. There was no error" (1993, 1336).[10] All three of these cases — *Grimsley* for involuntariness, *Kirkland* and *Roman* for insanity — assess the mental state of the alter committing the crime.

The second theory — that a multiple is insane if *any* of her alters meets the insanity test — is less well grounded in the language of the courts. Indeed, the two cases that appear to take this position — *State v. Grimsley* (1982) and *State v. Rodrigues* (1984) — also contain language suggestive of the first theory. In *Grimsley* (1982, 1076), the court suggests that it is relying on the second theory: "The evidence fails to establish by a preponderance that Ms. Grimsley's mental disorder had so impaired her reason that she, as Robin or as Jennifer or as both, either did not know that her drunken driving was wrong or did not have the ability to refrain from driving while drunk." Apparently, if either alter, Jennifer or Robin, met the insanity test, the defendant would be exonerated; it would not be necessary for Jennifer, the alter in control, to meet the test. While elsewhere *Grimsley* relied on the first theory to assess voluntariness, here the court suggests that the sanity of both the host and the alter personality is significant. Thus *Grimsley* appears to embrace both theories: the first in regard to involuntariness, the second in regard to insanity.

State v. Rodrigues (1984) is likewise equivocal concerning which theory it wishes to adopt. The court cites *Grimsley* and *Kirkland* for the first theory ("we will not begin to parcel criminal accountability out among the various inhabitants of the mind") but uses language strongly suggesting that it is adopting the second theory: "Since each personality may or may not be criminally responsible for its acts, each one must be examined under the American Law Institute (ALI) — Model Penal Code (MPC) competency test" (1984, 618). The court goes on to summarize at great length testimony from the various experts about the different personalities:

> Defendant had anywhere from one to three personalities; A could appreciate the wrongfulness of his acts and conform his behavior to the requirement of the law, but could not control B; B could understand the wrongfulness of his conduct but could or could not (depending on whose testimony was more persuasive) control his behavior to the requirements of the law; and C did not care whether what he did was right or wrong or about the consequences of his conduct. (1984, 620)

This language belongs to the second theory — the sanity of each alter is significant. Yet the court in *Rodrigues* fails to explain why it is necessary to examine the criminal responsibility of *each* alter. One interpretation is that if any alter is insane, the multiple meets the insanity test (the second theory); another is that the multiple meets the insanity test only when the alter who committed the crime is insane (the first theory). At one point the court's language suggests the latter interpretation: "[Responsibility] is a question for the jury where, as here, there are diverse opinions as to which personality performed the acts and whether that personality was sane or not" (1984, 621). On the other hand, it would be senseless for the experts to examine all of the alters — as the court requires — if the only relevant alter is the one who was in control at the time of the crime. While a dispute about which alter was in control may make an examination of all the alters necessary, it would be much more efficient to have experts testify as to which alter was in control and then go on to assess that alter for insanity (or, if the experts disagree as to which was in control, assess all the alters over whom there is disagreement). The *Rodrigues* court is creating a considerable amount of unnecessary work. Whatever the court had in mind, I shall take the *Rodrigues* opinion as an example of the second theory because it can reasonably be interpreted as such.[11]

The third position — that a multiple is insane if the host personality was unable to appreciate the nature and quality or wrongfulness of the criminal conduct — is found in *United States v. Denny-Shaffer* (1993), an extremely interesting and carefully reasoned decision from the Tenth Circuit. Denny-Shaffer, a nurse, kidnapped an infant from a neighboring hospital and, having feigned pregnancy, pretended to her boyfriend that the child was theirs. It appeared that defendant's irresponsible adolescent personality, Rina, and her "Mother Superior" personality, Bridget, were coconspirators in the offense. Her host or dominant personality, Gidget, was not present at the time of the abduction, although there was some evidence that Gidget was aware of having the infant in her possession at times after the abduction but before Denny-Shaffer was apprehended.

The federal insanity test relevant to *Denny-Shaffer* refers to the defendant's inability to "appreciate the nature and quality or the wrongfulness of his acts" (1993, 1004). The choice put to the court below in interpreting this statute was whether the test should be applied to the host personality or the alter in control. In the words of one expert, there were two possible ways of assessing Denny-Shaffer's responsibility:

> (1) that in light of the presence of a host personality and several alter per-
> sonalities, if the statute means that all alters, or at least the host personal-
> ity, must be fully aware of the nature, quality, and wrongfulness of an
> act, then Denny-Shaffer was not responsible at the time of the abduc-
> tion; and (2) on the other hand, if an MPD victim is viewed as a single in-
> dividual with varying personality components, and not divided as sepa-
> rate people, the issue changes; in such a case the question would be
> whether the personality in control at the time of the offense was unable
> to understand the nature, quality, and wrongfulness of her acts. If this
> is the proper interpretation of the statute, then the defendant did suffer
> from a significant mental illness, but it was not such as to render her un-
> able to understand the nature, quality, and wrongfulness of her acts.
> (1993, 1008)

The court below chose what has become known as the "specific approach" (as opposed to the "global approach")[12] by affirming the second way of assessing responsibility put forth by the expert: the multiple is insane only if the alter who was in control during the crime was insane. The lower court refused to submit insanity to the jury because there was no testimony indicating that the alter in control at the time of the kidnapping was insane.

The court of appeals reversed, holding that the correct standard is found in the expert's first manner of assessing responsibility, known as the "global approach." The global approach looks to the knowledge and control of the *host* personality. In favor of its interpretation the court invoked principles of statutory construction: first, that "literal application of a statute which would lead to absurd consequences is to be avoided whenever a reasonable application can be given which is consistent with the legislative purpose" (1993, 1014); and, second, that "penal statutes are to be strictly construed against the government" (1993, 1014). Taking the global approach, the court reasoned, would avoid absurd consequences while construing the statute in favor of the defendant. The court concluded that the host personality should be understood to be the defendant: "Both the historical purposes of the insanity defense, as well as the objectives of the Insanity Defense Reform Act, can be vindicated by construing 'defendant' in § 17(a) to permit consideration of evidence concerning the host or dominant personality and his or her appreciation of the nature, quality, and wrongfulness of criminal conduct" (1993, 1016). Thus, Denny-Shaffer ought to be permitted to submit her defense to the jury: "We hold that where the evidence would permit a jury to find that a defendant suffers from MPD and that the host personality was unaware of the criminal conduct at issue and did not participate in or plan that conduct, the jury may also find that the 'defendant' satisfied § 17's requirements and thus return a verdict of 'not guilty only by reason of insanity' pursuant to § 4242(b)(3)" (1993, 1016).

While the notion of the "host personality" is central to the *Denny-Shaffer* standard, its definition is somewhat unclear. The court refers to the "host" and "dominant" personality interchangeably; at one point it cites Braun's definition (" 'the personality that has executive control of the body for the greatest percentage of time during a given time period' ");[13] at another, expert testimony (the personality "recognized by society as the person, and . . . which interacts with the outside world and is identified 'officially' ") (1993, 1007). Nevertheless, the court leaves no doubt that the central issue is the host's mental state.

The court then comments on the relation between MPD and kidnapping in a very interesting way. Noting that the host may have "confined or held" the baby after the abduction, the court points to evidence that MPD victims tend to cover up acts committed by their alters. In the words of the concurrence, "If concealing evidence of the alters' activities is actually caused by MPD then it too fits into an insanity defense" (1993, 1022). Whether the host had an insanity defense for the acts of confining, holding, and transporting the infant after the abduction was a question of fact for the jury. The court then declined to apply an aiding-and-abetting theory to the host personality: " 'One must . . . aid or abet someone else to commit a substantive offense. One cannot aid or abet himself'. . . . We are not persuaded that in determining liability for aiding and abetting, alter personalities should be recognized as distinct legal persons with independent status under the criminal laws, who may be aided or abetted. As we have held, it is the host or dominant personality which must be the focus of the determination of possible criminal responsibility" (1993, 1020–21). Although *Denny-Shaffer* takes seriously the notion that the host personality is entitled to deference and respect, it declines to extend this status to other alter personalities.

Having delineated the three theories of insanity in the context of MPD, I now turn to the merits of each. The first view, that a multiple is nonresponsible only if the alter who committed the crime was nonresponsible, has been applied in the insanity and the involuntariness contexts. It is wanting in both.

It would be tempting to critique the first theory because it is internally inconsistent. According to this critique, if a finding of insanity must be based on the mental status of the alter in control — as the first theory requires — the alter in control is sufficiently personlike to be punished if guilty. Because there are no relevant differences between the alter in control and the other alters, a necessary corollary of the first theory is that other alters are likewise sufficiently personlike to be punished if guilty — *and to be spared if innocent*. As a consequence, this critique goes, the multiple must always be judged nonresponsible by the first theory should there be *any* innocent alters.

One could object to this critique by responding that being in control of the body distinguishes the acting alter from the other alters in a legally significant way. The alter in control is liable to punishment because, being united (if only temporarily) with a body, it is a person. The other alters, lacking a body, are nothing but ephemeral states of mind. The problem with this objection is that the other alters are not just ephemeral states of mind; they are at least personlike. Even if a body is necessary for personhood, it is not essential for criminality. As we noted earlier, if a disembodied entity commanded someone else to commit a crime, his lack of a body would not exonerate him. Similarly, I have no compunctions about punishing an alter who participated in a crime, even if he was not in control of the body at the time. This objection — that the alter in control of the body has a privileged status — does not answer the critique.

The first theory — that the determination of insanity must hinge upon the mental status of the acting alter — is misguided because it neglects facts about multiples. Looking only at the mental state of the alter in control during the crime neglects the other alters and their states of mind. If these alters are personlike — and that is partly an empirical question — this approach must fail. We should no more punish a multiple based solely on our assessment of the acting alter's state of mind than we would throw Siamese twins in jail based solely on the criminal twin's state of mind.

If alters are nonpersonlike parts of complicated people, the first theory remains wanting. If alters are nonpersonlike, the focus of our assessment should not be on the acting alter's state of mind, as the first theory would have it, but on the person's overall state of integration. That is to say, even if the alter knew what it was doing, the person as a whole may have been so unintegrated that he was nonresponsible for the reasons sketched out in the previous chapter — that significant parts of the individual were unavailable to the decision maker, and that no integrated executive performed the act.

To put the matter in more doctrinal terms, we could say that the involuntariness question should not focus on whether the alter in control was conscious, as the first theory demands, but on whether the person's consciousness was integrated enough, overall, to sustain responsibility. Given the uniqueness of MPD, however, we might simply set a rule for multiples' nonresponsibility, and abandon altogether the traditional language of insanity or involuntariness — a position I argue for later. For now, it is enough to say that if one wants to speak the language of involuntariness, the question is whether the multiple is sufficiently integrated, not whether her acting alter was conscious. Indeed, we have already seen that lack of integrated consciousness is the deeper explanation for why the phenomena called "involuntary" should give rise to exoneration.

The second view — that a multiple is insane if any of her alters meets the relevant insanity test — has more to commend it. This view makes sense both if alters are personlike and if they are not. If alters are personlike — the most natural way to see alters on this view — then it makes sense to treat each alter as an entity deserving of deference and respect. We must inquire into the sanity of each, because if any is insane, it is unfair to punish that personlike entity. If, in the alternative, alters are not personlike, significant parts of the person are not brought to bear on the act, and so the person should be held nonresponsible.

I believe that this second theory is sound, albeit with certain flaws. It does not make a great deal of sense to focus solely on the sanity of each alter. An alter may be innocent because he did not know either that the act was occurring or that it was wrong. He may also be innocent because he did not intend to commit the act and could not control its occurrence. The alter's sanity is relevant to the question of responsibility, but the alter's intent — or simple presence — is relevant as well. A second flaw is that these cases are misguided in asking whether each alter knew the act was wrong. Generally alters will know, for example, that murder is wrong. What an alter will not know is that *her* act is wrong, either because she is unaware an act is occurring (she is behind amnesia barriers) or because she believes — however delusionally — a separately embodied person is acting. If a person does not know she is acting — is under a delusion that another person is acting — she cannot be faulted for failing to prevent the act. A more minor problem with this view is that it requires all the alters to be sane, even though the only insane alters may be fragmentary and few in number. This and other such criticisms are really quibbles. The second theory — although not unambiguously embraced by any court — is sound.

The third view — the *Denny-Shaffer* view — is the most careful, well-reasoned position in the courts today. *Denny-Shaffer* says a multiple is insane if her host personality was unaware of the criminal conduct at issue and did not participate in or plan that conduct, in which case the host personality is "unable to appreciate the nature and quality or wrongfulness of the conduct which the alter controlled." *Denny-Shaffer* is clear — and correct — in its reasoning about multiples' responsibility: it is not enough that the alter in control during the act be sane if the host personality was unaware of what was happening. The host personality is a personlike entity — entitled to deference, respect, and *exoneration if innocent.*

The reasoning of *Denny-Shaffer,* however, errs in two ways: first, by focusing on the host; second, and complementary to the first error, by failing to appreciate the personlike status of the other alter personalities. Consider first the problem of focusing on the host, characterized as " 'the personality that has executive control of the body for the greatest percentage of time during a given time period.' "[14] Since the host is defined relative to a particular time period, its identity may change depending on how one defines that period. The crucial variable in the *Denny-Shaffer* approach may thus depend on arbitrary choices — which time period is the "given" time period? And whom do we designate to answer this question? The implausibility of this view is driven home when we consider that the prosecution will probably choose to define the "given time period" as the time of the crime, in which case the criminal alter is the host. Unless the criminal alter is independently insane, the multiple will always be guilty if the prosecutor has his way. In such a case the *Denny-Shaffer* test would reduce to the first test: we look to the sanity of the alter in control at the time of the crime.

We could get around this particular problem by setting the required time period more liberally: the host is whoever is in control the most during a year-long period. A fundamental difficulty remains, however, in identifying the "person" with whoever is present most during a given period of time, an approach that reduces the question to purely quantitative terms. Suppose the host is present 10 percent of the time, while other alters are present even less — yet, taken together, they are present 90 percent of the time. If the host didn't know about the crime, but 90 percent of the person (so to speak) did, a purely quantitative approach leads to precisely the opposite of the result reached by the court in *Denny-Shaffer*. While *Denny-Shaffer* would identify the person with the host and exonerate the multiple, the quantitative approach would lead to guilt.

We could further adjust the criteria for the host by requiring, for example, that she represent a certain substantial percentage of the person. Even with both of these qualifications, however, difficulties remain, primary among which is that the host personality can change. If the alter who was host at the time of the crime did not know about the crime, but the current host is the very alter that committed the crime, the multiple would be innocent. Conversely, if the host during the crime did know about it but the host now did not — was completely innocent — the multiple would be guilty. As these examples taken together illustrate, identifying the person with the host is not the best approach, precisely because the host personality does not remain the same. Finally, and perhaps most importantly, in many multiples it is impossible to identify who the host is — if indeed there actually is a host.

The second flaw with *Denny-Shaffer* is in giving the host personality a privileged status. The host has no more claim to be identified with the person than any other personlike alter. We cannot say that the host is due special status because it is present more often than any other alters during a particular period of time; we have seen how nettlesome that approach is. Nor can we privilege the host as "recognized by society as the person, and . . . identified 'officially' " (1993, 1007). Even if there is such an alter (I have not elsewhere seen this definition), the alter so identified can differ at different times, which again raises the problem of determining who — prosecutor, defendant, judge, or jury — is allowed to designate which alter is the host. In truth, society's perceptions may be quite superficial — who society sees and who the multiple is may be entirely different. The preceding quotation speaks to who "interacts with the outside world and is identified 'officially' " (1993, 1007); but unless the multiple does not switch at all in public — a very rare multiple — there is only someone "passing" as the person, not someone who always *is* the person. What you see may not be what you get.

The fundamental problem with identifying the person with the host is that the features that characterize the host personality *as the host personality* are accidental, not essential. The host has no more right to be identified as the person of a multiple than any other fully fledged alter. If the experts present good grounds to disagree with this position, and identify the host as the person, *Denny-Shaffer* takes the correct position; the issue should be the host's complicity in the crime. If, on the other hand, my position is adopted, then *Denny-Shaffer* does not go far enough — if *any* full-blown personality is not complicit in the crime, the multiple should be nonresponsible. Whichever path the courts choose to take, *Denny-Shaffer* has made great strides in understanding that it is wrong to punish innocent alters. *Denny-Shaffer* is absolutely correct in concluding that multiples who contain innocent, personlike alters ought to be held not guilty by reason of insanity.

There are some other, minor problems with *Denny-Shaffer.* The court's reasoning seems to require that the host not be aware of the criminal conduct. But we have seen other circumstances in which personalities who are aware of but do not actually participate in a crime lack blameworthiness — if, for example, they think that another, separately embodied person is acting. One cannot be faulted for failing to act if one believes — however delusionally — that another person is acting. Knowledge of the act alone does not make one blameworthy.

Denny-Shaffer is nevertheless right on a number of other points. It was correct, for example, to focus not just on the abduction but on what occurred after the abduction as well. *Denny-Shaffer* was also right to note that MPD victims tend to cover for the behavior of their alters and to conclude that "if concealing evidence of the alters' activities is actually caused by MPD then it too fits into an insanity defense" (1993,

1022). Finally, *Denny-Shaffer* was correct in labeling as a mistake a separate consideration of each alter under an aiding-and-abetting standard. Given the presence of multiple alters in one body, as well as the necessity of punishing the whole if guilty, one should make a global determination of innocence or guilt based on the guilt of the least guilty alter. The court was wrong, however, to take this (correct) position because it did not consider alter personalities sufficiently personlike.

While not without its flaws, *Denny-Shaffer* is a remarkable decision. It takes one of the alters — the host — seriously as a personlike entity that deserves deference and respect. Although *Denny-Shaffer* does not go far enough, the step from its position to the position recommended in this book is not great. And it is a step well worth taking.

I have two recommendations for the courts. First, the law should set a standard for the responsibility of multiples that does not try to fit MPD into the current doctrinal framework.[15] That framework was developed with far more common mental illnesses in mind, illnesses whose pathology does not match that of MPD. If, as an example, alters are personlike entities, then multiples are nonresponsible because the innocent alters were not complicit in the crime. While one can speak of their lack of appreciation, this book sets forth a simpler, truer way to make the case for their innocence. Its guiding principle is that the rule of law should speak to the psychopathology of MPD.

My second recommendation (which should come as no surprise) is that the law adopt my proposed rule. According to this rule, multiples are generally nonresponsible for their crimes. We depart from this rule in two situations that warrant an inference of guilt. The first arises when all of a multiple's personlike alters knew about and acquiesced in the crime. The exception to this exception comes when the only alters who failed to acquiesce were fragmentary and few in number relative to the total number of alters. The second situation that warrants an inference of guilt arises when three conditions are met: first, a multiple is sufficiently organized that a theory of group liability justifies an inference of guilt; second, the alter acted within the scope of his authority; and third, the alter acted with an intent to benefit the whole.

These principles can be adapted — albeit somewhat clumsily — to the language of traditional insanity and involuntariness rules. We might say, for example, that a multiple did not know or appreciate the nature, quality, or wrongfulness of her act if at least one personlike alter (or a significant number of fragmentary alters) was either unaware of the act or, if aware, believed a separately embodied person was acting (did not know the act's "nature or quality"). For jurisdictions that have a volitional prong, the question would be whether any of the personlike alters, or a significant number of fragmentary alters, could not control the behavior of the acting alter (e.g., by taking control itself). Sufficient organization of the multiple should defeat the inference that the multiple lacked either knowledge or control. While my recommended principle can be made to fit the language of the insanity test, the better way would be to adopt a rule that fits the phenomenology of MPD.

The case is somewhat different for the involuntariness defense. The problem is not the language of the test — there are no real words — but the manner in which the test has been interpreted: as requiring lack of consciousness or lack of conscious control. While MPD can be fit into this theory by asking if any personlike alter lacked consciousness, the wiser course would be to recognize that the involuntariness defense has not been well understood. The principle that best unifies the involuntariness cases is that action is involuntary if not performed by a sufficiently integrated consciousness. MPD fits squarely into this interpretation.

Some jurisdictions do not allow an involuntariness defense if it is based on mental illness, which might cause problems for jurisdictions that do not adopt a special defense for MPD. The reasoning behind this position is that involuntariness is a complete defense. There is no automatic civil commitment.

My response is twofold. First, if a jurisdiction wants the option of automatically committing multiples, it should go ahead and allow this option in the case of certain involuntariness defenses. Change the law. Second, the problem of automatic commitment is overrated. Many jurisdictions do not allow automatic commitment even when an insanity defense is successful. In these jurisdictions everyone, including those acquitted by reason of insanity, must be committed through the ordinary civil commitment process. The vast majority of people who are found not guilty by reason of insanity are civilly committable: they are mentally ill and, having committed a serious crime, dangerous. This will certainly be the case with multiples, who, unlike some mentally ill people who remit by the time of their trial, suffer a chronic illness that does not improve without treatment. In short, this problem is not very significant. Many jurisdictions have proceeded smoothly for years without a rule of automatic commitment.

The courts have had considerable difficulty with MPD. While certain standards are better than others, none is wholly adequate. My recommendation is that a special MPD defense should be adopted — namely, the one I have proposed — and that multiples who meet the defense be found not guilty by reason of insanity. Is this recommendation, as some psychiatrists have suggested, so countertherapeutic that we should not adopt it? We turn to this question now.

THE PSYCHIATRIC VIEW: CRIMINAL NONRESPONSIBILITY AND THERAPEUTIC EFFICACY

It has recently become fashionable to ask whether legal rules are therapeutic.[16] A new movement in mental health law, "therapeutic jurisprudence," recommends that the therapeutic implications of legal rules be seriously — albeit not exclusively — considered by legislatures. A number of psychiatrists argue that holding multiples responsible for their criminal acts is in their therapeutic interests.[17] They base their reasoning on the psychopathology of MPD, one prominent aspect of which is to disown, disclaim, and, in their view, put responsibility for unwanted impulses and feelings into a wholly other being. Also, many multiples see parts of themselves as wholly separate people. As this reasoning goes, the feelings multiples experience are *their* feelings, and these parts are *their* parts — not separate people. Multiples must come to accept their unity.

Some holding the therapeutic jurisprudence view believe that failing to hold multiples responsible strengthens their maladaptive picture of themselves and so is countertherapeutic. It allows multiples to disown their destructive parts — to disclaim responsibility for them — and entails the danger of accepting the patients' quasi-delusional belief that they are, or are as if, different people. According to this view, holding multiples responsible will encourage them to own all their parts and to see alters as parts for which they must take responsibility — alters are not separate people but rather repositories of unwanted feelings and impulses.

In what follows I shall, first, consider the therapeutic implications of holding multiples responsible or nonresponsible; second, question whether MPD differs significantly from other mental illnesses in ways that are germane to the therapeutic jurisprudence point of view; and third, argue that even if a rule of criminal nonresponsibility is counter-therapeutic, it should not be rejected for that reason alone. First, we simply do not know whether holding multiples nonresponsible is countertherapeutic. While advocates of this view have given theoretical reasons for suspecting it is, I know of no studies establishing — or even suggesting — that their position is correct. Yet, if people are rewarded for disowning feelings or parts of themselves, it does seem reasonable to think they will continue in these maladaptive — and perhaps criminal — behaviors. On the other hand, punishing a multiple for behaviors she cannot help may make her feel helpless and angry — and no more able to control her behavior. If a multiple holds firmly to the delusional belief that her alters are separate people, her belief may simply become entrenched when not recognized, or even acknowledged, by others. And while we do not know whether a rule of nonresponsibility will be therapeutic or countertherapeutic, it seems unlikely that behavior modification will prove an effective approach to MPD. The evidence suggests that "benign neglect" therapies of the past did not work. Pretending that there was no dividedness did not bring about unity — ignoring the "others" did not make them go away. Acting as if the multiple is responsible seems no more likely to make her so.

The best treatment researchers recommend helping the alters get to know each other, communicate better, and work through their individual difficulties and traumatic experiences. As alters get to know each other and develop better communication, their responsibility increases; as their responsibility increases, we hold them more and more responsible. Before they are responsible, holding them responsible seems more likely to cause only frustration and confusion. The principal point for now is that we just do not know; we need more research.

The second issue is whether MPD differs from any other mental illness in ways relevant to the therapeutic jurisprudence point of view. Many forensic psychiatrists say that one of the principal goals of treatment after a verdict of not guilty by reason of insanity is to bring the patient/inmate to accept responsibility for his act and feel remorseful. Put in other words, regardless of which mental illness the defendant suffers from, a therapeutic goal is for him to own and take responsibility for his act.

Accepting responsibility for an act does not mean that the legal system should hold one responsible for it. These forensic psychiatrists do not recommend otherwise. A defendant can come to realize and appreciate his essential involvement in an act without being held legally responsible. Mrs. Cogdon, for instance, may come to realize that she harbored hostile unconscious feelings toward the daughter she axed to death — and feel terrible about the badness in her that led to the act — without society holding her criminally responsible. However therapeutic it may be for her to own the act as hers, she was not legally responsible for it.

The theorists who recommend criminal responsibility may argue that MPD is different in two ways. First, when a multiple is held nonresponsible, society is sanctioning a distortion — that she consists of different persons or personlike entities — a distortion she must reject in order to get well. No analogue exists in the ordinary insanity cases. Second, simply thinking about oneself in a certain way is not going to make a schizophrenic well; the chemicals in his brain need to be changed as well. Thinking about herself in certain ways might, however, make a multiple better. As a consequence, how others encourage multiples to think about themselves is of utmost importance, and is different for MPD than for other mental illnesses.

Let us examine these claims in more detail. First is the claim that finding a multiple nonresponsible encourages her to think about herself in the very way that characterizes her illness. The multiple conceives of herself as having different selves, and this bears on her responsibility. So too the schizophrenic who hears a command to kill not as part of himself but as external — the voice of God. To say that his experience of these voices as externally derived is relevant to his responsibility is not to say — or reinforce — that the voices actually come from God. It is, rather, to acknowledge that his thinking is relevant to his criminal responsibility. Thus, the claim that the beliefs of a multiple bear a different relation to criminal responsibility than do the beliefs of individuals suffering from other mental illnesses cannot always be true.

Now consider the claim that the multiple's view of herself is the foundation for her nonresponsibility. Calling her nonresponsible reinforces the very beliefs that constitute her illness. The problem with this claim is that the multiple's view of herself — as consisting of different personlike entities — may be accurate. Her difficulty, then, is not having certain beliefs but being as she is. Put in other words, her very state of being — not her beliefs — constitutes her illness. There can, of course, be feedback loops, and the multiple's beliefs may affect how she is, so that if we change the beliefs we change her. But therapy may be geared toward getting her to change her beliefs — and, more important, her-self — without the judicial branch of the government denying her reality. To say that she is nonresponsible because there are different person-like entities in her is not to approve of that way of being or to diminish the importance of becoming whole.

There is a kernel of truth to the idea that beliefs may matter in the case of the multiple but not the schizophrenic. Telling the schizophrenic that the voices are his own unconscious projections is not likely to cure him of his delusions and hallucinations. Telling the multiple she is one person, on the other hand, may help her believe and eventually come to be that way. The distinction between the multiple and the schizophrenic, however, is not as sharp as it first appears. Schizophrenics are often reassured, at least somewhat, by being told that their scary beliefs are but delusions resulting from their illness. Coming to own an act as his will generally require a good deal of therapy for a schizophrenic, which consists of words — no medication brings people fully to accept and own unpleasant parts of themselves. I am not denying that psychotics need medication. I am denying that words play no part in their recovery. And, while multiples are helped by words alone, those words can vary. To tell the multiple that she may become one person with no personlike parts — whole — may be as effective as telling her that she is so. On some views the latter is a misrepresentation, and perhaps honesty is the better way. Once again, however, research that would provide a solid basis to answer our questions is decidedly lacking.

Assume, solely for the sake of argument, that holding multiples nonresponsible is countertherapeutic, and that such is not the case with other mentally ill people. What follows? The conclusion that multiples should therefore be held responsible unless the alter who committed the crime was criminally insane seems strained, at best. While the new movement of therapeutic jurisprudence considers whether legal rules are therapeutic, it does not make that consideration decisive. That a legal rule is countertherapeutic will yield to other considerations when justice so requires. MPD provides just such an instance. Even if it is countertherapeutic to hold multiples nonresponsible, a proper legal analysis shows that they *are* nonresponsible.[18] While it may be useful to hold people criminally responsible when they are not, it is also wrong. Principles of criminal law command us not to blame or punish persons who are innocent of mind.

Imagine a therapist putting an innocent patient in jail simply because he was thinking of doing something wrong. Incarceration, she tells us, will scare him enough that he will stop thinking that way. Imagine further that the therapist is right and that, without this "treatment," the patient will go on to offend and be incarcerated in the end anyway. Most people, I think, would still not want to put this person in jail.

The conflict is the classic conflict between utilitarian and deontological principles. Consider the commonly cited example of imprisoning an innocent person to further some good. At a certain point, our principles may collapse under the weight of the threatened harm — if we do not imprison the innocent person, the world will come to an end — but most people have strong intuitions that it is usually, if not always, wrong to imprison an innocent person, no matter what the threatened harm. Although the patient may benefit therapeutically from unjust imprisonment — although this is not clear in our scenario here — most people, I think, would say not to do it. On a deontological view, it is unjust to blame and punish the multiple for the act solely of her culpable part, regardless of whether doing so is therapeutic or not.

Mental health professionals who believe that failing to hold multiples responsible is countertherapeutic will have to counteract this harm and help multiples become well in other ways, perhaps not yet developed. Mental health professionals have lived with the *Tarasoff* rules and regimes permitting medication refusal in hospitals, and will no doubt be creative in their response to this rule as well. While it is unfortunate that justice requires us to do something which some mental health professionals believe does not serve the treatment interests of multiples, justice is simply more important.

Having discussed criminal responsibility, it is now time to look at an earlier phase in the criminal process and to ask whether multiples are competent to stand trial in the first place. And what happens *after* the trial? Can we commit multiples to mental hospitals if some of their alters are not mentally ill or dangerous? And what about multiples who are found guilty? Should their MPD lead us to mitigate their punishment, even if all of the alters knew about and acquiesced in the crime? What about the death penalty for multiples? It is to these questions we now turn.

7. Before Trial and After

WHY CONCERN OURSELVES with issues arising before and after trial, given that my proposed rule would hold the majority of multiples nonresponsible for their crimes?[1] Competency to stand trial is important for three reasons; first, the mere claim of MPD is not sufficient to warrant a disposition of not guilty by reason of insanity. A defendant must prove — by a full-blown trial if necessary — that he suffers from MPD. Second, even if a defendant can show he suffers from MPD, he must then establish that he does not fall under any of the exceptions to our rule of general nonresponsibility. Finally, my views on criminal responsibility may not be accepted, in which case a trial will be necessary to determine if the multiple meets the relevant standard for insanity. Competency to stand trial thus plays a pivotal role in our thinking about MPD and criminal responsibility.

Civil commitment and sentencing are likewise important to address, my proposed rule notwithstanding. Regardless of whether a defendant is found competent or criminally responsible, courts will have to arrive at a disposition — be it home, hospital, or jail. Which disposition is deemed most appropriate will depend on guidelines set forth by courts and legislatures. Civil commitment and sentencing are thus integrally related to our assessment of criminal responsibility.

MULTIPLE PERSONALITY DISORDER AND COMPETENCY TO STAND TRIAL

The requirement that the defendant be competent to stand trial can be traced back to the seventeenth century and has fairness as its central value. The defendant must be competent so that the results of the trial will be accurate, the proceedings dignified, and the imposition of sanctions morally justified.[2] So important are these values to our jurisprudence that the Supreme Court has held competence to stand trial a constitutional requirement.

In *Dusky v. United States* (1960, 402) the Supreme Court held that a defendant must have "sufficient present ability to consult with his lawyer with a reasonable degree of rational understanding — and . . . a rational as well as factual understanding of the proceedings against him." The two components of competence to stand trial — the ability to assist one's attorney and the ability to understand the proceedings — have been interpreted as implying various other capacities. The ability to assist one's attorney, for example, has been taken to require the capacity to consult with the attorney and to participate in the trial. The ability to understand the proceedings has been interpreted to require the capacity to follow what is going on in the courtroom and to comprehend the trial process.

As with criminal responsibility, simply having a mental illness does not render one incompetent to stand trial. A mental illness must affect a defendant's abilities — primarily cognitive — and not just his willingness to participate. Unlike criminal responsibility, the test refers to one's present ability, not an ability in the past. And while the test is flexible (a "reasonable degree of rational understanding"), most defendants, even if seriously ill, pass; the test sets a low level of competency.

Due process requires the trial court to order an inquiry any time there is a "bona fide" doubt about competency.[3] In most jurisdictions, any party — the defense attorney, the prosecutor, or the judge acting *sua sponte* — may raise the issue. If the court does find a bona fide doubt, an evaluation will be ordered, typically performed in a mental hospital over a period of several weeks to months. While virtually all defendants deemed incompetent to stand trial will be required to undergo treatment for the sake of restoring competency, there are limitations to the treatment's duration:

> A person charged by a State with a criminal offense who is committed
> solely on account of his incapacity to proceed to trial cannot be held
> more than the reasonable period of time necessary to determine
> whether there is a substantial probability that he will attain that capacity
> in the foreseeable future. If it is determined that this is not the case,
> then the State must either institute the customary civil commitment pro-
> ceeding that would be required to commit indefinitely any other citizen,
> or release the defendant. (*Jackson v. Indiana* 1968, 738)

Before the Court's holding, defendants who could not be restored to competency were sometimes held for decades after trivial offenses. Most jurisdictions now provide a formula for determining when such defendants must be either released or civilly committed.

Two characteristics of individuals suffering from MPD may impede their competence to stand trial: the *dividedness* inherent in MPD and *impairments secondary to this dividedness.* I turn first to the impairments — not as theoretically interesting as the issue of dividedness itself, yet able to vitiate competency nonetheless. Impairments secondary to dividedness consist of deficits in memory and confusion due to switching. Memory deficits and confusion may impede a multiple's ability to follow and understand the proceedings, to testify, and to consult with her attorney. Thus, impairments secondary to dividedness are relevant to both prongs of the *Dusky* standard.

Memory deficits, as the reader may recall, are part of the diagnostic criteria for MPD and range from trivial to profound. The more profound impairments arise when alters are amnestic for each other — Eve White had no knowledge of, and hence no memory for, what went on when Eve Black was in control. If an alter is in control for a large stretch of time, the multiple's amnesia may be severe: she can have lost hours or days or, less commonly, months or years. If alters are staying out for shorter periods of time, each new alter may be amnestic for what occurred even immediately prior to her arrival — as if a series of new people happened on a scene and had to orient themselves. Deficits in memory can impair a multiple's competence to stand trial in two ways: first, the memory deficit may be *acute,* in which case the multiple may not remember the crime and thus be unable to assist her attorney; second, *ongoing* memory problems may impair a multiple's ability to follow and participate in the trial process.

Acute memory deficits, such as amnesia for a crime, are common in all manner of defendants. Some defendants suffer injuries during their crimes, as in a crash after a high-speed chase, while others have psychogenic amnesia — the crime is so disturbing that it is repressed for psychological reasons. While forgetting a crime, or the events surrounding a crime, would seem to render a defendant incapable of assisting her attorney in every instance — a defendant amnestic for a crime can hardly provide an accurate rendition of events — the District of Columbia Court of Appeals, having written the classic case on this issue, has applied a somewhat different analysis.

In *Wilson v. United States* (1968) the court held that a defendant amnestic for his crime is not necessarily incompetent to stand trial. The defendant in *Wilson* suffered amnesia as a result of head injuries — ruptured blood vessels in his brain — sustained when fleeing the police. The court reasoned that the defendant was competent to stand trial because he could perform the functions that, in the words of the majority, "are essential to the fairness and accuracy of a criminal proceeding." The court cited as factors to be considered in assessing the defendant's competency to stand trial the extent to which the amnesia affected the defendant's ability to consult with and assist his lawyer; the extent to which the amnesia affected the defendant's ability to testify in his own behalf; the extent to which the evidence in the suit could be extrinsically reconstructed; the extent to which the government assisted in this reconstruction; the strength of the prosecutor's case; and any other facts and circumstances indicating whether or not the defendant had a fair trial.

While a vigorous dissent convincingly argued that the effect of the court's ruling was "very much as though [the defendant] were tried in absentia notwithstanding his physical presence," the majority's opinion is not without its rationale. If amnesia is an absolute bar to trial, defendants with permanent amnesia for their crimes — who could be both dangerous and deserving of punishment — will never be tried. Moreover, trying such defendants may not be unfair, their amnesia notwithstanding, if all the conditions the court put forth are met. Finally, amnesia is so easy to feign that if it were sufficient to bar suit we should expect an epidemic among criminal defendants, a possibility that seems a reasonable basis on which to put amnestic defendants on trial when doing so would not be unfair.

Is there something special about amnesia as it is experienced by multiples such that their amnesia should automatically bar trial? Multiples will often have more profound memory loss than the typical amnestic defendant. The alter on trial may not remember months or years surrounding the crime, while most criminal defendants will have memory loss for the events surrounding the crime only. Moreover, multiples will have *changeable* memories, because different alters will remember different things. Neither of these differences, however, sets multiples apart from other criminal defendants in a way that is likely to be legally cognizable. Some criminal defendants without MPD will have profound memory loss (perhaps amnesia for their entire past), and the problem of alters having different memories can be addressed by caution in questioning and by proper instructions lest juries think changeable stories necessarily imply prevarication. There thus seems nothing about the way multiples are amnestic for their crimes that would warrant a special analysis under *Wilson*. *Wilson* does not, however, say that all amnestic defendants — multiple or nonmultiple — are competent to stand trial. The more severe the memory loss, the less ability the defendant will have to consult his lawyer and testify, and the less possible it will be extrinsically to reconstruct the evidence.

The *ongoing* memory problems experienced by multiples are a different matter and do set them apart from other criminal defendants. A highly dissociating defendant, for example, may "wake up" midtestimony having no idea where she is or what is happening and thus be unable to assist her lawyer by listening to and evaluating testimony. In *State v. Badger* (1988) the court suggested that should an amnestic alter come out at trial the lawyer could merely fill the client in on what had been happening. There are multiples for whom special accommodations such as the *Badger* court suggested will be appropriate. A multiple whom I recently interviewed had one alter whose function it was to act as "the representative." This alter, who was not always present during court proceedings, had the ability to reorient himself quickly upon returning and claimed that he could inform his attorney if and when he needed to be filled in on what he had missed. The *Badger* suggestion will, however, be inadequate for the great majority of multiples. The lawyer will often have no way of knowing that a switch has even occurred, and the client — being completely disoriented — will not know to ask the lawyer what has gone on. Alter personalities may switch frequently enough that informing each new alter would be disruptive, and it is possible that a multiple will switch from "the defendant" to an alter who had nothing to do with the crime. While the lawyer can inform the amnestic alter of what the witness has just said, he cannot report what the prior alter — who may have been on the brink of an insight — was thinking about that testimony.

Ongoing memory problems may also impede a multiple from testifying effectively. Alters may have different information about the crime and thus give the appearance of inconsistency or, worse, of lying. If the multiple has difficulty following questions posed by an examining attorney, she may not be able to answer in any coherent fashion; imagine trying to answer a question the beginning of which you have already forgotten. Coherent, cohesive, and consistent testimony can be crucial to the outcome of a trial, testimony which multiples with ongoing memory problems will not be able to provide. Although ongoing memory problems are not found in all, or even most, multiples, when present such memory deficits — little different in a severely dissociating multiple than ongoing short-term memory loss — should vitiate competency to stand trial.

In addition to acute and ongoing memory deficits, rapid switching of alters may render a multiple incompetent to stand trial. Imagine a multiple on trial for murder as she listens intently to the prosecutor's opening statement. A child alter sees the witness as an abuser and starts screaming. Another child alter thinks she is playing a game of "lawyers" and, having appeared, starts objecting to the testimony. Eventually switching occurs so rapidly that the multiple has no understanding of what is going on. One confabulated scenario soon follows another with utter disorganization as the result, little different than the confusion typically found in acute psychotic states. Although rapid switching is not a common phenomenon in MPD, when switching among alters does produce a psychotic-like confusion the multiple should be found incompetent to stand trial, as people in such states normally are.

While *impairments secondary to the dividedness* inherent in MPD — rapid switching and memory deficits, both acute and ongoing — may vitiate competency in quite practical and concrete ways, the *dividedness* itself raises issues of a more theoretical ilk. If, for example, we conceive of alters as persons, or even personlike, do we violate an alter's right to be present at trial when he or she is not coconscious during the entire proceeding? We can, it seems to me, resolve this issue by looking at the reasons behind the right to be present at trial: to convince the public that the trial is not a sham, to provide the defendant with the sense that he is being heard, and to ensure that the defendant can *defend* himself against the charges by hearing the testimony against him. The public will be satisfied as long as a competent alter is present; this end will be frustrated only if there is no competent representative at the proceeding. While the second goal would be best met if each alter were coconscious, the defendant should be satisfied if at least one competent alter is present to hear what transpires. Finally, on the model of a class action suit, a defendant can hear and respond to the testimony as long as a competent representative is present to act on his behalf.

A more provocative problem arising from the dividedness inherent in MPD looks to the very identity of the defendant. If alters are persons who disagree about fundamental trial strategy, which alter will decide what to plead? To whom should the defense attorney defer when alters cannot agree whether to take the stand? Assessing the impact of disagreement among alters on competency to stand trial is made some-what easier insofar as this competency, unlike most others, is not primarily about decisional autonomy. Competency to stand trial is mostly about the defendant's ability to *assist* his lawyer — lawyers have most of the autonomy during the trial. Indeed, once fundamental aims are agreed upon, what remains is a matter of strategy — not value questions but technical questions such as which witnesses to call in which order, how to examine and cross-examine, and what objections to raise, questions about which the lawyer will have the expertise. Moreover, it would be extremely disruptive if the attorney consulted with her client each time a matter of import requiring a decision arose during the trial.

Standard doctrine does, however, reserve certain especially im-portant decisions for the defendant, primarily because the client — not the lawyer — will have to live with the verdict. The defendant may choose her lawyer — and exercises some control even when the attorney is a public defender — and may make decisions fundamentally affecting the course of the trial such as whether to testify and what to plead. The client guides the lawyer by making fundamental value choices, which will implicate competency to stand trial when the alters disagree.

Fortunately, most of these are choices on which interalter consensus is likely. If, for example, the prosecution has a strong case and the charge is a serious one, the multiple's best bet is probably to plead not guilty by reason of insanity, and a lawyer would likely be able to convince each of the alters to so plead. When alters do disagree about an issue over which the defendant retains control, the lawyer should first attempt to negotiate among the alters. If the lawyer's best attempts at consensus fail, she must then decide to which alter she should defer. Put simply, the lawyer must decide who her client is.

Disagreements among alter personalities on matters over which the defendant retains control are a matter of concern in assessing competency to stand trial regardless of whether we conceive of alters as persons, personlike centers of consciousness, or nonpersonlike parts of complicated people. Our assessment will, however, depend on which of these conceptualizations we choose. Our analysis for the first two conceptualizations — that alters are persons or personlike — is the same, insofar as lacking a body, the principal reason one could argue that alters are not persons, is irrelevant to competency to stand trial. Indeed, alters conceived of as distinct personlike apperceptive centers are moral agents, fully entitled to the autonomy and respect we accord to persons.

If we conceive of alters as persons or personlike, and the alters disagree over trial decisions that implicate competency to stand trial, we have three options. We could, first, simply declare the multiple competent, and either develop some rule for determining which alter gets final say or cede to the attorney decisions normally reserved for the defendant; second, find a multiple competent by treating the alters as distinct people and giving each a separate trial; or third, find a multiple incompetent for a predetermined length of time deemed reasonable for the alters to reach some accord, after which time we fall back upon one of the first two possibilities as a default position and either declare the multiple competent or give each alter a separate trial.

The first possibility that arises when we conceive of alters as persons or personlike — simply declaring the multiple competent even if the alters disagree about matters over which they retain control — seems to go against everything I have argued for thus far. My position has been that one alter's decision to commit a crime should not be used as a basis to imprison a multiple, since innocent alters would then be unfairly burdened with the punishment. Why should one alter be allowed to impose its choices — and the possible consequences of those choices — on the others? Being a person, after all, means having the liberty to make important personal choices, choices that should be allotted to each alter if we conceive of alter personalities as separate people.

Yet are choices that arise during the course of a trial of the same magnitude as the choice to commit a crime? Consider the following argument, based on the premise that the ultimate disposition of a trial will turn much more on what the lawyer does than on what the defendant decides, even when the defendant's decision concerns what plea to enter: giving defendants choices over even a few — albeit concededly important — trial decisions indicates deference to their feelings, but not much beyond that. The choice to testify, for example, is no more important than the choice of which witnesses to call and sometimes less important than developing and executing a strategy for direct and cross-examination. Letting defendants decide whether to take the stand makes them feel better but is not all that important as a personal right.

If this line of reasoning is persuasive, perhaps we should be obliged to give defendants authority to make important trial decisions only when we can do so with relative ease. Disagreements among alters would then be of much less consequence. This argument is buttressed when we consider that many choices in the trial process are equally consequential as the decision to testify, yet the authority to make these decisions is given to the lawyer. Presumably it would be unduly burdensome for the lawyer to interrupt the trial process to ask his client in what manner to proceed each time a decision of consequence arose, and we may think that in most instances the lawyer will have a good sense of what his client would want anyway.

This way of thinking does have its merits, particularly when we consider the administrative advantages: it allows us to proceed with the trial. We may nevertheless hesitate at the thought of giving defendants authority to make important decisions only when we can do so with relative ease. Even were we to concede that lawyers are important — crucial — to a trial's outcome, that many decisions in the trial process are as important in a tactical sense as how to plead, and that administrative convenience plays *some* role in determining when to give defendants decisional authority, we could not conclude on these bases alone that decisions like the choice of plea should be ceded to the attorney — or to the most outspoken alter — when alters disagree.

The decision to plead innocent or guilty is crucial, and perhaps even different in kind from other trial choices. The lawyer may exert considerable influence over which plea the defendant enters and the charges to which the defendant pleads, but the choice of plea is finally the defendant's — and is probably his most consequential choice. The plea is the defendant's public declaration of guilt or innocence, and it is the defendant who must ultimately bear the consequences of that plea. Recognizing the plea's practical and symbolic import, a number of courts set the standard for pleading guilty higher than the standard for competency to stand trial — although the Supreme Court has now rejected that view.

My sense is that certain decisions in the trial process are important enough that we should require competency. The difficult question, however, is whether a given choice is important enough that unanimity — except among the most trivial number of the most fragmentary alters — is required. Perhaps the importance of the lawyer, the likelihood of consensus among alters over most of the decisions, and administrative interests counsel us to require a different rule — a rule, for instance, that when alters disagree we simply declare the defendant competent and follow the choice of the majority of alters who can be elicited.

Even where the practical and normative context of a decision is such that we could relax the requirement of near unanimity among alters, competency to stand trial does not strike me as a context in which the requirement of unanimity, or near unanimity, should be waived, for two reasons. First, the costs of finding the multiple incompetent because alters disagree on matters over which the defendant retains control are not high. Finding a multiple incompetent in such a case entails what should be a relatively brief delay; greater interalter cooperation, not necessarily integration, is needed. Such interalter agreement usually occurs early in treatment. While the costs are insignificant, the advantages of waiting until agreement is reached are profound. Waiting for competency based on unanimity, or near unanimity, shows respect to and confers dignity upon a defendant who, given a brief delay, may be perfectly able to choose how to plead before a court. Our first option, simply declaring the multiple competent despite interalter disagreement, lacks the very respect we are trying to preserve.

Our second option, which deals with disagreements in a quite different way, is to try each of the alters separately, thus allowing alters who disagree to make their own choices. In Billy Milligan's case, Adalana can plead guilty, Arthur innocent, and Billy himself not guilty by reason of insanity. Arthur — with his own attorney — can take the stand, while Billy, after consulting with *his* attorney, may decline to do likewise. If alters are different people, why not try them as such? For convenience, the alters can be tried in the same proceeding, although each would be given his or her own trial, as were the Menendez brothers.

Would giving each alter his or her own trial work administratively? If we cannot punish alters separately, why do we think we could try them separately? Some problems with separate trials are easily resolvable. We could, for example, avoid a multitude of lawyers by treating all alters with the same plea as a class, in which case there would be at most three attorneys. If alters within a class disagree over a matter of import, the class could be subdivided, and additional attorneys assigned if necessary, much the same as happens in class actions. Evidence and objections would not need to be duplicated — the Menendez brothers did not have each of their witnesses testify separately.

Other administrative problems arising from separate trials are not so easily surmounted. It is often difficult to distinguish one alter from another and to ensure that, once out, a given alter will stay out long enough to complete a given task. While alters will have incentives to come out and stay out — when out they can hear witnesses, help their attorney formulate defenses, and suggest questions for cross-examination — often alters lack the ability to come out at will, especially when more forceful, perhaps less benign, alters are present. Moreover, the lawyers on the class action model will not easily consult with their clients, since usually only one alter can be out at a time. These problems are not entirely dispositive — alters can, for example, identify themselves when they appear at trial, so that the jury can keep them separate — but they are more than minor inconveniences.

At first glance the concept of separate trials, while logistically problematic, is at least theoretically sound. If, after all, alters are people, or even personlike, how better to respect their personhood than to judge each separately? Each alter can make its own decisions: if an alter believes himself guilty, he can plead guilty without subjecting the others to his plea; if another alter believes herself innocent, she can plead innocent; and so with a plea of not guilty by reason of insanity. Two problems, however, are apparent. First, according to my proposed rule, most multiples will be found not guilty by reason of insanity. As a consequence, the majority of these trials will hinge on whether the defendant is a multiple. Granting each alter his own lawyer, and the ability to make his own trial decisions, may strongly bias the jury in favor of finding that the defendant does suffer from MPD. This problem can be dealt with in a fairly straightforward way: try the MPD question first. Trying the question of MPD, with a single lawyer, will not prejudice each alter's individual decision concerning what to plead. If certain alters deny that they are MPD, they can so testify. Since the MPD issue will be dispositive only if the disorder is found *not* to exist — in which case the MPD plea cannot stand — being found to suffer from MPD will not unduly harm the alter claiming sanity: she may still be found guilty or innocent, and she may still plead as she wishes. Thus the first problem — that granting alters separate trials will prejudge the MPD question — dissolves if the MPD issue is tried first.

The second problem with trying alters separately is more serious: even if tried separately, alters are still denied footing equal to that of ordinary criminal defendants. Consider that if an ordinary defendant pleads innocent and prevails, he will be found innocent. He may go where he pleases. If he pleads not guilty by reason of insanity, and prevails, he will be found NGRI; if he pleads guilty he will, of course, be found guilty. When alters disagree, a multiple is in a much different situation. If any alter pleads guilty, then an alter who pleads innocent, even if she prevails, cannot be part of a multiple who, as a whole, is found innocent; at best the multiple will be found NGRI because she will have one guilty alter and one innocent alter. The alter pleading innocent in this scenario thus has no chance of achieving her desired disposition.

The problem is clear: if we try alters separately, an alter may not achieve the outcome she desires even if she prevails on her plea. The ultimate disposition — be it prison, hospital, or home — is determined, at least in part, by the decisions of other alters. Allowing disagreeing alters to make their own decisions is thus as unfortunate to a particular alter as if either the state interposed a plea or we simply let one alter impose its decision. The very purpose of retaining control over the decision-making process has been lost. While an alter pleading guilty could achieve her desired disposition should alters pleading innocent be found guilty, no such possibility exists for those alters who wish to plead innocent — the guilty pleas will prevent them from being set free. Requiring NGRI pleas will not solve the problem, insofar as alters wishing to plead innocent or guilty will necessarily be dissatisfied. An NGRI plea would be, at best, a compromise, the very sort of compromise other defendants need not make.

While a tempting comparison, the defendant whose coconspirator pleads guilty is in a different position entirely. Although such a defendant will certainly want his coconspirator to plead innocent, the possibility of an acquittal is not foreclosed if his partner enters a guilty plea. By contrast, one alter's guilty plea does make it impossible for the alter pleading innocent to prevail — to walk away. The very purpose of retaining control over the decision is lost.

At the heart of the matter is that, while alters may have different views about what *should* happen to them, only one thing *can* happen to them — even if alter personalities are different persons, they share one body. They can make separate pleas, but there can be only one overarching disposition for the multiple as a whole. This does not mean that the multiple is one person (she may be one group of people), but she is a group that cannot be separated and so, in certain circumstances, must be treated as one. Trying alters separately — our second option — therefore does not provide separate decisional authority, defeats the very purpose of retaining decisional authority, and renders any such decisional authority illusory.

Having thus rejected the option of trying alters separately, and having concluded that the cost of finding a multiple incompetent, at least until some measure of integration is achieved, is small, we come to the following rule, captured by our third option: when alters disagree about matters over which they retain decisional control, a multiple is found incompetent to stand trial for a period of time (say six months), or as long as she is holdable based on other competency rules, whichever is more. Should the alters still disagree at the end of that period, the majority of alters is allowed to make the decision, unless they wish to keep working toward agreement and can be expected to reach an accord within a reasonable period of time. If the alters refuse to state a preference, if there is no majority, or if the wishes of the majority cannot be ascertained, decisional authority is ceded to the attorney, who must decide what a reasonable defendant would decide.

This compromise serves three purposes. First, it states that trying a multiple in a state of internal accord is the best option. Second, it acknowledges that ceding authority to the majority of alters or to the attorney is a second choice — the closest we can come to what the multiple as a whole would choose — a choice acceptable when the cost of achieving complete accord is too high. Finally, it recognizes how easily disagreements among alters can be feigned, how readily interalter agreement can usually be achieved through a brief therapy, and how infeasible it would be to provide separate trials for alter personalities.

Disagreement among alters conceptualized as nonpersonlike parts of a complicated person requires a different analysis. Amnesia will not provide a basis for finding incompetency in this instance insofar as we are now considering multiples whose alters, while disagreeing over trial strategy, are not very amnestic for one another. Thus arguing, as we did in regard to criminal responsibility, that parts behind amnesia barriers are not brought to bear on the decision-making process is somewhat problematic. Parts are nevertheless excluded from the decision-making process — not by amnesia, however, but by the defense attorney. When there is disagreement, the defense attorney will, by necessity, adhere to the wishes of certain alters and disregard the wishes of others. If a multiple is criminally nonresponsible because amnesia prevents all parts of the self from being brought to bear on the decision-making process, a multiple should be incompetent to stand trial when a defense attorney prevents certain alters from being brought to bear on the decision-making process.

An objection to holding a multiple incompetent to stand trial on these grounds is that such a defendant differs little, if at all, from a criminal defendant who continually changes his mind about what to plead. His attorney is in no less a quandary about which part he listens to and which part he disregards. Two points answer this objection. First, a nonmultiple criminal defendant can make a decision representative of him at a given time — that is, a decision which, when it must be made, takes into consideration all his conflicting parts. The multiple, by contrast, is divided at a given time; the decision is not the sum of all her parts — it is not *her* decision. A multiple is like a person acting under posthypnotic suggestion, when one aspect of a person wonders why another is acting as it is. This is not to say, of course, that dividedness *over* time is not important; but such dividedness is common enough that we have agreed-upon rules about how it should be handled — the person as she exists at a certain moment makes the decision, and how she thinks about the choice before or after is given little, if any, weight. This way of thinking about multiples fails in virtue of their "cross-sectional" dividedness.

The second answer to the objection that multiples whose nonpersonlike alters disagree are no different than criminal defendants who cannot make up their minds is that sometimes we should declare such defendants incompetent. Consider a defendant who, every few seconds during the first meeting with her attorney, yells out a different choice as to her plea — Guilty! Not guilty! Not guilty by reason of insanity! It would seem arbitrary to pick a particular choice, no less so the last choice before the trial begins, as her final plea. This defendant has not made a choice we can defer to; in a sense, she has not made a choice at all. Such a defendant, of course, is much like a multiple. There is little difference between a defendant who manifests three choices in rapid succession and someone who manifests three choices simultaneously. If we declare incompetent to stand trial a nonmultiple who in rapid succession manifests three mutually contradictory choices — as commentators in other contexts sometimes suggest we do — a multiple whose alters cannot agree on a plea, even when alters are conceptualized as nonpersonlike parts, should be held incompetent to stand trial as well.

Having discussed pathologies specific to MPD that vitiate competency, we should not forget that criminal defendants suffering from MPD may be incompetent to stand trial for the very same reasons nonmultiple defendants are held incompetent — they fail to meet the *Dusky* standard. To meet the *Dusky* standard, at least one competent alter must be present at all times; if, for example, only a psychotic or a child alter is present, the multiple will be incompetent in the same way and for the same reasons that a child, or a psychotic individual, is incompetent, and so should not be tried.

We have concluded that MPD vitiates competency to stand trial in three circumstances: first, when ongoing memory impairments render multiples unable to follow the trial proceedings or assist their attorney; second, when rapid switching produces a psychotic-like confusion; and third, when alters cannot reach agreement about matters over which defendants retain decisional authority. If alters cannot agree on such matters the multiple is deemed incompetent for six months, or as long as she is otherwise holdable, whichever is more. At that point decisional authority is ceded to the majority of alters or to their attorney, unless they wish to keep working toward accord and it seems likely they will achieve accord in a reasonable amount of time. To ensure that the multiple meets the *Dusky* standard, at least one competent alter must be present at all times.

Our position is consistent with *Jackson v. Indiana* (1972, 738), which says that a defendant declared incompetent to stand trial can be held no more than a "reasonable period of time necessary to determine whether there is a substantial probability that he will attain . . . capacity in the foreseeable future." The standard for attaining capacity under *Jackson*, however, must be applied differently to multiples than to nonmultiple criminal defendants. By and large, ordinary criminal defendants cannot control the time necessary for treatment; medication works, or not, irrespective of their wishes. Cooperation, while helpful, cannot ensure the efficacy of an antipsychotic agent; likewise, lack of cooperation cannot prevent an antipsychotic agent from working.[4] MPD is different. Psychotherapy — not medication — is the treatment of choice. The efficacy of psychotherapy — unlike that of medication — *does* depend on the patient's motivation. An uncooperative patient in psychotherapy will simply not get better — at least this is what our best guess tells us. A multiple can therefore virtually guarantee that she will not be restored to competency, which, in turn, means that under the *Jackson* standard she must be either civilly committed or released, with her charges eventually dropped. It would seem that, in this way, a criminal multiple could potentially evade trial and go free after committing a crime.

At least three reasons would prevent an uncooperative multiple from escaping confinement and evading criminal charges altogether under *Jackson*. First, a multiple who committed a dangerous crime would be committed to a psychiatric hospital. *Jackson* creates problems when a defendant who is *not* mentally ill is incompetent to stand trial, as, for example, a deaf-mute who cannot learn to sign. Such a person may well be dangerous yet not mentally ill. A multiple who commits a dangerous crime is both dangerous and mentally ill, and so committable. There is no danger under any reading of *Jackson* that an uncooperative multiple can evade confinement altogether. Second, while the Supreme Court has suggested that it would be unfair to hold charges indefinitely over the head of an individual who is incompetent to stand trial, there is hardly a question of fairness if the defendant has chosen to remain incompetent or will not comply with efforts to make him competent. Such a defendant has chosen his own lot and hence has no cause for complaint. A third reason an uncooperative multiple would not be able to avoid trial and evade criminal charges is that, even if not civilly committable, a multiple who refused to cooperate with treatment could nevertheless fall under the *Jackson* standard. There is a "substantial probability" that such a person, who is able but unwilling to get better, will attain capacity "in the foreseeable future," insofar as at any time he could come to see competency, and his subsequent trial with its final adjudication, as in his best interests.

We could, if necessary, create a presumption that any multiple who can get better will get better in the foreseeable future. This presumption fits squarely into the framework of *Jackson*'s central value, fairness to the defendant who cannot be tried and so *cannot* prove his innocence. It is constitutionally and morally permissible to hold uncooperative defendants indefinitely as incompetent to stand trial. Defendants will thus have an incentive to cooperate with treatment, to attain competence, and to prove their innocence. Indefinite confinement, even if not prison, is a significant sanction.

An objection to holding incompetent defendants indefinitely on the grounds that they fall under the *Jackson* standard is that a defendant should not be able to evade trial simply by refusing to cooperate. Trial is not his choice; it is society's choice. Thus, when a defendant remains incompetent to stand trial for a significant time because he refuses to cooperate in treatment, the proper disposition would not be continued confinement but rather a trial — the administration of justice ought not to be thwarted. Nevertheless, it could be countered, a defendant's incompetence is incompetence. The values underlying the doctrine behind competence to stand trial are undermined if we try incompetent defendants, whatever the reason for their incompetence.

Uncooperative defendants thus may be seen as incompetent or unwilling, depending upon one's point of view. Fairness cuts both ways. It is fair to put an individual on trial who lacks certain capacities because he refuses to take the steps, even when offered, necessary to acquire those capacities. On the other hand, the values behind competency — promoting the accuracy and the dignity of the process — will be violated if we try such a defendant. After all, uncooperative defendants suffer from an impairment — albeit one that is self-imposed — and therefore stand in contrast to defendants who, like the multiple whose alters feign disagreement, do not suffer from any true impairment.[5] While I myself would prefer to hold uncooperative defendants indefinitely, the question is a close one and I am happy to let others decide.

We now have some idea of what should happen before the trial. But what about after?

DISPOSITION OF MPD
INSANITY ACQUITTEES

What then happens when a multiple is deemed competent to stand trial and is subsequently found not guilty by reason of insanity? Ordinarily an insanity acquittee would be committed to a psychiatric hospital for treatment until he either recovers or is no longer dangerous, although in some jurisdictions states are required, even after an acquittal by reason of insanity, to prove that the defendant meets civil commitment criteria. If we conceptualize alter personalities as nonpersonlike parts of one complicated person, this way of doing things makes perfect sense; the individual as a whole is mentally ill and dangerous, despite the fact that some alters may be neither. If, however, we conceptualize alters as persons, or even personlike, the disposition of multiples found NGRI raises the same problems as does the disposition of multiples found guilty: as it is not fair to blame and punish one alter for the crimes of another, so it seems unfair to institutionalize one alter because another is dangerous and mentally ill. Put another way, how can we justify civilly committing an alter who is neither mentally ill nor dangerous, solely in order to treat and protect the public from one who is? Civil commitment must therefore be distinguished from imprisonment if multiples can be treated in the same manner as other defendants acquitted by reason of insanity.

While the similarities are perhaps most striking, five differences set civil commitment apart from imprisonment. First, blame, by general consensus, is necessary for punishment — it is universally accepted and acknowledged that to be imprisoned an individual must have done something wrong, in the sense of being morally blameworthy. What is necessary for civil commitment, on the other hand, is opaque at best; experts themselves disagree on what is normatively required, and the general public would hardly be expected to have a good sense of what is necessary to commit someone to a psychiatric hospital. Thus, innocent alters who are incarcerated will suffer more public condemnation than will nondangerous alters committed to psychiatric hospitals.

A second difference between civil commitment and incarceration is that the stigma of wrongdoing — *blame* — is more onerous than the stigma of illness, even when the illness entails the possibility of danger. While people who are mentally ill and potentially dangerous may scare us, dangerous criminals have intentionally harmed us.

A third difference is length of confinement. With appropriate treatment, MPD can often be cured or significantly ameliorated within several years. Several years in a psychiatric facility is far less burdensome than a long, perhaps life, term in prison. On this ground alone commitment of a healthy alter is less troublesome than imprisonment of an innocent alter.

A fourth difference is that while blameworthiness, in and of itself, is both a necessary and a sufficient condition for imprisonment, dangerousness, when coupled with mental illness, is sufficient, but not necessary, for commitment. Put another way, we commit when dangerousness is intermittent. We could, for example, confine an asymptomatic person with a contagious illness if, by the time symptoms appeared, it would be too late to protect others. We could also confine a mentally ill person who makes threats — even in the absence of evidence that she would carry out those threats. Dangerousness need permeate neither time — a person need not be dangerous every moment — nor every aspect of the person, in order to justify civil confinement. Dangerousness may not be needed at all: many mental health professionals believe that the need for treatment, or the inability to care for oneself, is adequate justification for commitment. We come back to the issue of stigma: because the threshold for civil confinement is lower than that for criminal confinement, the stigma attached is correspondingly less.

A fifth difference is that society pays a greater price for failing to confine the nondangerous or non-mentally ill alter than it does for failing to imprison an innocent alter. When we fail to imprison an innocent alter, whose fellow alter has committed a dangerous crime, we sacrifice one function of punishment — retribution. Nevertheless, through civil confinement, we can meet other ends of punishment such as rehabilitation, deterrence, and incapacitation. When, on the other hand, we fail to confine a nondangerous and non-mentally ill alter whose fellow alter is dangerous, much is lost. There is no way of protecting the public other than confinement. Put in other words, failing to punish a guilty alter costs society some retributive satisfaction and costs the multiple the respect of being treated like a person; failing to confine a dangerous alter may cost lives. Much is at stake when we fail to confine an alter — even a nondangerous alter — when dangerous alters are present.

Having discussed five distinctions between imprisonment and civil commitment that are consistent with confining nondangerous alters —

even though we would not imprison innocent alters — I would now like to examine the concept of dangerousness as it applies to multiples. The idea that alters may be innocent even when a fellow alter commits a heinous crime is compelling; alters can be as different in their degrees of blameworthiness as people can be. The idea that the alters may not be dangerous in a multiple when a fellow alter commits a dangerous act seems somehow different; our intuitions seem to say that in a dangerous multiple *all* the alters are dangerous and mentally ill.

That all alters in a multiple are mentally ill seems straightforward. While individual alters may not be clinically depressed, anxious, or psychotic, the very condition of sharing a body with other personalities is a mental illness suffered by each alter. The usual criteria for mental illness are met — distress, disability, abnormality, and treatability. While, of course, none of these four, taken alone, would be sufficient to merit a diagnosis of mental illness, together they strongly suggest the presence of psychopathology. Without embarking upon a full-scale discussion of the concept of mental illness, I will accept that the presence of all four indicates mental illness for each individual alter.

The argument that all alters are dangerous is more complex. Why does the mere condition of sharing a body with a dangerous alter make other, perhaps quite docile, alters dangerous? Consider the following three analogies. First, if a bomb is in one room of a house, all the rooms in that house are dangerous; none is safe. Second, if my waving a flag regularly provokes another person to become violent, then my flag-waving, even when done with the best of intentions and without malice, is dangerous. Third, an individual unknowingly suffering from a seizure disorder, like epilepsy, may be dangerous, especially if she has a seizure while driving a car or while engaged in some other potentially dangerous activity such as using a sharp knife. A multiple with a dangerous alter seems a case in point, insofar as her body itself is lethal.

Denying dangerousness may be tempting because, as a label, danger may imply stigma and blame. The flag-waver and epileptic may be innocent of malice or intent to harm; violence results from the actions of the former because another person acts; harm comes from the actions of the latter because his body — not his person — acts. If, however, "danger" is not understood to apportion blame but rather is taken to mean "increases the likelihood that harm will occur," both the flag-waver and the epileptic are dangerous. Our thinking is in terms of base rates — the base rate of personal injury is higher in the proximity of such people. This analysis "de-links" the concept of dangerousness from the concept of blame, and it is this sense of dangerousness that provides the basis for civil commitment. We commit psychiatric patients not because they are blameworthy for the danger they pose but because we wish to protect both the public and the patients themselves, in whose presence harm is more likely to occur.

In this regard innocent alters are dangerous — inextricably bound to dangerous alters, their presence is a predictor of harm. They are, if you will, "infected" with a dangerous form of MPD. No more blameworthy than an individual suffering from tuberculosis, innocent bystanders are nevertheless more likely to be harmed when these innocent alters are near than when they are absent. There is another way in which innocent alters are dangerous as well. I have suggested that alters have an obligation to intervene and prevent acts of other alters if they can do so without undue effort or danger. If they cannot, whether because of amnesia barriers, insufficient control over switching, or the violence of other alters toward them, they are, in a sense, passively dangerous because they fail to prevent a harm perpetrated by their very own body.

We conclude from this analysis that alters — even peaceable alters — are dangerous precisely because they are mentally ill. They are dangerous in one sense because, infected with the disease of MPD, they share a body with other dangerous alters, such that their presence is a predictor of harm. They are dangerous in another sense because, in virtue of their MPD, they have amnesia and insufficient control of other alters, and so are passively dangerous. An individual who is dangerous because she is mentally ill is precisely the person we deem fit for civil commitment.

Consider again the individual suffering from a seizure disorder. If her seizures regularly caused harm, we would impute to that person a moral obligation to seek treatment. If, for whatever reason, the person were unwilling to seek treatment, we would impose treatment upon her, perhaps as a kind of just penalty for not volunteering to be cured. If, for whatever reason, this person were unable to seek treatment, we would impose treatment upon her not as a penalty but because she presented a danger to innocent others. People have a moral obligation to stop being dangerous when they are able, and society takes it upon itself to prevent their dangerousness when they are not able.

What of the objection that innocent alters, when confined because dangerous alters have been acting up, are being treated as nothing other than means to an end? The objection becomes more forceful when we tell the peaceable alters that, although entirely blameless, they have a moral obligation to be civilly committed for treatment, thus adding insult to injury. Two responses answer this objection. First, when an individual is dangerous because mentally ill, treatment makes all the sense in the world, especially when the illness is treatable in a relatively short time. Given the risk of nontreatment — harm to innocent others — a brief treatment, even though mandated, does seem morally acceptable, if not morally appropriate. Second, it is permissible to harm an individual who presents a clear and immediate danger. If an epileptic lunges toward you with a sword, you would shoot him to protect yourself. Even though you may feel bad afterward, your act will have been morally acceptable. By contrast, it would not be morally permissible to kill another person whose organs you need to save yourself. Unlike the lunging epileptic, potential organ donors pose you no danger. Peaceable alters are more like the lunging epileptic than the potential organ donor, in that their very bodies are lethal to innocent others. It is permissible to do what we can to deprive the alter of that lethality, especially when the intent of our intervention is to benefit, not to harm.

The two broad rationales given for confining dangerous mentally ill people apply to individuals suffering from MPD. The first is that we treat dangerous mentally ill people. This rationale, of course, makes sense only if the mentally ill person is treatable, and individuals suffering from MPD are eminently treatable. The second rationale is that dangerous people who are not mentally ill can respond to the sanctions of the criminal law, while dangerous mentally ill people often cannot. This rationale argues for committing people who would be found not guilty by reason of insanity should they commit crimes. Most multiples who commit crimes will be found not guilty by reason of insanity. The civil commitment of multiples thus does not cause the intractable problems that arose from their imprisonment.

There may be those who object and argue that we should apply the same analysis to civil commitment as we did to imprisonment. Consistency, the reasoning would be, demands that we not subject innocent alters to civil commitment, just as we would not subject them to imprisonment. I do not agree with this way of thinking, and would be quite comfortable confining the epileptic who cannot, or will not, seek treatment on his own, and who continues to engage in dangerous behaviors. Nor, however, do I agree with those who, on the opposite end of the spectrum, would relax the commitment criteria for multiples who have dangerous alters, on the basis that such multiples will be found not guilty by reason of insanity if the dangerous alters act. The argument here is that the dangerous alter is, as it were, "lying in wait," capable of great harm. While I once found this argument persuasive, it now seems to me that we should not deviate from our normal practice. Many dangerous people will be found not guilty by reason of insanity if they commit a crime, and of many we can be sure that danger lurks even when not patent. Predicting dangerousness is always precarious, no less so when the prediction concerns an alter who has not emerged for a period of time; the alter may have integrated, its danger may have muted, or it may no longer come out. We should commit multiples only for the same reasons we commit other dangerous mentally ill individuals: because the danger has reached a certain level of urgency.

Civil commitment of MPD insanity acquittees is thus acceptable. While we will not imprison innocent alters, civil commitment differs in several important regards, most of which center on the concept of blameworthiness. The commitment standards for multiples should not be relaxed. We should apply the same standards to multiples as we do to all other mentally ill individuals.

MPD, SENTENCING, AND THE DEATH PENALTY

/ SENTENCING, CAPITAL AND NONCAPITAL /   The sentencing of multiples is important for two reasons. First, jurisdictions may adopt a narrower standard for criminal responsibility than the one I have proposed, in which case fewer multiples will be judged insane. The sentencing issue will arise correspondingly more often. Second, even on my view the sentencing issue will inevitably arise, insofar as I have set forth several situations in which multiples will be judged responsible for their crimes. The question I will address is whether MPD ought to be considered a mitigating factor, a question that is especially pointed in the death penalty context.

Consider a standard for criminal responsibility according to which a multiple whom I would hold innocent is found guilty. In my way of thinking, MPD would serve as a mitigating factor in this jurisdiction for two reasons. First, if alters are different persons or personlike centers of consciousness, innocent alters render the multiple as a whole less guilty. Mitigating the sentence is a way to recognize the multiple's nonculpable "pockets." If, in the alternative, alters are nonpersonlike, the lack of integration lessens the multiple's culpability, a lessening that likewise calls for mitigating the sentence. My position on this score should hardly be surprising; given that I think the multiple should be exonerated entirely, I could not think other than that her sentence should be mitigated. Second, MPD should serve as a mitigating factor because it is a severe mental illness — indeed, the most severe of the dissociative disorders. The presence of a severe mental illness was often taken into account in indeterminate sentencing schemes, and even determinate schemes allow reduction of sentence for severe mental illness. In certain cases, such as provocation, extreme emotional states are considered a mitigating factor; MPD should act in this way as well.

Although jurisdictions administer the death penalty in quite different ways, all consider aggravating and mitigating circumstances in determining which defendants convicted of a capital crime will be executed. While most jurisdictions call for weighing aggravating and mitigating factors and allow the death penalty to be imposed if the former outweigh the latter, the Model Penal Code allows the fact finder to consider a death sentence only if she finds "no mitigating circumstances sufficiently substantial to call for leniency" (ALI 1985, sec. 210.6 (2)). Connecticut has the strictest standard, prohibiting imposition of the death penalty if any statutory mitigating criterion is found. While statutes' aggravating factors are exclusive, any mitigating factor may be considered, so that the fact finder will be open to the "possibility of compassionate or mitigating factors stemming from the diverse frailties of humankind."[6]

To be sufficiently "aggravating," a circumstance "must genuinely narrow the class of persons eligible for the death penalty and must reasonably justify the imposition of a more severe sentence on the defendant compared to others found guilty of murder."[7] One mental illness-related aggravating circumstance is "dangerousness": whether "there is a probability that the defendant would commit criminal acts of violence that would constitute a continuing threat to society."[8] Typically several mental illness-related mitigating factors are found in death penalty schemes. In the language of the Model Penal Code, they are (1) whether the defendant was "under duress or under the domination of another person"; (2) whether the defendant was suffering from "extreme mental or emotional disturbance"; (3) whether "the capacity of the defendant to appreciate the criminality (wrongfulness) of his conduct or to conform his conduct to the requirements of law was impaired as a result of mental disease or defect or intoxication"; and (4) whether "the murder was committed under circumstances which the defendant believed to provide a moral justification or extenuation of his conduct."[9] Each of these mitigating factors is a weak version of actual defenses in criminal law (duress, provocation, the insanity defense, and self-defense, respectively).

Perhaps, given the person's lessened ability to prevent violence, MPD should be considered an aggravating factor. It could be argued that, by virtue of her MPD, there is "a probability that the defendant would commit criminal acts of violence that would constitute a continuing threat to society."[10] The qualifier "continuing," however, disqualifies MPD per se as an aggravating factor. While untreated MPD may indeed lessen an individual's ability to abide by the law — although there is no evidence that multiples in general are less law-abiding than nonmultiples — the danger, if any, abates with treatment; alters come to know and cooperate with each other, so that control over behavior increases. More important, a few years of treatment are sufficient in most cases to achieve integration, in which case any danger presented by the MPD will no longer exist. MPD, in and of itself, ought therefore not to be considered an aggravating factor.

Multiples who commit capital offenses will virtually always be able to establish several mitigating factors. Can it be said that multiples, in the words of the first factor, are under duress or the domination of others? Yes — such is the defining characteristic of MPD, in that one alter takes control of the body and hence of the other alters. In terms of the second factor, multiples suffer extreme mental or emotional disturbance by virtue of having MPD. In regard to the third factor, insofar as innocent alters may neither know about nor have the capacity to control the acts of other alters, the multiple as a whole may be less able to appreciate the wrongfulness of his acts or to conform his conduct to the requirements of the law. Finally, capital defendants often raise histories of child abuse as a mitigating factor. In most studies, over 90 percent of multiples report such a history. While not a mitigating factor in most schemes — too few people diagnosed with

MPD have been sentenced to death for legislatures to have encoded it as such — the best reason not to execute multiples is that they contain personlike centers of consciousness who are innocent of wrongdoing. Even should we reject this reasoning as a basis for exoneration from criminal responsibility, we should accept it as a mitigating factor in the capital sentencing context. Put in other words, even though we deem the multiple as a whole guilty of a capital crime, we should not put the innocent alters to death.

Should we go one step further and say that, in cases of MPD, the mitigating factors outweigh the aggravating factors as a matter of law? I would do just this when, despite the presence of innocent alters, multiples are found guilty. The reasoning is that we should not execute innocent alters even if their guilty alters deserve as much. At the least, the innocence of an alter should be an explicit mitigating factor. We could likewise conclude that multiples meet enough of the illness-based mitigating factors that the death penalty should never be imposed, an alternative equally acceptable to my way of thinking.

What should happen in cases in which, under my standard for criminal responsibility, the multiple would be guilty? When, by definition, all the alters are complicit in the crime, mitigating factors may nevertheless be present. An extreme emotional disturbance may have had an impact on the crime; while all the alters participated, perhaps the integrated person would have had a different configuration of personality traits, possibly more benign. As a result, this multiple's capacity to appreciate and control his conduct may indeed have been lessened. Despite the arguable presence of such mitigating factors, this is not a case where we would want a rule that the mitigating outweigh the aggravating factors as a matter of law. The guilt of this multiple approaches that of a "normal" person, the pathology notwithstanding, even should we consider MPD a mitigating factor in and of itself. Multiples, then, will not always escape the penalty of death.

/ COMPETENCY TO BE EXECUTED / The United States Supreme Court has yet to articulate a standard for competency to be executed. While the Court did in *Ford v. Wainwright* (1986) constitutionalize the common law rule that it is not permissible to execute someone who is incompetent, the only guidance as to what constitutes incompetency in this regard is found in Justice Powell's concurring opinion: "The Eighth Amendment forbids the execution only of those who are unaware of the punishment they are about to suffer and why they are to suffer it" (1986, 422). In interpreting the concept of competency to be executed, some states have set standards that focus on an inmate's ability to understand his situation, while others require that an inmate be able to assist his lawyer in the appeals process as well. In the latter jurisdictions, multiples will be incompetent to be executed for similar reasons they are incompetent to stand trial, in addition to the ways they are incompetent in the former jurisdictions. In the former — and more common — jurisdictions, the matter is less straightforward.

Consider first jurisdictions that have rejected my rule for criminal responsibility and have adopted instead a rule that allows for a finding of guilt even though some personlike alters did not know about or acquiesce in the crime. Should this jurisdiction's standard for competency be that an inmate must understand his situation, and should alters be conceptualized as persons or personlike, all of the alters must understand that they are to be executed and why. Put in other words, because separate people, or personlike entities, are being put to death, each must understand this fact and the reasons behind it.

If alters are conceptualized as nonpersonlike entities, parts of one complicated person, our analysis changes little: given the finality of death, all the multiple's parts should understand the situation, not just a majority or an outspoken few. This case can be likened to an inmate who has a part of himself — perhaps a delusional part — that denies he is about to die. While it might not be unusual for someone in a situation as stressful as death row to have parts of himself that deny the reality of his impending fate, suppose the delusional part takes over to the point where, for significant periods of time, this inmate denies he is to be executed. In a jurisdiction where competency to be executed turns on understanding, he is incompetent at those times. Perhaps, over time, his "sometime competency" will become so inconstant that we would declare him incompetent to be executed altogether.

The case becomes even stronger if this inmate suffers from delusions that he is separate people, some of whom accept, while others reject, that he is about to die. If alters are conceptualized as nonpersonlike, the multiple is in precisely this position — he has delusions of being different people. If it is not permissible to execute an inmate who does not know that he is to die, it seems equally impermissible to execute someone who thinks he is a separate person from the death row inmate and is about to die for reasons he cannot fathom. Any way of looking at the situation leads to the same conclusion: all parts of a multiple must understand both that he is to die and the reasons why the death penalty has been imposed.

Variations on this scenario become increasingly complex. Would the statement of an innocent alter, "I did not commit the crime, and so cannot understand why I am to be executed," render the multiple incompetent to be executed? In the alternative, would we deem the multiple competent if the alter could comprehend our reasoning, namely, that the multiple as a whole is guilty? In such a case the alter, while not agreeing, would at least understand our reasoning. While there is some tendency to read competency to be executed in this bare manner, the death penalty may be one context in which a finding of competency should require a fuller appreciation of the situation.

If we conceive of alter personalities as nonpersonlike, the alter's belief is in the nature of a delusion, the sort of delusion that should lead to a finding of incompetency. Consider a psychotic person who has the delusion that another person — not he — committed the crime. This person cannot understand why he is to be executed and so cannot come to terms with his punishment; remorse, repentance, the respect and dignity of being treated as a person capable of choosing right and wrong — all will be lost on him. His punishment will be an accident of fate, "fear and pain without comfort of understanding."[11] His understanding that society thinks he committed the crime will not change our analysis; as long as he believes in his innocence, punishment cannot be experienced and understood as punishment, the sine qua non of competency to be executed. If we conceptualize alter personalities as nonpersonlike, the multiple whose alter claims innocence is in the very same position as the psychotic person, and should be deemed not competent to be executed.

The scenario calls for a different analysis if we conceptualize alters as persons or as personlike. In this case the multiple and the state agree on the facts — this person (i.e., the alter) did not commit the crime for which the death penalty has been imposed. The multiple and the state disagree, however, on the normative conclusion to be drawn. Put another way, the question no longer turns on what role a delusion should play in our assessment of competency, insofar as the disagreement stems not from different perceptions of reality but from different views on when the death penalty is justified.

At first glance this sort of disagreement would not seem to affect competency. After all, many death row inmates feel that the death penalty is always wrong (as have Supreme Court justices), that their role in the crime was too small to warrant execution, or that a history of child abuse makes the death penalty inappropriate. Disagreement with the state on such matters should not be recognized as having a role in determining whether an inmate is competent to be executed. In at least two ways, however, these kinds of disagreements seem different from the disagreement that arises when the alter conceived of as a person claims innocence. First, inmates who, for example, consider their role in a crime too trivial to warrant the death penalty disagree with the state on purely philosophical grounds. The multiple whose alter claims innocence disagrees with the state for reasons intimately connected with her MPD. Put another way, there would be no disagreement were it not for her mental illness, in the absence of which she would have no alters to claim innocence. While giving mental illness this sort of causative role in competency is not without its problems (Saks 1993, 751–58), many commentators on competency and responsibility do so, and it does seem significant that the disagreement, though normative, could arise only in virtue of a severe mental illness, MPD.

A second distinction seems deserving of more weight. Differences arising over matters of jurisprudence — the mitigating role, say, of an abusive past — are unlike differences over culpability *vel non*. Disagreement over normative matters may cause upset, even anguish — I may object, vehemently, that you have sentenced me to death on the basis of my relatively trivial role in this crime. Disagreement over culpability, however, renders punishment devoid of precisely the characteristics we wish to preserve — the person cannot experience punishment as a response to his wrongdoing, a recognition and consequence of his moral culpability, a stimulus to or opportunity for remorse and repentance. And it is not that he refuses to do so — he cannot, for he firmly believes, and the state agrees, that *he did not commit the crime*. To put the matter another way, disagreements over whether one is sufficiently guilty to merit the death penalty are qualitatively different than disagreements over whether one is guilty at all. The latter disagreement — arising between the state and the alter who says "I did not do the crime, and so should not be executed" — may therefore give rise to a finding of incompetency even though the former does not. In this latter situation, the defendant is not arguing for a different system of rules but is challenging the application of society's own rules — one does not punish the innocent; therefore he, innocent, ought not be punished.

Alters may render a multiple incompetent in a variety of ways. They may be too young to understand the concept of death; psychotic in their own right; unable to achieve coconsciousness, in which case they will not know about their own execution; or, most often, innocent of the crime and so unable to understand the reasons why the death penalty has been imposed. In each of these ways multiples may be incompetent to be executed even though, given a standard for criminal responsibility narrower than my own, they would be held guilty. While most incompetency, in virtue of MPD's treatability, can be resolved in a relatively short time, this form of incompetency cannot be resolved at all. It cannot be resolved because no degree of integration achieved after the criminal law has intervened will render the multiple able to understand his impending punishment; like the innocent alter, the integrated multiple did not commit the crime and cannot understand why he is to be punished. The death penalty is therefore not an option for multiples in whom all of the alters did not acquiesce in the crime.

In jurisdictions that have adopted my standard of criminal responsibility, guilty multiples may be found competent to be executed. Given that a multiple can be found guilty under my standard only if all the alters knew about and acquiesced in the crime, there are no "innocent" alters. There may, of course, be alters in virtue of which such a multiple would be deemed incompetent if, as the execution drew near, young children or psychotic alters emerged; this sort of incompetency can be resolved by treatment. Multiples will therefore be found incompetent to be executed less often if my standard is accepted.

Our analysis for competency to be executed applies equally to competency to be punished. Regardless of whether a jurisdiction adopts my standard for criminal responsibility, most multiples will not be competent in either way and should therefore be confined to psychiatric institutions. While statutes and cases of a number of jurisdictions suggest a competency-to-be-punished requirement,[12] I know of no jurisdiction that implements such a requirement in practice. Inmates generally find their way to psychiatric hospitals not because they do not understand their punishment but because they are unmanageable by virtue of their mental illness.

Having looked at issues before and after the trial of multiples, we now turn to the other dissociative disorders. MPD is the most severe of these disorders. Do other forms of dissociation raise the same thorny, at times intractable, problems for the criminal justice system? It is to this question we now turn.

8. Criminal Responsibility & Other Dissociative Disorders

N EARLIER DISCUSSIONS we distinguished the dividedness of MPD from the more ordinary dividedness of neurotic conflicts and everyday ambivalences. Based on the distinctions we drew, we concluded that the dividedness most people encounter in their day-to-day lives does not vitiate criminal responsibility, while the dividedness of MPD does. How does our analysis apply to other dissociative disorders? Are individuals suffering from derealization, depersonalization, dissociative amnesia, and the like responsible for their crimes, and, if so, are they competent to be punished?

DEREALIZATION

Derealization entails losing one's sense that the external world is real. While the capacity for reality testing is not lost, familiar people and places seem strange, unreal.[1] The individual experiencing derealization knows that the external world is real — it just *seems* strange. Should the experience of derealization vitiate criminal responsibility? In virtually all cases, no. Derealization does not share any of the characteristics of MPD that speak to whether an individual is responsible for his crimes; it implies neither different persons, different personlike centers of consciousness, nor a significant lack of integration.

One argument for holding derealized individuals nonresponsible is that a person suffering derealization does not fully appreciate that he is harming a real person with real feelings. Not appreciating the "realness" of other people gives one less incentive to respect their interests. And it is precisely this lack of appreciation and respect for what one is doing that serves as a common basis for the insanity defense.

The flaw in this argument is that while the derealized person may not have the fullest appreciation possible of the external world and the people in it, she never loses touch with reality. The knowledge that other people are indeed people, with their own interests, needs, and capacities to feel pain, remains intact. Indeed, it can be argued that it is precisely this quality—empathy, if you will—that psychopaths, whom the law does hold criminally responsible, lack. To "lack substantial capacity to appreciate" what one is doing requires more than the estrangement from the external world brought on by derealization; indeed, it requires even more than the lack of appreciation for other people as other people that characterizes psychopathy. If the experience of derealization becomes so intense that it approximates a loss of reality testing, then an individual should have the insanity defense available. But this will happen rarely, if ever at all.

DEPERSONALIZATION

Depersonalization involves losing the sense of reality *of oneself*—the "feeling that one's body or self is unreal" (Steinberg 1994a, 8). Depersonalization, recognized as a clinical entity in its own right, is "characterized by a feeling of detachment or estrangement from one's self. . . . The individual may feel like an automaton or as if he or she is living in a dream or a movie. There may be a sensation of being an outside observer of one's mental processes, one's body, or parts of one's body" (APA 1994, 488). Individuals suffering depersonalization report feeling as if they are hovering above, watching themselves go through the motions of living. Often they describe an "observing self" and a "participating self." As with individuals experiencing derealization, depersonalized individuals do not lose contact with reality; they know they are real and they know who they are, yet they feel unreal and unfamiliar to themselves. While sometimes occurring separately, most often depersonalization and derealization occur together.

Should someone who commits a crime while in a depersonalized state be found nonresponsible? In many regards the analysis applied to derealization seems apt. Feeling things less real — whether what is felt as less real is the self or other people — is not enough to vitiate criminal responsibility. If anything, feelings that the *external world* is unreal (derealization) would be more significant from the perspective of the criminal law — hence more likely to vitiate criminal responsibility — than would feelings that the *self* is unreal (depersonalization). Perhaps, though, the attenuated sense of self should distinguish depersonalization from derealization in a legally cognizable way. If an individual appreciated less well her own values and interests — her humanity, if you will — she would likely act in a less human way. On the other hand, feeling oneself less real does not necessarily mean feeling less human. The sense of living in a dream or a movie is only a sense for the depersonalized individual; she does not literally believe that she is so living. *Fully* appreciating one's acts has never been considered a sine qua non of criminal responsibility.

Of what significance to the criminal law is the often reported experience of a split between an observing and a participating self? Does this experience suffice to warrant a finding of nonresponsibility because, as in the case of MPD, we have two persons or personlike entities, or at least a significant lack of integration? There are striking — and legally relevant — differences between the "selves" of depersonalization and the "selves" of MPD. The "selves" of depersonalization are not different persons, or even different personlike entities. The observing self does not have its own unique characteristics, nor are there amnesia barriers between the observing and participating selves. Moreover, nothing suggests that the observing self conceives of itself as a different self from the participating self; indeed, depersonalized individuals speak of watching *themselves* from a distance. And they conceptualize their experience of depersonalization as involving a split in their experience of *the* self — not as involving a split between *different* selves, the sort of experience reported by multiples.

Applying Dennett's criteria, we see that the observing "selves" fall woefully short of what is needed for personhood. These selves are not self-conscious, and they can be considered language users and the subjects of Intentional predicates (the sole criteria they can be reasonably argued to meet) only because the observing self is part of the self as a whole. Criteria for personhood other than Dennett's six, such as not being too ephemeral and being relatively versatile, do not apply to the observing selves at all. The selves of depersonalization thus cannot be categorized either as persons or as personlike entities, the basis for our first two theories of criminal nonresponsibility in the case of individuals suffering from MPD.

What about the basis for our third theory of criminal nonresponsibility, that individuals suffering from MPD lack an integration sufficient to impute a cohesive agency? While depersonalization does entail a lack of integration, it is hardly profound. The observing self, which has neither its own unique characteristics, its own sense of self, nor barriers that separate it from the participating self, is less a way of naming a separate self than a way of describing an experience of detachment. Unlike with MPD, the participating and observing selves of depersonalization are not necessarily in conflict, nor does each have its own separate wants and needs. For these reasons we cannot speak of discrepant parts of the individual not being brought to bear on an act, at least no more so than with neurotically ambivalent individuals. The third basis for finding multiples nonresponsible — lack of integration — thus does not apply to depersonalized individuals. The case of depersonalization so profound that splits are experienced as they are in MPD, or that a person feels like an automaton carrying out someone else's command, may sometimes amount to nonresponsibility but will occur rarely, if ever.

DISSOCIATIVE AMNESIA

Dissociative amnesia is "typified by the inability to recall important personal information . . . usually of a traumatic nature. The amnesia must be too extensive to be explained by ordinary forgetfulness and must not be due to . . . the activities of alter personalities" (Steinberg 1994a, 7). In its discussion of dissociative disorders, the DSM-IV distinguishes among five different types of amnesia. An individual suffering from *localized amnesia* "fails to recall events that occurred during a circumscribed period of time, usually the first few hours following a profoundly disturbing event"; in *selective amnesia* "the person can recall some, but not all, of the events during a circumscribed period of time"; in *generalized amnesia* "the failure to recall encompasses the person's entire life"; *continuous amnesia* refers to "the inability to recall events subsequent to a specific time up to and including the present"; finally, *systematized amnesia* is the "loss of memory for certain categories of information, such as all memories relating to one's family or to a particular person" (APA 1994, 478).

To illustrate the difference between these five types of amnesia, consider the following scenario. A man returns home after a long day at work, only to be met by his partner, who intends to end their ten-year relationship on the basis of a new, intense love affair. The partner, having disclosed both the affair and the intent to end the relationship, leaves the house to spend the night with the new love, a neighbor who lives only a few doors away. The man, devastated by this news, sits at home for several hours, alone in the dark, and begins to consider various means by which he might kill himself. As the night goes on, however, he becomes increasingly enraged at his partner and the neighbor, and sometime before dawn enters the neighbor's house, goes up to the bedroom, takes a heavy lamp, and bludgeons the pair to death. He then returns to his house and sits in the living room, mute, covered with blood, until the police, having been notified by neighbors that something appears amiss, arrive later that morning.

If this man suffers from *localized amnesia,* he may remember coming home from work and being found by the police, but nothing in between. The intervening hours will be completely lost to him. If he suffers from *selective amnesia,* he may remember something of what happened during those hours. He may, for example, recall hearing his partner tell him of the affair, entering the neighbor's house, and having the lamp in his hand, but he may also recall nothing of the actual murders or his departure from the house after the killings. If the person suffers from *generalized amnesia,* he will remember nothing of his entire life — who he is, what he does, whence he comes. If he suffers from *continuous amnesia,* he will be unable to recall anything from a given point in time — perhaps hearing of the affair — up to the present. Finally, if he suffers from *systematized amnesia,* he may recall nothing at all about his partner, about the house in which he and his partner were living, or about the neighbor with whom his partner was having the affair.

Consider first what should happen to this man — call him Steve — if any of these five types of amnesia follows the murders. Should Steve be held criminally responsible? Certainly. Each of these amnesias *post-*

dates the murders. Put in other words, the impairment had no effect on the crime; any psychopathology that follows the crime cannot be argued to have been a factor contributing to the commission of the crime. While Steve was sufficiently traumatized by the murders to repress his memory of them, traumatization can stem from a number of sources. Perhaps he was horrified at what he had done and felt a keen sense of remorse. Or perhaps he was terrified by the intensity of his rage, or by the prospect of spending the rest of his life in prison. In any case, traumatization would speak to mitigation at sentencing, not to criminal responsibility.[2]

Can it be argued that any, or all, of these amnesias vitiate competency to be punished? Is the person who cannot remember himself committing the crime in the same position as the innocent alter ("I did not do the crime; how can you punish me for it?") whom we deemed not competent to be punished? Consider first the difference between not *remembering* and not *believing* that you did something. Steve, even though he does not remember committing the crime, may well concede that he committed the murders when presented with sufficiently persuasive evidence, such as his fingerprints on the lamp, blood on his shirt, and so on.

Someone who accepts that he committed a crime, whether or not he remembers it, is competent to be punished. He can come to terms with his punishment. He can feel remorse, repent, and feel the respect and dignity of being treated as a moral agent. Acceptance will suffice to achieve these ends; actual memory is not necessary. Yet what does it mean to accept having done that which one cannot remember having done? What would it mean for Steve to accept having murdered his partner and the neighbor if he had no recollection of having committed the crime? While I can believe I did something without actually remembering having done it, can I truly own such an act as my own? Can I say with any force, "This was *my* act," when I have no recollection whatsoever of what I did? Certainly the way I "remember" things I have been told I did is very different from the way I remember things I can actually see myself doing in my mind's eye. The latter remembering comes with an experiential feel that the former lacks; there is greater depth to the latter, and the memory connects with other of my experiences.

This discussion about competency to be punished is somewhat academic in two respects. First, as long as an individual believes he committed a crime, a rich appreciation of the deed is unnecessary;[3] individuals suffering derealization lack a rich appreciation for the external world, but they are criminally responsible nonetheless. Second, the facility with which memory loss can be feigned is alone reason enough to deem competent to be punished criminal defendants whose sole claim to incompetency is amnesia.

Should the law make a special case for individuals suffering from generalized amnesia? Put in other words, should someone who loses his entire life history be deemed not competent to be punished for his crimes? A person suffering from generalized amnesia has lost who she is, what she does, whence she comes; if there can be a person without a history, an individual with generalized amnesia is she. It is virtually impossible to imagine what such a state must be like; almost by definition it would be accompanied by confusion, disorientation, and fear. Perhaps it would simply be too cruel to punish an individual who is suffering in this way.

We said previously that belief, defined as acceptance — and as contrasted to memory or appreciation — was a sufficient basis for competency to be punished. Why should the case be any different for someone suffering from generalized amnesia? Perhaps if we could bring her to believe that she had committed a crime, she should be deemed competent to be punished. While persuasive, a caveat needs to be made. Belief may need special consideration in the case of generalized amnesia. Individuals with this sort of amnesia may be so distraught that they cannot assimilate any, much less complex, information of the sort that would be required to recreate a life history. And even after the acuity has passed, such individuals may still be likelier not to believe they are the person who committed the crime. Note that, in the case of localized amnesia, the necessary belief is the belief of having committed a particular act; with generalized amnesia, the necessary belief is the belief of *being a certain sort of person,* as well as being *the particular person who committed this particular act.*[4] The estrangement from the information is much more profound, and we may conclude that acceptance is not sufficient to establish competency in the case of generalized amnesia. We need more empirical research on the quality of the "belief" in the case of the generalized amnesiac to determine whether he is competent. The arguments, then, are tentatively in favor of competency to be punished, with the possible exception arising for those who suffer generalized amnesia.

Now consider a person suffering from *continuous amnesia,* who cannot lay down new memories subsequent to a particular time and up to the present — literally as if he has no ongoing memory. Such a person would not remember at any given time *that* he was being punished, much less *why* he was being punished. Surely the point of punishment is lost, and it would make little sense to hold this person competent until his memory has been restored. Continuous amnesia thus provides the one clear instance in which dissociative amnesia vitiates competency to be punished.

Our discussion of amnesias following the crime has been straightforward. Criminal responsibility is unaffected; the pathology follows the crime and so cannot be a cause of, hence the basis for an exoneration for, a criminal act. Competency to be punished was, with a wrinkle or two, equally direct. Localized, selective, and systematized amnesias do not affect competency to be punished. Generalized amnesia may, depending upon what we come to know about the "beliefs" such a person can have about his life and crimes. Continuous amnesia vitiates competency to be punished.

We now turn to amnesias that occur *before* or *during* a crime. At first glance it is easy to imagine how localized, selective, or systematized amnesia could be relevant to criminal responsibility. Albeit concededly a rare occurrence, someone with these amnesias could, for example, marry, having forgotten that he already has a spouse. Such a possibility would exist whenever a particular memory is necessary for mens rea.

What about generalized amnesia? Is a person who commits a crime while amnestic for his entire life criminally responsible? Clinicians have suggested to me that this scenario is not clinically realistic, insofar as such a person will be too distressed, distraught, or disorganized to commit a criminal act. Consider, though, the following three scenarios: first, individuals who have just lost their memories; second, individuals who have lost their memories some time ago, so that they have a continuous memory of themselves since the time of the memory loss but not before; and third, those who have lost their memories some time ago, have continuous memory for the events subsequent to the memory loss, and have had the events prior to the memory loss filled in by loved ones. The most disturbed will almost certainly be those in the first category; having just lost their memories, they will be extraordinarily confused and distraught. Still, even hopelessly deteriorated psychotics and young children commit crimes,[5] so it does not seem possible to rule out this category of generalized amnestics as potential criminals. Those in the second and third categories seem quite able to commit criminal acts — they can engage in a host of other activities, and there seems no obvious reason to believe they could not engage in crimes as well. The empirical question of whether a generalized amnesiac can commit a crime thus remains open, and the question retains its theoretical interest regardless.

Let us begin by discussing criminal responsibility for the person in the first category of generalized amnesia, the person who has just lost his entire past. To think about whether this person is responsible for criminal acts he may commit, we need to distinguish between different ways in which one may "lose" one's past. A person who has lost his past may lack conscious access to *information;* lost may be items such as name, address, occupation, education, and birthplace. Another way in which one may lose the past is to lose all access to what may be referred to as character: likes, dislikes, morals, dispositions, preferences, aims, wishes, dreams, fears, goals — the things that make this person who he is. A final way of losing the past may refer to a much more complete — insidious, if you will — loss: the past irretrievably disappears, as if it never happened. Character, in this instance, ceases — the person can no longer be said to have characteristic likes, dislikes, morals, dispositions, preferences, aims, goals, and the like.

Consider now the person in our first category of generalized amnesia, a person who has just lost his entire past. If losing his past entails losing *information* about himself, the nature of the information lost is unlikely to be relevant to criminal responsibility. Not knowing my name or occupation, for example, would hardly seem to exonerate me from criminal responsibility. What, though, if the forgotten information pertains to the sort of person one is — that one is, for example, generous, kind, and gentle? The argument for criminal responsibility is that dispositions of this sort remain operative even if conscious access to them is lacking; the characteristically honest person's disposition to be honest will prevent him from stealing, even if he is not able to recite to himself, "I am characteristically honest and do not steal." Yet there undeniably are people for whom such knowledge will aid in their conforming to a set of norms, such as the criminal law. Cases that find acts following posthypnotic suggestion nonvoluntary are consistent with the view that conscious access to disposition or character is relevant to criminal responsibility. While some have argued that a hypnotized person will not act contrary to his character, so that hypnosis should not be a basis for exoneration from criminal responsibility, others have argued — and courts have agreed — that society punishes an individual not for having a bad character but for failing to restrain himself in circumstances where the ordinary means of restraint are available. Hypnosis, a state of heightened suggestibility, makes it more difficult to resist a command, and so renders one less blameworthy for not restraining oneself. Thus, being in an ordinary, waking state of consciousness may be important for — and legally relevant to — an individual's capacity to conform his actions to the strictures of the law.

The challenge regarding the first category of generalized amnesia is to determine the nature of the forgotten material, whether information or dispositions, and whether, if the latter, generalized amnesia then vitiates criminal responsibility. I do not have an answer, although it does seem that most of what we do is a matter of dispositions, having to do with our wishes, dreams, fears, goals, predilections, and tastes, at least to a significant degree. It is difficult to imagine that someone who retained these dispositions and, at the same time, lacked knowledge of or conscious access to them, would act contrary to such character traits. I tend to believe that this sort of generalized amnesiac would be criminally responsible, although the question of whether such a person would act contrary to his dispositions is an empirical one.

The person who has just lost his entire past in the sense of lacking even *unconscious* access to his dispositions is really a variant of the other ways of thinking about losing one's past, and so does not require a separate analysis. Put in other words, if the dispositions are operative regardless of whether a person has access to them, consciously or unconsciously, then awareness of the dispositions is irrelevant to how the person behaves. The amnesia makes it neither less nor more likely that such a person would commit a crime. If, on the other hand, a person who loses his past in this way loses his dispositions in the sense that they no longer have any influence over his behavior at all, this person, in effect, is now in the situation of having no morals, dispositions, likes, dislikes, preferences, goals, and so on. Such a person has lost his character. Can he ever be criminally responsible?

If I lose my past in the sense of losing — definitively — those things we call character, what shall restrain my behavior? An argument for criminal responsibility is that if I know an act is wrong, the law expects me not to do it, regardless of whether I have lost the disposition to behave as I normally would. This argument, however, involves an exceedingly cramped view of what determines behavior. Habits, dispositions, tendencies — the kind of person one is, aspects of the superego, if you will — these are what restrain people, not mere knowledge. Having no character thus makes a particularly strong case for nonresponsibility. The person with no character is, in a sense, not a person at all but an amalgam of momentary thoughts, feelings, and desires. The person who commits a crime in this state will not know what he is doing because he will be so confused about himself. The crime will be no more than an accident, and this may be the sense in which the clinicians who deny these people can commit crimes are right: their acts are almost random. The character-based theory of responsibility, however one considers its merits, and traditional theories of criminal responsibility agree that criminality is more than a bad act. Criminality requires a state of mind, and perhaps a certain sort of character as well. A person without a character who commits an act is like someone who stumbles, not like a moral agent choosing to do wrong.

Whether someone who has just lost his past is criminally responsible thus depends upon how we define "losing." If losing one's past means losing access to information, or losing access to dispositions that nevertheless continue to exert their influence, then generalized amnesiacs who have just lost their past would be criminally responsible. If, on the other hand, losing one's past is no different than losing one's character, the generalized amnesiac who has just lost his past may well be deemed not responsible for his crimes, insofar as he has lost those parts of his person that play a central role in governing how he behaves.[6]

Now consider the second category of generalized amnesiac, the person who lost his memory for his past at time t and commits a crime at some later time, $t + n$. Suppose, in other words, he forgets his entire past — in the third sense above — due to a traumatic event in January 1994 and commits a crime in January 1995. Is he responsible for his act? Our analysis depends upon empirical information that is not currently available. The question in this instance would be whether within that year he had developed a character sufficient to hold him responsible for his crimes. Put another way, the question is whether in January 1995 he would be in a characterologically different position than he was in January 1994, when he would not have been responsible for his crime. My inclination is to say yes, he would be, and to hold him criminally responsible.

The third category of generalized amnesiac is the person in the second category who has now been told of his pre–January 1994 life by his loved ones. This case seems straightforward. If the person in the second category is responsible, so is the person who, having information about his life, falls into the third category. Indeed, the only way these two individuals differ is that the person who has been told about his life has more information, which would serve to enhance, rather than diminish, his criminal responsibility. Thus, generalized amnesiacs in the second and third categories, who have lost their memories and committed a crime at some later point in time, will be responsible for their crimes,[7] while those who have just lost their memories may or may not be responsible, depending upon what we come to know about how one's past is really "lost."

Continuous amnesia once again requires a separate analysis. Individuals who suffer continuous amnesia while they are committing a crime should not be held criminally responsible. During the commission of the crime the person would not know what he was doing, much like the person who, in the middle of a sentence, cannot remember its beginning. It could be argued that such a person is worse than the typical criminal, insofar as he must continually renew his criminal intent; in each moment, as it were, he starts the crime afresh. But this argument misses the point. The person suffering from continuous amnesia would not consciously know what he was doing so that, even if his acts were to be somewhat coordinated in the manner of an automaton, the intent to complete a criminal act of any complexity would be missing. Any action that revealed a good deal of planning would, by definition, rule out the diagnosis of continuous amnesia, leaving the possibility of criminal responsibility only for those acts that could be completed with the span of memory left to a continuous amnesiac — on the order of a few seconds. In all other cases the person suffering from continuous amnesia will not be responsible for his crimes.

In sum, unlike derealization and depersonalization, dissociative amnesia of certain kinds may thus vitiate both criminal responsibility and competency to be punished.

DISSOCIATIVE FUGUE

Dissociative fugue is characterized by "sudden, unexpected travel away from home or one's customary place of daily activities, with inability to recall some or all of one's past. . . . This is accompanied by confusion about personal identity or even the assumption of a new identity" (APA 1994, 481). While most fugues do not involve the assumption of a new identity, new identities that are formed are "usually characterized by more gregarious and uninhibited traits than characterized the former identity" (APA 1994, 482). The person in a dissociative fugue who does form a new identity "may assume a new name, take up a new residence, and engage in complex social activities that are well integrated and that do not suggest the presence of a mental disorder" (APA 1994, 482). Recovery from dissociative fugue is usually spontaneous and rapid.

Are people suffering from dissociative fugues responsible for crimes they commit while in a fugue state? The answer may depend on whether, during the fugue state, a new identity is formed. Consider first those fugues in which a new identity is not formed. In these cases dissociative fugue is distinguishable from dissociative amnesia of the generalized form by two characteristics: wandering and confusion about one's identity, neither of which is relevant to criminal responsibility. If a person's mental state warrants a finding of criminal responsibility — which generalized amnesia may often do — the fact that she was wandering when the crime was committed hardly changes matters. Nor would confusion alter the analysis we applied to dissociative amnesia; if a person loses the memory of who she is, her confusion, in and of itself, is not sufficient to vitiate responsibility. Thus the analysis for dissociative fugues in which a new identity is not formed tracks our analysis for dissociative amnesia.

Does a fugue state in which a new identity *is* formed vitiate criminal responsibility? The answer rests, in part, on an empirical question: Are the identities that arise in fugue states like the alter identities of MPD? While their differences need to be studied further, we can nevertheless make some salient observations. If the formation of a new identity entails merely assuming a new name and occupation — the more superficial aspects of identity — there are important and legally relevant differences between the identities of MPD and the identities of dissociative fugues. If, on the other hand, a new *character* is formed, the situation is quite different and much more closely approximates MPD.

If the identity formed in a dissociative fugue has it own character — its own memories, wishes, dreams, fears, and goals — the analysis for criminal responsibility tracks the analysis set forth and applied to MPD when the fugue identity commits a crime. Put simply, if the identity is a person or personlike — the first two ways in which we conceptualized the alters of MPD — the individual should be nonresponsible. If, in the alternative, we judge the new identity not to be a person or personlike, the individual is nevertheless nonresponsible because she lacks sufficient integration. That is to say, if we conceptualize the identities during a fugue state in the same manner we conceptualize the alters of MPD — whatever that conceptualization may be — our rule of nonresponsibility holds.

The analyses of MPD and dissociative fugue diverge at this point, in virtue of differences between the nature of the identities formed in each. Dissociative fugue usually consists of a single episode without recurrence: the new identity appears, then disappears, never to emerge again. For all practical purposes, that personality no longer exists. As a consequence, in the case of dissociative fugue there is good reason to do precisely what the court did in *Denny-Shaffer* — identify the "defendant" with the "host personality." Although we rejected this approach for MPD, we accept it for dissociative fugue; while we worried about protecting all the alters in MPD, dissociative fugue gives us only one "alter" to worry about, an alter that is ephemeral and, by its very nature, stands in stark contrast to the dominant personality, which is clearly identified as the true person. In dissociative fugue, then, our concern lies with protecting the main personality from the acts of the identity that arises during the fugue state. Put in other words, when a multiple commits a crime, we need to worry about how punishing the criminal alter might entail punishing innocent alters. No one alter is identified as "the person" — not even the host — so that each alter stands on the same footing as the others and should be afforded equal protection. When, on the other hand, the main, or dominant, personality of someone suffering from a dissociative fugue commits a crime, we don't need to be worried in the same way about protecting the "alter" — an alter that will likely disappear, never to resurface again. We will not impute criminal responsibility until the main personality again takes control, but this should mean waiting only a relatively short while. We therefore formulate a rule of nonresponsibility designed to protect the main personality from the acts of the new identity: if the person suffering dissociative fugue commits a crime while in the new identity, he is not responsible. We elaborate this rule by stating that if this person commits a crime while in the main personality he should be judged criminally responsible when that personality returns.

To sum up, our analysis of criminal responsibility for people in fugue states depends upon whether or not a new identity is formed. Sometimes people suffering from fugue states will be criminally responsible, sometimes not.

DISSOCIATIVE DISORDER NOT OTHERWISE SPECIFIED

Dissociative Disorder Not Otherwise Specified (DDNOS) is a catchall category for disorders "in which the predominant feature is a dissociative symptom (i.e., a disruption in the usually integrated functions of consciousness, memory, identity, or perception of the environment) that does not meet the criteria for any specific Dissociative Disorder" (APA 1994, 490). Examples include clinical presentations that are similar to MPD but fail to meet MPD's full criteria; states of dissociation resulting from brainwashing; dissociative trance disorder; Ganser syndrome (the giving of approximate answers to questions — e.g., "2 plus 2 equals 5"), as well as other dissociative states.

In this section I focus on disorders that are the most common form of DDNOS, disorders that are similar to, yet fall short of, full-blown MPD. Clinical presentations may be similar to MPD but fail to meet the full criteria when individuals lack amnesia, or when the personalities or personality states are not adequately developed. The latter may occur either because the personalities are not sufficiently elaborated or distinct, or because the personalities never take full control of the individual.

Are individuals suffering from such forms of DDNOS criminally responsible? Consider first the individual whose personalities are complete and distinct from one another, take control of the person at different times, yet are not separated by amnesia barriers. Lack of amnesia could be relevant to criminal responsibility in two ways: first, it might determine whether the alters can be considered different persons or personlike entities; second, it could bear on whether the person is sufficiently integrated to be held responsible for criminal behavior.

Does lacking amnesia barriers imply that alters are not different persons or personlike entities? Criteria of personal identity typically refer to continuity of memory — a single person has his or her *own* memories. Put another way, our memories are our very own; while we may choose to share them with other people, they belong to us in a way they belong to no one else. Conversely, to the extent that different entities share memories, they are not like different persons — different people do not have access to one another's memories. On the other hand, we saw that alters read another's memories *as* another's, and that did not disqualify alters from the status of persons, or personlike entities, at least in our earlier analysis. That alters could share memories would not seem on its face to change this analysis. Indeed, lack of amnesia barriers may also simply mean being present simultaneously, not reading another alter's thoughts. The question is a close one, but if the alters in a DDNOS patient have all the other characteristics of personhood that we have discussed, lacking amnesia barriers would not seem a sufficient basis to take away their status as persons or personlike. It will be necessary in patients of this kind to scrutinize carefully whether their alters are personlike in other respects. If so, then my inclination would be to deem such patients nonresponsible.

How do such DDNOS patients fare if we adopt the third theory of criminal nonresponsibility, that individuals lacking integration are not responsible for their acts? Amnesia barriers place impediments to different parts of the self influencing an act, and are one characteristic of multiples that distinguishes them from neurotic individuals. Amnesia barriers, however, are only one such impediment. Other impediments include the manner in which the personality in control may conceptualize different alter personalities as people, with interests, wants, and needs quite separate from his own. He may take special care not to listen to the other alters, and even to thwart their interests. Lack of amnesia notwithstanding, integration in this case is quite clearly compromised. By the same token, the problem of no executive self among the alters, an executive self who can represent the whole, seems fatal to the notion of an integrated self, regardless of whether or not alters are amnestic for one another. While I tend to favor a finding of nonresponsibility for such DDNOS patients (unless, of course, all the alters acquiesce in the crime), a careful case-by-case determination is necessary to see if the DDNOS patient's symptomatology matches the features of MPD closely enough in other regards that a finding of nonresponsibility makes sense.

Are DDNOS patients whose alters are not elaborated or distinct enough to meet the DSM-IV criteria for a personality or personality state responsible for their crimes? Michelle, for example, believed that she housed many people in her body, but she could describe them only as the "little people" and the "big people." They had neither names, unique personality characteristics, nor their own memories.[8] While existing for Michelle, these "little" and "big" people had, as it were, no flesh on their bones and would almost certainly not meet Dennett's — or anyone else's — criteria for personhood. Simply because Michelle conceptualized them as people would not make them so. Michelle, it would seem, would be held responsible for her crimes under our first two theories of criminal responsibility. How would Michelle fare on our third theory? Can her crimes truly be imputed to her as an autonomous agent, or does she lack sufficient integration to be held responsible for her criminal behavior? Since the "little" and "big" people are not described as having wishes, desires, and interests of their own, they could hardly have *discrepant* wishes, desires, and interests. As a consequence, we could not say that an act failed to reflect these various and competing interests — Michelle is responsible on the third theory as well. It is conceivable that DDNOS patients would have alters that, while not sufficiently distinct and elaborate for MPD, would suffice to vitiate criminal responsibility. Such cases, however, will be rare, and would have to be examined with great care on an individual basis.

Now consider a DDNOS patient whose alters never take full control of her behavior. Because these alters never "come out" and so remain, in a manner of speaking, behind the scenes, the full criteria for MPD are not met. At first glance this patient would seem responsible for her crimes; her configuration of alters does not present the problem presented in the ordinary multiple, in whom one alter commits the crime for which another alter must suffer the punishment. In a DDNOS patient of this sort, whoever commits the crime suffers the punishment, insofar as only one personality is ever out — we need have no moral concerns about punishing the innocent. Such, however, is a shortsighted interpretation of a case that, upon further consideration, becomes enormously complicated.

Analysis of DDNOS patients whose alters never take control implicates a wide range of issues, including the nature of alter identities, the nature of the role the identities play in an individual's external behavior, and the nature of the identities' experience.[9] In terms of their experience, there is no reason to suppose that only the alter who is "out" experiences what goes on in the patient's life. Nor does there seem a good reason to suppose that only the alter who is out affects the patient's behavior. Presumably the submerged alters could be complicit in — or wholly innocent of — the crime. Likewise, submerged alters may well be able to suffer the punishment, as coconscious rather than as "out" alters. On the other hand, while coconscious alters suffer the loss of liberty and any restrictions the person is under, they are not seen as subjects of punishment, insofar as they never present themselves to the external world. As a consequence, they never suffer the stigma of being punished.

Perhaps these considerations fail to address the most important question, which is whether alters who are never out and never take control are sufficiently personlike for us to concern ourselves with their interests. Put another way, is an entity that is fully developed, has its own sense of self, and is separated from other like entities by amnesia barriers disqualified from the status of person or personlike because it never takes control of the body? Arguing against person or personlike status is the fact that such an entity never has intercourse with the external world; other people cannot relate to it, any more than it can relate to other people. Such an entity would seem to fail Dennett's "stance" and "reciprocation" criteria for personhood. On the other hand, intercourse with the external world, in and of itself, hardly seems the sine qua non of personhood. Imagine an individual who has an accident that prevents all communication and movement. If we could somehow determine that he nevertheless remained conscious and self-conscious, as well as rational, and retained his capacity for language, we would still continue to think of this individual as a person. And, to the objection that we would do so only because of loved ones and friends who remembered him *as* a person, we could reply that even should those people die, we would still think of him as a person.

Consider another analysis that would find these patients responsible for their crimes regardless of how we conceptualize their alters. Even if the alters who never come out are personlike, they are much less personlike than the alter who is always in control — the alter who does have intercourse with the external world, relationships with other people, and obligations as well as rights. If we had to choose which alter best captures who the person is, we would certainly designate the alter always in control. *Denny-Shaffer* gave that status to the host personality in a multiple; we disagreed with the *Denny-Shaffer* position, arguing that no one alter in a multiple merits that station. Our reasoning was that, in a multiple, the host is distinguishable from the other alters only quantitatively, and changes from time to time. That alter in the DDNOS patient under discussion differs from the other alters in a *qualitative* respect and remains the *same* over time. Thus, there are crucial differences between a multiple's host personality and the alter always in control of a DDNOS patient — so much so that there are compelling reasons for identifying the alter in control with "the person," regardless of whether the other alters are persons or personlike.

If we take this position and identify the alter always in control as the person, we have only a short step to holding such DDNOS patients responsible for their crimes. Our reasoning would be as follows: the patient is responsible if the alter always in control committed the crime; none other than this alter *can* commit the crime; the alter in control — the "person" — is responsible. The only exception to this rule easily fits into current doctrine, arising when the alter in control is the innocent agent of a submerged alter. In this case, to which even the narrowest rule of nonresponsibility would apply, the DDNOS patient is nonresponsible.

This position, however, which identifies the alter in control as the person and strongly suggests a holding of criminal responsibility in virtually all cases, is not as persuasive as it may seem at first glance. Even if the alter in control has the most robust claim to be "the" person, other alters could be at least person*like* and, as personlike entities, should hardly have to suffer for something they did not do. If we cannot punish a guilty person or personlike entity without punishing innocent persons or personlike entities, then we should withhold punishment. Nor is it obvious that the leader of a group should be able to subject members of the group to harm. Of less force is the position that the alter in control, as the group's representative, is acting on behalf of the group — after all, the alter in control was hardly elected to that position. Moreover, even if alters are not conceptualized as persons or personlike, our third theory of nonresponsibility may be available. While there is an executive self making decisions in DDNOS patients of this sort, this self may not have access to the submerged alters' interests, wants, and needs, either because of amnesia barriers or because the alter in control identifies them as other selves (even though we may not). A careful inquiry into the nature of and relationships among the alters will be necessary to determine whether this patient is sufficiently integrated to be held responsible.

Clinical experience shows that people who initially appear to be DDNOS patients are often later diagnosed as suffering from MPD. Two reasons may help to explain why a diagnosis of MPD is not made initially: first, DDNOS may be a condition on the way to MPD — a prodromal phase of MPD, if you will; second, patients may come to know better, and so trust more, their therapists over time in a way that allows them to share their true symptomatology after the initial phases of therapy have passed. If the former reason holds true, the analysis of this section applies;[10] if the latter, the MPD rule of nonresponsibility governs.

DDNOS, then, provides a weaker basis for nonresponsibility than does MPD, and more so than with MPD a careful inquiry into the symptomatology will be required. Nevertheless, certain DDNOS patients will not be judged responsible for their criminal behavior.

In conclusion, patients suffering from dissociative disorders other than MPD will sometimes be responsible, sometimes not. Note, as a final comment, that if many people suffering from dissociative disorders other than MPD are responsible for their crimes, so will people suffering from the milder forms of dissociation such as daydreaming or divided attention. People suffering from such everyday sorts of dissociation will rarely, if ever, receive the benefit of a nonresponsibility defense. Only the most extreme form of dissociation — MPD — generally gives rise to a finding of nonresponsibility. Other forms of dissociation require close scrutiny into the exact nature of their pathology.

9. Conclusion

D R. JEKYLL'S TRIAL: What should the outcome be? Under my proposed rule, most multiples will be held criminally nonresponsible. Ironically, Dr. Jekyll will almost certainly be found guilty. Indeed, my proposed rule will support a finding of responsibility when the alters acquiesce in a crime — Jekyll drank the potion with the knowledge that Hyde would commit some heinous deed. Both my proposed rule and justice favor punishing Jekyll.

How would Norman Bates fare? Norman, as common sense would suggest, is different from Dr. Jekyll. He had, as far as we know, no potion, no magic word, no trigger under his control that would bring out his mother. According to the story, Norman did not even know that his mother was part of himself. For these reasons my proposed rule would hold Norman nonresponsible for crimes his mother committed. I would thus favor sending Norman to a hospital for treatment rather than a prison for punishment. Norman's horror upon discovering what his mother had done is both consistent with a finding of nonresponsibility and propitious for his treatment.

It may be that crowded dockets and misplaced fears of malingering will tempt some courts and lawyers to disregard evidence of MPD — evidence that makes the administration of justice more complex and more expensive. Yet only by forcing ourselves to pay careful attention to the way multiples present themselves can we achieve the fairness that our criminal law is designed to produce. Sometimes, as in the case of Dr. Jekyll, that will mean a finding of guilt and life in prison. Other times, as in the case of Norman Bates, careful attention to MPD will mean a finding of nonresponsibility and a stay in a psychiatric hospital.

What makes MPD so very difficult, and so very different from other psychiatric disorders, is the radical dividedness with which these patients present. In this book I have attempted to grapple with how the law should think about this dividedness. Whatever conclusions we have come to, one thing is clear: the law's way of assessing criminal responsibility in the case of other mental illnesses and other mental states does not provide a good fit for MPD.

The dividedness of MPD manifests itself in alter personalities. Philosophy, it seems, offers us three ways of conceptualizing these singular entities: as persons; as personlike centers of consciousness (what Stephen Braude calls apperceptive centers); and as mere parts of deeply fragmented people. It would be a mistake to commit ourselves prematurely to any one of these three conceptualizations. Indeed, the research on the nature and phenomenology of MPD is still in its infancy. We can, however, examine how the law should assess criminal responsibility under each different conceptualization.

Most multiples will be found criminally nonresponsible. If alters are different persons, punishing a guilty alter would inevitably entail punishing innocent people. If alters are different personlike centers of consciousness, punishing a guilty alter would entail punishing, and hence causing to suffer, blameless centers of consciousness. And if alters are nonpersonlike parts of complex people, the individual suffering from MPD is not sufficiently integrated to execute criminally responsible acts. Only in those unusual circumstances in which the alters either participate or acquiesce in the crime will we deem the multiple guilty. In the case of the other dissociative disorders, sometimes the defendant will be responsible, sometimes not; in each instance a case-by-case analysis is necessary.

What does the future hold for research on MPD? In addition to more research on the phenomenology, etiology, assessment, and treatment of MPD, we need more research into whether the disorder is a genuine clinical entity in its own right. Similarly, research into how best to understand alter personalities is indicated. We will need to explore, for example, the extent of interalter amnesia, the degree to which alters share personality traits, and the extent to which alters capture the richness and complexity of true personalities. Also helpful will be neurophysiological studies of personality and psychoanalytic studies of the etiology of personality. There is no less a pressing need for better ways to assess whether an individual — perhaps a criminal defendant — actually suffers from MPD, as well as better ways to judge the degree to which alters have acquiesced or participated in a particular course of action.

Finally, the future calls for a deeper exploration of legal issues. Should the analysis of competency track the analysis of criminal responsibility, even though the contexts are quite different? Does the presence of one competent alter making a decision preclude finding the multiple incompetent as a whole? After all, finding him incompetent would simply add one more decision maker — the guardian — to the mix. Perhaps, though, a guardian could mediate among disagreeing alters, and so would be indicated. Yet again, a guardian might not be necessary should the alters agree, as a rule, to follow whatever conscionable course a competent alter decides upon. Quite apart from responsibility and competency, MPD raises other legal questions. What does "reasonable accommodation" in the workplace entail? How can educators respond to the challenge of schooling and testing children who may switch personalities abruptly? How should we respond to iatrogenic creation or amplification of MPD?

MPD will, no doubt, continue to fascinate the public. Part of the fascination comes from the fears and fantasies the disorder raises; part as well comes from the challenges MPD poses to the way we think about ourselves and the people around us. This book will provide, I hope, a step toward bringing order to our conceptual world in the face of this strange and exotic disorder.

Appendix: Assessment, Empirical Studies, and Treatment

Assessment techniques, empirical studies of differences among alter personalities, and treatment are technical areas in the study of MPD with which it is worth having some familiarity. Each bears on the issues with which we are struggling. For example, assessment and the empirical studies should provide some reassurances to people worrying about malingerers of MPD in the criminal justice system. If there are reliable techniques for diagnosing MPD, we need worry less that these patients are malingering. And if studies of differences among alters can distinguish true alters from malingering controls, we have another means to ferret out malingerers in the criminal justice system. As a result, these first two issues also bear on skepticism about MPD. The existence of reliable and valid assessment instruments puts MPD on a similar footing to other mental disorders. And if controls cannot replicate empirically verified differences among alters, we would have further evidence that the skeptical position is off the mark.

The treatment studies are relevant to our concerns in two ways. First, they should be of interest to those who wonder about the rationality of hospitalizing for treatment multiples who are found nonresponsible. Second, they, too, bear on the skeptical position, inasmuch as effective treatment is evidence for the reality of the disorder. We now turn to these various studies.

ASSESSMENT

The area of assessment of MPD is making great strides. In addition to face-to-face individual diagnostic interviews, the methods most often relied upon to assist in the diagnosis of MPD are screening instruments for dissociation, psychological tests such as the MMPI and the Rorschach, and structured interviews. Screening instruments such as the Dissociative Experiences Scale (DES) (Bernstein and Putnam 1986), the Perceptual Alteration Scale (PAS) (Sanders 1986), and the Questionnaire of Experiences of Dissociation (QED) (Riley 1988) are cost-effective tools, and thus particularly useful in large-scale studies.[1] Unfortunately, their use as diagnostic tools is limited; while screening instruments can indicate the degree of dissociation an individual experiences, dissociation in and of itself is not sufficient to warrant a diagnosis of MPD — follow-up interviews are necessary for this purpose. Psychological tests such as the MMPI and the Rorschach are useful to look not only at dissociation but also at other psychological characteristics associated with MPD. Once again, however, diagnoses cannot be made on the basis of projective tests alone; clinical interviews are necessary for follow-up. Finally, structured interviews, such as Marlene Steinberg's SCID-D, have been designed specifically for the purpose of diagnosing MPD. The SCID-D has shown enormous promise and has been revised to follow the various editions of the *DSM*.

The most well-studied screening instrument for the dissociative disorders is the Dissociative Experiences Scale (DES), a twenty-eight-item self-report measure that asks about various kinds of dissociative experiences such as depersonalization, derealization, and amnesia, as they are experienced when the examinee is substance-free. The DES also inquires into dissociative experiences that are common in normal populations such as gaps in awareness (e.g., listening to someone speak and suddenly realizing that you did not hear all or part of what was said); absorption (e.g., becoming so involved in a movie or television show that you are unaware of what is happening around you); and imaginative involvement (e.g., not being sure whether some activity occurred in a dream or in reality). Studies have shown that the DES has good internal and test-retest reliability, good convergent and discriminant validity, and that there is an absence of differences associated with gender, race, religion, income, and education. Studies have also shown that the DES relates well to routine clinical diagnoses, as well as diagnoses from structured interviews (Carlson and Armstrong 1994).

Scores on the DES range from 0 to 100; higher scores indicate a greater likelihood that the individual is suffering from a dissociative disorder. Patient scores on the DES are what one would predict: individuals diagnosed with MPD score highest on the scale, with individuals suffering from other dissociative disorders and PTSD scoring higher than other samples. Bernstein and Putnam (1986), for example, report that normal adults and alcoholics scored about 4, phobics about 6, college students approximately 14, schizophrenics 20, PTSD patients 31, and multiples 57.[2] Individuals with a history of abuse — another predictor of dissociation — also score high on the DES.[3] A consensus seems to be emerging that a cutoff score of 30 maximizes accurate classifications,[4] although the DES alone should not be used as a diagnostic tool.

The DES suffers from several limitations. First, factor analyses have failed to reach any consensus on precisely what the subscales of the DES measure; while one general dissociation factor has been identified in a recent study,[5] how — or whether — this factor can be broken down is not clear and is the subject of much debate.[6] Second, North and her colleagues (1993, 104), commenting on Gilbertson's study, concluded that scales of dissociation, including the DES, "are very transparent to individuals taking the test and thus are easily faked in either direction." Current dissociation scales are, as a consequence, highly susceptible to malingering. Finally, the DES has been shown to have poor ability to discriminate between dissociation and the effects of substance abuse (Steinberg 1995). These limitations notwithstanding, the DES remains an important clinical and research tool in the investigation and treatment of dissociation, perhaps the most prominent feature of MPD.

The MMPI and the Rorschach have also been relied upon to assist in the diagnosis of MPD. On the MMPI, individuals suffering from MPD tend to have seven to nine clinical scales elevated to T-score 70 or higher — with the Schizophrenia scale elevated highest of all — and an elevated F scale as well.[7] North and colleagues (1993, 99) suggest that the Schizophrenia scale "can be understood as a reasonable first pass at an MPD scale," and Carlson and Armstrong (1994) have pointed out that the F index may also measure dissociative experiences. The MMPI has not, however, been shown to distinguish MPD from other syndromes such as Briquet's and borderline personality disorder. At the moment, scores on the MMPI can be interpreted as consistent with, but not indicative of, MPD.

Armstrong and Loewenstein (1990) have conducted a promising study on the Rorschach.[8] Relying on a new manner of administering this projective test, Armstrong and Loewenstein invite all the alter personalities to participate. Having found that individuals suffering from MPD display complexity, human relatedness, and highly developed self-observing capacities, Armstrong and Loewenstein have concluded that their personality style reflects a capacity for "internalization, . . . ideational organization of anxiety, . . . taking analytic distance from themselves, . . . and viewing and relating to others in a complex and empathetic fashion" (Armstrong 1991b, 544). These findings, suggestive "of what developmental psychologists call a 'strange' development, i.e., an atypical developmental pathway created by unusual interactions with the world" (Armstrong 1991b, 544), have allowed Armstrong and Loewenstein to distinguish between MPD patients and individuals suffering from PTSD and borderline personality disorder. Most striking in this regard, Armstrong and Loewenstein found that individuals suffering from MPD appear obsessional, rather than hysterical, on the Rorschach. While Rorschach studies on dissociation suffer from several limitations (Carlson and Armstrong 1994), Armstrong and Loewenstein, among others, have underscored their promise as an aid in the diagnosis and treatment of MPD.

Structured and semistructured interviews designed for the purpose of diagnosis include the Dissociative Disorders Interview Schedule (DDIS),[9] Loewenstein's (1991a) Office Mental Status Exam for Dissociative Disorders and, the most well-studied and promising of the diagnostic instruments for MPD, Marlene Steinberg's Structured Clinical Interview for *DSM-IV* Dissociative Disorders (SCID-D). Created in 1984-85, the SCID-D has undergone various incarnations to keep pace with changes in the *DSM*. The SCID-D is designed to assess the severity of five dissociative symptoms and diagnoses the dissociative disorders according to *DSM-IV* criteria. A semistructured interview, the SCID-D uses open-ended questions that allow for follow-up when symptoms are endorsed and contains sections for exploring specific aspects of identity disturbance such as mood changes and internal dialogues. Patients are asked about similar symptoms in a variety of ways, to ensure that they do not fail to endorse symptoms that are present merely by virtue of how questions are phrased.

The five core symptoms assessed by the SCID-D are amnesia, depersonalization, derealization, identity confusion, and identity alteration. Steinberg explains that amnesia, "the inability to recall a significant block of time that has passed, and/or the inability to recall important personal information," is often difficult to assess because patients may have "amnesia for their amnesia."[10] She defines depersonalization as involving "the experience of detachment from one's body or self; for example, feeling the self to be strange or unreal, feeling a sense of physical separation from the body, detachment from emotions, or feeling like a lifeless robot" and derealization, which often occurs along with depersonalization, as "the sense that the physical and/or interpersonal environment has lost its sense of familiarity or reality" (Steinberg et al. 1993, 5). Identity confusion is "a sense of uncertainty, puzzlement or conflict regarding personal identity"; identity alteration "refers to objective behavior that indicates the assumption of different identities" (Steinberg et al. 1993, 5). While nonpsychiatric patients may be aware of different roles or demeanors that are in their control, and psychiatric patients may report such differences that are not in their control, patients with MPD experience identity alterations which represent distinct personalities that appear to take control. Each of the dissociative disorders listed in DSM-IV is associated with a particular graph representing the severity of these five dissociative symptoms; MPD shows severe-level elevations in all five.

The SCID-D thus far appears to have excellent interrater reliability for the five dissociative symptoms and for the diagnosis of dissociative disorders.[11] Others have replicated these findings.[12] Steinberg and her colleagues (1990) have concluded that the results achieved with the SCID-D are comparable to those achieved using similar instruments with clinical samples in other major diagnostic categories.

The SCID-D has many important uses.[13] It permits early diagnosis of MPD and the other dissociative disorders; as we have seen, misdiagnosis of these patients, and consequently cost-ineffective treatment, is all too common. The SCID-D also permits monitoring of dissociative symptoms, as well as treatment planning. It permits one to focus on dissociative symptoms in nondissociative disorders as well as in dissociative disorders, and may permit differential diagnosis in complicated cases. It permits a determination of which among many comorbid diagnoses is primary. Record keeping is facilitated by such a test, and documentation of baseline dissociative symptoms may have legal value, say in cases involving hypnosis. Finally, the SCID-D may be of use in forensic cases.

Like screening instruments, structured clinical interviews such as the SCID-D also have their limitations. Structured clinical interviews depend on patients' ability to answer questions fully and honestly, an ability that may be lacking or limited in certain individuals. The SCID-D also lacks internal mechanisms for detecting lying, exaggeration, or dissimulation — it has no validity scales. Thus it may not be able to detect malingering. Despite these flaws, the SCID-D is a state-of-the-art instrument for diagnosing the dissociative disorders.

The existence of these instruments, with their impressive levels of reliability and validity, should prove helpful in the criminal justice context, where malingering (and false-negatives) is always a concern. The instruments also help to allay concerns over the reality of MPD. We turn now to empirical studies of differences among alter personalities.

EMPIRICAL STUDIES

A growing body of literature examines the phenomenology of alter personalities from psychological, memory, and physiological perspectives. This literature is in its infancy and its studies are limited in a variety of ways: few rely upon blind raters, sample sizes are typically small, and controls are often lacking.[14] Nevertheless, research examining alter personalities offers perhaps the most promising avenue for investigating the nature and phenomenology of MPD.

Erickson and Rapaport (1980, 274), in one of the earliest studies[15] administering psychological tests to individuals suffering from MPD, found that the alter personalities of one of their two subjects showed a "distinct separateness."[16] While the alter personalities of the other subject seemed less distinct, the personalities of each subject tested consistently throughout the tests, both within individual tests and from one test to another. The examiner, who was blind to the treaters' clinical impressions, made findings consistent with those of the clinicians.

Ludwig and his colleagues (1972) administered a modified version of McDougall's Classification of Emotions; the MMPI; the Adjective Checklist; and the Draw-A-Person. Their subject's four personalities tested consistently with clinical impressions of each personality.[17]

Larmore, Ludwig, and Cain (1977, 38) found that their subject's MMPI and McDougall's Scale of Emotions scores differed in ways "remarkably consistent with the clinical data." Loewenstein and his colleagues (1987) described the application of experiential sampling, a time-sampling method, to the assessment of rapid state changes in a woman with MPD. They found that the alters displayed certain characteristics that were as different as those occurring between separate individuals studied previously with the method. Alpher (1991) described the application of the Bell Object Relations Reality Testing Inventory to the host and three alters of an MPD patient. The personalities differed in striking ways; while the host appeared normal, one alter appeared disturbed, another very disturbed. Confer (1984, 413) examined his MPD patient on the MMPI, both before and after integration, and found that the "profile of each personality fragment [was] consistent with client report and therapist observation, and markedly different from the other personality fragment." Studies in which the Rorschach was administered have found that alters have personality structures that are "remarkably different."[18] In contrast, nonmultiples test consistently on different sittings,[19] a finding substantiated by at least one study using blind judges to compare Rorschach protocols (Danesino, Daniels, and McLaughlin 1979).[20]

Memory tests have been used to measure the extent of amnesia and transfer of information across alter personalities. Silberman and his colleagues (1985) tested nine subjects with MPD and ten controls. Their hypothesis was that if MPD patients were truly dissociated — if alter personalities stored and processed their experiences separately — patients suffering from MPD would show supernormal ability to discriminate two highly confusable sets of stimuli. They were unable to confirm their hypothesis; while the patients reported no awareness of hearing stimuli read to a disparate alter, "there was considerable 'leakage' of information across states" (Silberman et al. 1985, 258). In studies with similar findings, Ludwig and colleagues' (1972) subject experienced a clear practice effect across personalities, and Nissen and colleagues' (1988) subject, while disclaiming explicit recall of information, had implicit recall for information presented to another alter.

What is interesting is that the latter two studies also contained certain information that did *not* leak across personalities — in Ludwig et al.'s (1972, 302) paired word test, for example, there was "essentially no transfer of memory from any one personality to the other three."

Ludwig and colleagues (1972) and Nissen and colleagues (1988) accounted for these findings by noting that the material that did not leak across personalities was affectively laden, while information that did leak was more neutral. Nissen and colleagues conducted another study in which alter personalities again did not recall affectively laden information presented to other alters. In one part of the study the authors read a story to five personalities in turn and found that the alters did not systematically improve their performance as they attempted to recall the story. In another aspect of the study, subjects were given a stem-completion test in which there were ten possible answers, some of which were highly charged in terms of affect — no repetition priming effect occurred.[21] In a third test, requiring the subjects to interpret ambiguous sentences and texts, material previously shown to one personality did not help another personality interpret the same or highly related material. Thus, while in these studies certain information did make its way across personalities, other information — that appearing to be more charged with affect — did not.

Physiological and neurological tests measure such things as galvanic skin response and brain wave activity.[22] Some commentators have objected to the entire project of investigating physiological differences among alter personalities (Ross and Weissberg 1991). Their claim is that the best outcome for such studies would be to discover multiple minibrains in the heads of individuals suffering from MPD. Such a suggestion — bizarre on its face — misses the point entirely. Studies investigating physiological differences among alters do not seek to show that alters are different people.[23] Rather, the purpose is to show that MPD is grounded in deviant biological processes — much in the same way researchers have explored the physiology of schizophrenia or manic-depressive disorder.

Miller (1989) studied optical differences among nine MPD patients and nine controls role-playing MPD. Multiples showed significantly greater variability in visual functioning across alters than did the controls, although Miller's outcome measures have generated some debate over his conclusions (1989, 485). In a later study Miller and his colleagues (1991, 132) were able only partially to replicate these findings; they concluded that differences among alters may be more labile than initially thought.

Mathew, Jack, and West (1985) measured regional cerebral blood flow in a patient suffering from MPD while the patient was in two different personalities, and subsequently after she had recovered. Three control patients were included in the study. Mathew and his colleagues found that the personality change of the MPD patient was associated with right temporal hyperfusion; no other significant alterations in cerebral blood flow were noted.[24]

Putnam, Zahn, and Post (1990) investigated differential autonomic nervous system (ANS) activity using peripheral indices of skin conduction and heart rate across nine multiples. Five controls who produced "alters" by simulation and by hypnosis or deep relaxation were also included in the study. Eight of the nine MPD subjects exceeded the chance number of significant effects for personality state, while three of the five controls exceeded chance levels. The authors found that the patterns of significant differences in the MPD and control groups were different, which, in their thinking, suggested that the two groups may arrive at differences in ANS activity between alter personality states in different ways.

Ludwig and his colleagues (1972) conducted a series of studies in which they administered psychophysiological tests. In one such study galvanic skin reactions were measured when the experimenter showed the patient emotionally laden words.[25] The results appeared consistent with true differences among the personalities: "The greatest GSR values [for a particular emotionally laden word] are found for that particular personality with very little response by the others" (Ludwig et al. 1972, 303). Unfortunately, Ludwig and his colleagues did not compare these results with those of subjects simulating MPD. Moreover, Larmore, Ludwig, and Cain (1977, 38–39) conducted a study in which no GSR changes attributable to switching between personalities were found.[26]

An early study looking at alter personalities with an electroencephalogram — those of the patient "Eve" — showed only "slight or inconclusive" EEG differences among the personalities (Thigpen and Cleckley 1957, 149). Cocores and his colleagues (1984) also found that the EEG is not changed by dissociation. Other studies, in contrast, have found differences among alter personalities. Braun, for example, found that the visual evoked potential topographical maps of two patients differed before and after integration,[27] and Dick-Barnes, Nelson, and Aine (1987), utilizing event-related potentials, found that alter personalities were differentially processing relevant versus irrelevant words. Ludwig and his colleagues (1972, 305) noted "definite qualitative differences in the VER records in the different states" of their patient, and Larmore,

Ludwig, and Cain (1977, 39) found that the average evoked visual responses for each personality of their patient were "quite different" from one another. Pitblado and Cohen (1984) studied the average evoked visual responses in five different personalities of a thirty-two-year-old woman, repeated at intervals over a two-year period: "Results showed significant and longitudinally stable differences among the five personalities in amplitudes, latencies, and right-left asymmetries of their AER's." Frank Putnam (1982) has used EEGs and computers to compare measurements in ten multiples and ten controls of average evoked potentials — brain wave activity produced in response to specific stimuli such as flashes of light. Controls simulating multiple personalities could not change their evoked potentials simply by pretending to be someone else: "The alternate personalities of the people suffering from MPD, in contrast, showed statistically significant differences in their averaged EPs. This indicates that alternate personalities are not merely an elaborate act, but are actual shifts in personality accompanied by significant changes in brain activity."[28] Nor, in another study, did an actor portraying MPD evince the differences between alter personalities on a topographical brain map that a genuine multiple did (Hughes et al. 1990, 207). Coons, Milstein, and Marley (1982), on the other hand, found that frequency analyses of an EEG were not able to distinguish between individuals suffering from MPD and a control.

How do these empirical studies of differences among alter personalities bear on the question of MPD's existence? Those skeptical of MPD's existence are not persuaded by the empirical studies. They point out that the research is, at best, equivocal, and that malingerers could produce many of the results that proponents will rely upon to support their position. Most MMPI scores, for example, show that a large percentage of multiples have elevated F scores,[29] and other studies have shown that people wishing to malinger psychotic disorders are able to do so on tasks even as unstructured as the Rorschach.[30] To date, there have been no controlled studies to establish that malingerers cannot produce the same variability in test results as true multiples. Nor, from the vantage point of a skeptic, do the memory tests indicate much; that neutral information leaks across alter personalities while affectively laden material does not can again be explained by malingering — certainly malingering of a more sophisticated sort, but malingering nonetheless.[31] The skeptics will go on to say that the physiological tests, whose findings are equivocal to begin with, suffer from a variety of methodological shortcomings such as a lack of controls, small sample sizes, and subjective outcome measures. Positive findings, such as those based on alpha activity, do not necessarily set multiples apart from normals, and hypnosis itself can produce striking physiological changes.[32] Differences between and among alters could, as a consequence, be a purely mental, autohypnotic phenomenon, not the result of distinct neurophysiological states. In short, the skeptics will argue that while empirical studies do not disprove MPD's existence, they certainly do not prove it either.

The skeptics are certainly correct in pointing out that empirical studies do not prove the existence of MPD. To say that the studies do not show everything, however, is a far cry from claiming they show nothing. Empirical studies, albeit in their infancy, are more consistent with the existence of MPD than with its nonexistence. Virtually all the psychological tests noted important differences among alter personalities, and nearly all physiological tests did so as well. The memory tests noted amnesia for affectively laden material, with the one qualification that, claims for amnesia notwithstanding, neutral information did cross personalities on implicit memory tests. Even this qualification is hardly dispositive — after all, patients with organic memory deficits display implicit memory on a variety of tasks, yet no one doubts that their memory loss is genuine. The bulk of the evidence — tentative though it may be — weighs in favor of MPD's existence.

We turn now to evidence about the treatability of MPD.

TREATMENT

There is near-universal consensus that the ideal goal of treatment of MPD is integration into a single, unified whole. There is also general agreement that integration may not be possible for a number of MPD patients. Horevitz and Loewenstein (1994), for example, divide patients into three groups: high-functioning patients, patients whose cases are complicated by comorbid conditions, and enmeshed patients. Only patients in the first group can realistically be expected to work toward integration; treatment for patients in the third group consists mainly of symptom stabilization and crisis management — worthy goals in and of themselves, given the level of distress and chaos many enmeshed patients experience.

Kluft (1993) presents a variation on this theme, dividing therapists into integrationalists, personality-focused, and adaptationalists. Integrationalists are explicit in working toward integration. Personality-focused MPD therapists, while willing to pursue integration if the patient so desires, believe that dividedness is acceptable if the alters are functioning together smoothly — personality-focused MPD therapists do not press for an unwanted integration of separate personalities. Adaptationalists have as their goal helping MPD patients manage their lives more smoothly. Adaptationalists believe that integration, while desirable, is not a practical goal for every patient, often because time, money, or motivation to work through early traumas is lacking. In such cases the primary goal of therapy is symptom relief. Aside from Kluft's helpful categories, Caul has been cited for his baldly pragmatic approach: "It seems to me that after treatment you want a functional unit, be it a corporation, a partnership, or a one-owner business" (Putnam 1989, 301).

Intensive, psychoanalytically oriented psychotherapy, because it holds the greatest promise for integration, is considered by many the treatment of choice for most MPD patients.[33] While cognitive (Fine 1993)[34] and behavioral therapies (see, e.g., Kohlenberg 1973) have also been advocated, 95 percent of MPD treaters ranked psychoanalytically oriented psychotherapy as their first choice in treatment; in describing the stages of treatment, Braun (1990), Putnam (1989), Horevitz and Loewenstein (1994, 306), and Coons (1986b) — five of the best-known MPD experts — all see integration as occurring in the latter stages of such an intensive psychotherapy. Horevitz and Loewenstein provide an excellent example of how a psychotherapy is broken into three stages. Their schema sees the treatment consisting of, first, stabilization; second, working through the trauma and resolution of the dissociative defenses, a working through that culminates in integration; and third, postintegration treatment. The first stage consists of setting forth the goals, modalities, and techniques the treatment will employ; the second of abreaction and integrating dissociated aspects of the self into a single identity; the third of grieving the many losses entailed by a life of trauma. The treatment focuses on bringing dissociated, split-off, and splintered aspects of the self into a unified whole that will be experienced as such, and on solidifying or cementing the unity.[35]

The treatment of MPD entails special challenges, seen perhaps most acutely in the transference and countertransference. The intensity of the transference has been remarked on by a number of commentators;

treaters are seen, to name only a few of the paradigms, as the abuser, the witness who failed to intervene, and the wished/longed-for good parent. No less intense — or complex — is the countertransference in the treatment, a phenomenon that has been written about extensively. Kluft (1992) describes how therapists are initially fascinated by and overinvested in their MPD patients, a situation that leads to exasperation, fatigue, anger, the eventual wish to discontinue treatment, and the possibility of suffering from a secondary PTSD through counteridentification with their patients. Putnam (1989) details the difficulty in maintaining neutrality given the overwhelming volume of material, and he points to the demands made upon the therapist, which range from dealing with the patient's seductiveness, to warding off wishes to reparent a badly abused child alter, to experiencing the patient's possibly public denigration of the treatment and the treater. Loewenstein (1993) has written of the transference-countertransference field, which he sees as fundamentally dissociative and posttraumatic. For Loewenstein, both patient and therapist will, during the course of the treatment, experience episodes of dissociation, amnesia, and altered perceptions. Marmer (1991, 681) introduces the concept that "the treatment setting [is] a dramatic transferential reenactment in which the therapist sometimes plays the part of a figure in the patient's past; sometimes plays the patient while the patient plays the part of a past figure; sometimes plays the patient while the patient plays the therapist; and sometimes experiences dissociation and confusional states as the patient evokes in the therapist what the patient has experienced."[36]

The intensity of the transference and countertransference has caused a number of authors to suggest special techniques and rules for the treatment of multiples. Virtually all caution against the seemingly irresistible pull to violate one's usual boundaries and norms. Chu (1994) warns against becoming preoccupied with individual personalities and recommends relating to the patient as a whole. In Kluft's (1992) list of twelve rules of thumb for a successful treatment, he emphasizes the importance of maintaining a strong therapeutic alliance; the patient's mastering, as opposed to merely reexperiencing, the trauma; reducing separateness and conflict among the alters; and pacing the therapy in order to avoid the patient's becoming overwhelmed by the amount and intensity of material.[37]

A number of commentators have remarked on the dearth of good outcome studies.[38] Coons (1986b) and Kluft (1982, 1984b, 1986b) have published results of their research, which, while not based on controlled studies, are certainly helpful in assessing the efficacy of treatment. Coons studied twenty patients from state hospitals. The patients had, on average, less than a high school diploma and were treated by trainees, most of whom were seeing an MPD patient for the first time. The trainees saw the patients at less than the optimal frequency. Despite these conditions, Coons reported that thirty-nine months after intake, 64 percent of the patients indicated moderate to great improvement, with 25 percent reporting complete integration. Kluft's sample, by contrast, consisted of patients in the private sector who had already achieved a measure of integration. The patients were all treated by Kluft himself, who determined how often each patient would be seen. Kluft reassessed the patients over time and concluded that, on average, patients achieved integration after twenty-two months of treatment. Kluft found that approximately 90 percent of the patients who continued in treatment achieved integration and that all of the integrated patients but two were doing much better later in life.

Differences between the results reported by Coons and Kluft can almost certainly be explained, at least in part, by differences in their samples (Kluft 1994). Kluft examined patients who had already achieved a measure of integration, which means that patients whose conditions made integration impossible or unlikely were probably excluded from his study. In a later work Kluft (1994) has claimed it possible to predict treatment progress. Putnam (1989, 305), summarizing his and Coons's views, relates a good prognosis to

> the patient's emotional commitment to treatment and resolution of separateness; a lack of investment in the separateness of the alters; the patient's willingness to try nondissociative coping skills; and the establishment of a therapeutic alliance in which the patient trusts the therapist sufficiently to relinquish control to him or her. Fewer alters, lesser degrees of internal complexity, and the absence of severe concurrent personality or developmental disorders (Axis II) psychopathology are also positive prognostic indicators. Coons's (1986b) study would add one more issue: the role of retraumatization during the course of therapy.

In sum, the treatment of choice for MPD is an intensive psychotherapy, the goal of which is integration. For a variety of reasons, however, integration is often not a practical outcome. For such multiples, cooperation among alters, or a reasonable adaptation to life circumstances, is a perfectly acceptable end. Studies suggest that MPD is indeed treatable, although commentators are increasingly sober about the prospects of treatment, given the constellation of factors that correlate with good or poor prognoses. Still, one can feel assured that, in committing nonresponsible multiple personality patients to psychiatric hospitals, we are acting to the benefit of both the multiple and society.

Notes

NOTES TO CHAPTER 1

1. See Reisner and Slobogin (1990, 521), mock dissenting opinion in *Pollard* case.

NOTES TO CHAPTER 2

1. While the 1994 version of the *Diagnostic and Statistical Manual, DSM-IV,* has changed the name to Dissociative Identity Disorder (DID), the earlier nomenclature seems more descriptively informative, and that is how I shall refer to this unique disorder.

2. See, e.g., Loewenstein 1994; Murphy 1994; Nakdimen 1989a; and Ross 1991.

3. An Appendix addresses diagnostic techniques, empirical studies of differences among alters, and treatment.

4. For an interesting article discussing the meaning of "dissociation," see Cardeña 1994.

5. Kluft 1984a, 23, cited in Putnam 1989, 103–4.

6. Kluft 1988b, 51, cited in Loewenstein and Ross 1992, 15.

7. See, e.g., Ludwig 1984, 161: The concept of a personality is "exemplified almost in caricature in the manifestation of multiple personality." See also Greaves 1980, 591: alters are "woefully incomplete as personality systems." As Braude (1991) notes, however, even people have the kinds of personality limitations invoked by MPD writers to justify their claims that alters are not personalities — and these do not detract from their personhood, let alone their personality-hood.

8. The quotations herein are taken from two sources. The first consists of eighty hours of videotapes compiled by Dr. Marlene Steinberg of Yale University, in which Dr.

Steinberg and her research assistants interview patients suffering from MPD (cited herein as *SCID-D interview, unpublished transcript*). The second source consists of interviews I have conducted of patients on a dissociative disorders unit at Del Amo Hospital in Torrance, California (cited herein as *Del Amo interview*).

James Glass has conducted a number of interesting interviews with patients suffering from dissociative disorders. The transcripts of these interviews provide an excellent illustration of Glass's point that, postmodern romanticizations of multiple selves notwithstanding, dissociative disorders entail enormous suffering. See Glass 1993.

9. *SCID-D interview, unpublished transcript*.

10. *SCID-D interview, unpublished transcript*.

11. *SCID-D interview, unpublished transcript*; italics added.

12. *SCID-D interview, unpublished transcript*.

13. *SCID-D interview, unpublished transcript*.

14. *SCID-D interview, unpublished transcript*.

15. Steven Frankel and Todd O'Hearn (in press) build an interesting typology of alter personalities based on social groupings in the ghettos of Warsaw during World War II.

16. *SCID-D interview, unpublished transcript*.

17. *SCID-D interview, unpublished transcript*.

18. *SCID-D interview, unpublished transcript*.

19. *SCID-D interview, unpublished transcript*.

20. *SCID-D interview, unpublished transcript*.

21. *SCID-D interview, unpublished transcript*.

22. *SCID-D interview, unpublished transcript*.

23. *SCID-D interview, unpublished transcript*.

24. *SCID-D interview, unpublished transcript*.

25. *SCID-D interview, unpublished transcript*.

26. *SCID-D interview, unpublished transcript*.

27. *SCID-D interview, unpublished transcript*.

28. *SCID-D interview, unpublished transcript*.

29. *SCID-D interview, unpublished transcript*.

30. *SCID-D interview, unpublished transcript*.

31. Although it is widely believed that multiples are highly hypnotizable and that dissociation and self-hypnosis are linked, in a recent article Putnam and Carlson (in press) carefully marshal the evidence showing that this may not be so.

32. See also Allen 1993, emphasizing triggers, the switch process, and the nature of altered experience in the gap, the endpoint, and the amnestic barrier; Andorfer 1985, proposing a neodissociationist model of MPD; Elin 1995, proposing a comprehensive developmental model for the identification and treatment of MPD; Kroonenberg 1985, offering a three-mode principal components analysis of MPD; and Li and Spiegel 1992, applying Rumelhart's theory to MPD.

33. For other psychoanalytic theories of MPD, see, e.g., Arlow 1992; Barach 1991; Berman 1981; Brenner 1994; Ferguson 1990; Garfinkle 1989; Lampl-De Groot 1981; Lasky 1978; Lovinger 1983; Mollinger 1984; Noll 1989, 1993; Reis 1993; Rose 1987; Roth 1992; Schwartz 1994; Sciali 1982; and Smith 1993. For a detailed description of the psychoanalytic treatment of a "typical" MPD patient, whose course of treatment and transference issues were also presumably typical, see Fink 1992. For a detailed description

in the same volume by a psychiatric resident of the difficult psychoanalytic therapy of a patient hospitalized in a long-term unit at the Sheppard and Enoch Pratt Hospital, see Lyon 1992. The remainder of this issue of the *Psychoanalytic Inquiry* is dedicated to discussing this case from a variety of perspectives. For more general discussions of the psychoanalytic treatment of MPD, see Kline 1990; Wilbur 1984, 1988. For a discussion of the analytic treatment of incest survivors in general, which focuses on the need for more "provisions" at the beginning of therapy and on the unfolding of a merger transference, see Perlman 1993.

34. In a later article, Marmer (1991) discusses the characteristic triad of aggression, dissociation, and repetition seen in MPD patients in terms of Freud's concept of the death instinct, using MPD to reciprocally shed light on Freud's concept.

35. Some even see MPD as a mere nonspecific psychiatric *symptom* of another disorder. See, e.g., Bruce-Jones and Coid 1992; Dinwiddie, North, and Yutzy 1993; and Fahy, Abas, and Brown 1989.

36. Buck 1983; Clary, Burstin, and Carpenter 1984; Kirsten 1990; Pohl 1977. There may be a base-rates problem in cases in which MPD seems to coexist with other particular disorders; psychiatric patients in general may have a higher rate of dissociative disorders, so the apparent connection between, for example, a dissociative disorder and an *eating* disorder may be somewhat misleading.

37. Branscomb 1991; Hyer et al. 1993. See also, e.g., Young 1987, who describes a case of possibly adult onset of MPD following a traumatic war experience. Because treatment of the patient terminated prematurely, it was not possible to rule out earlier dissociation. Indeed, Young suggests that the patient's history of abuse requires a high index of suspicion that dissociative defenses may have been called upon earlier (Young 1987, 253).

38. Bowman and Coons 1992; Coryell 1983. A related phenomenon occurs when aspects of MPD seem to mimic other disorders. See, e.g., Marcum, Wright, and Bissell 1986, who report a case of affective disorder that responded to treatment only when symptoms of MPD were discovered and addressed; and Satel and Howland 1992, who report a case of a patient who appeared to suffer from postpartum depression but turned out to suffer from MPD. The patient's symptoms abated on treatment of the MPD.

39. See, e.g., Arbetter 1992; Coons and Bowman 1993; Demitrack et al. 1993; Levin et al. 1993; Torem 1990; Wetsman 1992; Zerbe 1993.

40. Bliss 1980, 1984a; Hoff 1987; Ross, Heber, Norton et al. 1989; Saxe et al. 1994. Pribor and Dinwiddie (1992) note symptoms of somatization disorder in abuse survivors generally.

41. Ghadirian et al. 1985; Hersh and Atlas 1993; Nakdimen 1990; Rathbun and Rustagi 1990.

42. Ahern et al. 1993; Benson, Miller, and Signer 1986; Drake, Pakalnis, and Denio 1988; Mesulam 1981; Rosenstein 1994; Schenk and Bear 1981; see also Loewenstein and Putnam 1988, and Ross, Heber, Anderson et al. 1989, differentiating MPD from complex partial seizures on two dissociation scales.

43. Goff et al. 1992; Ross and Anderson 1988.

44. It is not always entirely clear which concept of "borderline" a particular commentator intends; I hope not to inadvertently misclassify.

45. Benner and Joscelyne 1984; Gruenewald 1977, 1984. See also Brenner 1994; Grotstein 1984, 280-82; Nakdimen 1989b; and Stoller 1973. Others, by contrast, see MPD

as a higher-level, hysterical phenomenon that takes place at the Oedipal level. See, e.g., Bliss 1980, 1396; Cutler and Reed 1975; Jorn 1982; Lovinger 1983; Moss, Thompson, and Nolte 1962; Prasad 1985; and Prince 1978.

46. For another very interesting account of the differences between borderline splitting and MPD dissociation, see Young 1988.

47. Others point out that it may be easy to mistake borderlines for multiples given the identity diffusion of the borderline patient. Such an error may itself lead to a new pathological identity and inappropriate treatment. See Ogata et al. 1990.

48. See also Boon and Draijer 1993; Fink 1991; Horevitz and Braun 1984; Kemp, Gilbertson, and Torem 1988.

NOTES TO CHAPTER 3

1. See also Clancy, Yates, and Cadoret n.d. (unpublished paper on file with author).

2. See, e.g., Modestin 1992; Piper 1995.

3. See, e.g., Bowers 1991.

4. See, e.g., Kenny 1981.

5. See, e.g., Merskey 1992.

6. See, e.g., Fahy 1988; Gelb 1993; Simpson 1989; Tozman and Pabis 1989; Weissberg 1993. Some of these commentators may believe that iatrogenesis, while a problem, does not account for all of MPD.

7. See e.g., Bowers 1991.

8. This sounds as if Spanos is saying that multiples are conscious malingerers, but Spanos explicitly denies this interpretation.

9. Merskey 1992. For a more moderate but still somewhat skeptical position, see Hacking 1992, 4 (MPD is a "parasite that requires a host. The host provides a way to experience or express mental anguish; the parasite thrives only in a peculiar conjunction of medical and social conditions." Hacking does not unequivocally deny that MPD is real, but he does believe that "these specific forms of pain and dysfunction [which constitute MPD] exist only at a time and place"). See also Hacking 1995.

In addition to this skeptical literature, there is also an MPD literature responding to this skepticism. See, e.g., Barton 1994a, 1994b; Chande 1992; Cohen, Berzoff, and Elin 1995 (see especially Martínez-Taboas and Spiegel; Coons 1990; Dunn 1992; Fahy 1992; Fleming 1989; Fraser 1992; Huapaya 1994; Kluft 1992; Leavitt and Braun 1991; MacIlwain 1992; Mindham, Scadding, and Cawley 1992; Nakdimen 1989a; Novello and Primavera 1992; Putnam 1992; Ross 1990a; Van der Hart and Boon 1989.

10. I am not suggesting that the psychological antecedents of diseases work their effects without producing physiological changes in the brains of the sufferers; mind-brain identity theories seem to me to be true. Rather, I am suggesting that requiring certain kinds of detectable biological antecedents for a psychological condition to qualify as a disease is implausible.

11. See, e.g., Tozman and Pabis 1989, 708 (report seeing no cases in thousands of patients over forty people-years). See also Chodoff 1987 (reports seeing only one "very doubtful" case in forty years of practice; reports informal poll of colleagues claiming no cases, or not more than one or two); Thigpen and Cleckley 1984 (team of psychiatrists

who had diagnosed Eve [1957] report only one further apparent case out of tens of thousands of patients seen over three decades, hundreds diagnosed or self-diagnosed as multiples). Most of the claims that follow are made by a number of different commentators; I simply select one or two for the sake of brevity.

12. See, e.g., Ludolph 1985.

13. See, e.g., Chodoff 1987; Hilgard 1988.

14. See, e.g., Goff and Simms 1993. See Armstrong's (1993) response to this claim as well.

15. See, e.g., Weissberg in Ross and Weissberg 1991.

16. Weissberg seems to approve of this argument. See Ross and Weissberg 1991.

17. Others argue that there is evidence that hypnosis can produce multiple-like personalities, without suggesting *how* it might do so. They cite, for example, Morton Prince's famous Miss Beauchamp (see Prince 1978) and Leavitt's induction by hypnosis of a second personality in a twenty-year-old soldier who was being treated for hysterical hemiplegia on the right side (see Leavitt 1947).

18. See, e.g., Weissberg in Ross and Weissberg 1991.

19. Kluft makes this point. See, e.g., Kluft 1986c.

20. See, e.g., Coons and Milstein 1986, 107.

21. Compare, e.g., Putnam et al. 1986 with Ross, Norton, and Wozney 1989.

22. See Appendix.

23. Ross (1995) makes the point that this is the scientific way to establish diagnoses as well.

24. See, e.g., Wilbur and Kluft 1989 (comparing results of debunking therapies with those of intensive psychotherapy geared to MPD).

25. See, e.g., Coons 1986b; and Kluft 1984b, 1988b.

26. One bit of evidence that some may find compelling are the tapes of Marlene Steinberg in which patients, some of whom have not been given the diagnosis of MPD, and perhaps even deny they have MPD, endorse a variety of MPD symptoms. These patients, who seem not yet to have been educated about the disorder, present a convincing picture of the syndrome. One young man, for example, who claimed to have manic-depressive disorder rather than multiple personality disorder, when asked whether anyone had ever called him by a different name or said that he acted like a different person, stated that his lover had complained of precisely such behavior. The lover had even taken a videotape in which the patient was acting quite differently than he had ever known himself to act and was calling himself by different names. The patient said that he found watching the tape to be extremely disturbing.

27. See Appendix.

28. See Appendix.

29. E.g., Piper 1995.

30. A compromise would be that judges determine this issue as a matter of law. Judges share some of the virtues of legislators, and at least their decisions can serve as precedents for other courts.

31. See, e.g., Ellsworth 1989.

32. *Daubert* is arguably more liberal because "general acceptance," one of several criteria the Court lists for determining the reliability of the evidence, is not necessary for admissibility. General acceptance may, however, be sufficient if we reason that the

scientific community would generally accept a theory only if it were scientifically respectable.

NOTES TO CHAPTER 4

1. The present work deals only with the criminal law issues. I plan another work to deal with the civil law issues raised by MPD, principally, how we should understand the various civil competencies as applied to MPD.

2. Philosophers, by contrast, tend to be much more open to the view that alters are different persons or selves. See, e.g., Anderson 1976; Humphrey and Dennett 1989; McInerney 1985; Moor 1982; Radden 1996; Wilkes 1988.

3. Radden (1996), in her approach to multiplicity, uses a much different way of speaking. Rather than talk about different persons, personlike agents, or parts of people, she speaks of different *selves*. Radden gives four criteria, what she refers to as "conditions," for multiplicity, or the state of having multiple selves: agency, personality, continuity, and disordered awareness. Radden suggests that, in addition to multiples, who clearly meet all four conditions, individuals suffering from manic-depression and schizophrenia might meet them as well. She even suggests that there may be people free from mental illness, such as acratics (i.e., those suffering from weakness of will), who meet her criteria. My discussion of personhood, on the other hand, is such that only multiples' states could be considered different persons. As a consequence, the arguments I give for criminal nonresponsibility apply only to multiples — not to individuals suffering from the more common mental illnesses.

4. At least the audience at the Oprah Winfrey television show which discussed this case approved of this disposition.

5. A related point has to do with the relation between the responsibility (moral agency) and personhood questions. I take the former to turn to some extent on the latter, while Dennett takes the latter to turn to some extent on the former. For an interesting discussion of the interdependence of metaphysical and moral intuitions in dealing with such issues, see Radden 1996.

6. *SCID-D interview, unpublished transcript.*

7. *SCID-D interview, unpublished transcript.*

8. See Appendix.

9. This is because, if I must have the same body to be the same person, it follows that, to be a person, I must have a body, but the reverse is not true: if I need not have the same body to be the same person, I may nevertheless need to have a body to be a person — it just does not *follow* that I do. Thus, it seems possible to hold a psychological theory of personal identity and at the same time a bodily theory of personhood — that personhood must make reference to a body. Imagine that one person's brain traces are transplanted into another person's brain (for more on this example, see below). So long as he has a body in both cases he is a person — the theory of personhood. But the new body with the old brain traces may be the same person by the psychological criterion even if he has a *different* body, provided he has *a* body. Thus, a bodily criterion of personhood may be compatible with a psychological criterion of personal identity.

10. Indeed, it may even be that the colonial view is right; people are all originally split, and multiples defensively fail to bring their parts together.

11. Wilkes's (1981) observation is equally problematic for the view that alters are person*like*.

12. See, e.g., LaFave and Scott 1986, 650: "*A* is guilty of murder if he is actually the agent of *B*'s death, notwithstanding the fact that he acted at *B*'s request."

13. See, e.g., LaFave and Scott 1986, 651-52: "At one time many jurisdictions held [aiding or soliciting suicide] to be murder, but a great many states now deal specifically with causing or aiding suicide by statute, treating it either as a form of manslaughter or as a separate crime." There is a movement in some places to decriminalize certain cases of physician-assisted suicide, but bills introduced to further this end are generally quite strict; for example, they permit physicians to assist in suicide only if, among other things, the patient is terminally ill and likely to die within six months. The case of multiples would not fall under such bills.

14. Similarly, the new person will have many more memories than the original alters alone, although each alter's memories will survive the integration. Because the resulting person will have many more memories, some incompatible (an integrated person cannot have been both composing a song and studying for finals at the same time), it is a little hard to know what the memories of the integrated person are like and how the integrated person conceives of her past. In any case, the psychological traits of the integrated personality will be vastly different from those of the prior individual alters, so the alters would not seem to survive the integration.

15. Or so at least the law holds. See, e.g., LaFave and Scott 1986, 444: "The Model Penal Code commentaries suggest that the defense [of necessity] is available . . . [when] a person intentionally kills one person in order to save two more." See ALI 1985, sec. 3.02, 14–15. In finding that killing one innocent person to save more is justified, the law seems to be presuming some version of utilitarianism. The question whether such an act is so justified is, of course, controversial.

16. Annas 1987, 27–29.

NOTES TO CHAPTER 5

1. For the literature on this question, see, e.g., Abrams 1983; Allison 1981, 1982-83; Appelbaum and Greer 1994; Beahrs 1994; Braude 1996; Coons and Kanovitz 1994; Dinwiddie, North, and Yutzy 1993; Finkel and Sabat 1984; French and Shechmeister 1983; Hall 1989; Halleck 1990; Hindley 1994; Howe 1984; Lewis and Bard 1991; Moore 1984; Ohberg, Haring, and Marsh 1982; Perr 1991; Piper 1994; Radden 1996; Radwin 1991; Rubenstein 1991; Sands 1981; Savitz 1990; Slovenko 1989; Steinberg, Bancroft, and Buchanan 1993; Watkins 1976, 1978.

2. Radden (1996) would find the other alters nonresponsible, at least in the moral realm, because they did not remember the crime. It seems to me that the inability to remember — a mental state that postdates the crime — does not really speak to responsibility. More important is that the other alters did not *participate* in the crime. Put another way, the touchstone for responsibility in this context is whether an alter participated in the crime, not whether an alter remembered it.

Of course, just being a different person is not enough for nonresponsibility. As is clear from accomplice liability law, one must also be noncomplicit in the crime. This doctrine applies not only to the ordinary case of two people but also to the science fiction case of a person committing a crime and then splitting into two. Arguably, his two clones would both be guilty of the crime because, though different people, they participated. If we prefer to deny that they both participated, we shall simply have to take the position that a different person from the criminal, who was noncomplicit in his crime, is not guilty *unless he is a clone of the criminal.*

3. Blackstone 1897 (vol. 4) 358.

4. Robinson v. California (1962, 667).

5. See Exod. 20:5. See also Gen. 3:12–19; Exod. 12:12-13; Judg. 9:56.

6. See United States v. Salerno (1987, 746–47); Kennedy v. Mendoza-Martinez (1963, 168–69).

7. *Salerno.* Radden (1996) observes — correctly, I believe — that theories which see intent as a defining characteristic of punishment go well with retributive theories of punishment. Relying on the doctrine of double effect, Radden argues that because we do not intend to punish innocent alters when we punish the guilty alter, imprisonment or, presumably, any other disposition, would not be to punish the nonoffending alters. That is to say, the absence of punitive intent renders the disposition nonpunishment, and so morally permissible when necessary to carry out legitimate punishment. Radden points out that punishment often harms innocent individuals as, for example, when we imprison a husband or father. Nevertheless, we do not say that the other family members have been punished.

It seems to me that Radden's example is not entirely dispositive on this question. She is certainly correct that there are instances in which aversive treatment without punitive intent is not punishment. It is quite another matter, however, to say that aversive treatment without punitive intent is *never* punishment. Whatever theory of punishment one holds — and a full theory would be necessary to settle this question — treatment of the kind described in the text would seem to me to count as punishment.

8. Radden (1996) suggests that criminal responsibility is problematic to assess for *successive* selves. In this section I hope to show that *simultaneous* selves — or parts of selves — present a challenge to our conception of criminal responsibility as well.

9. While jurisdictions are split over whether to consider hypnosis and posthypnotic suggestion involuntary, the Model Penal Code does.

10. See, e.g., Hart 1968; LaFave and Scott 1986; Moore 1993; Robinson 1984; Schopp 1991; Williams 1978.

11. On the other hand, standard doctrine states that when it can be proved that strong feelings, such as anger, do overwhelm other aspects of the self, the criminality of an act may be mitigated. See, e.g., classic provocation doctrine.

12. But not necessarily all such people; see chapter 8.

NOTES TO CHAPTER 6

1. See note 5 for more on why I now believe this.

2. Accessory-after-the-fact liability is a special case with multiples, and is worthy of note. At common law and later, families were excepted from accessory-after-the-fact liability, an exception that some jurisdictions continue today. The reasoning — that the law should not expect family members to take actions adverse to a blood relation —

applies even more so to alter personalities. As a consequence, alters should not be held to this liability. If, however, we decide to follow the jurisdictions that do not keep the exception, it remains that accessories after the fact are not ordinarily liable to the same degree as principals and other accessories; usually they are punished only for a crime like "obstruction of justice," which carries a lesser penalty than the underlying offense. If certain alters are only accessories after the fact, then the multiple as a whole should be liable only for this lesser offense. To hold him accountable for the greater offense would be to punish innocent alters — innocent, insofar as their guilt extends only to the lesser crime.

3. For this reason I would not impose an affirmative obligation to intervene on an alter if he (delusionally) believes another alter is a separately embodied person; people cannot be faulted for failing to stop a wholly separate person from acting.

4. Indeed, many believe that they will not suffer even if they kill an alter sharing their body.

5. Nevertheless, as noted, I no longer believe that the overwhelming majority of multiples will be innocent. The reason is that most multiples who commit crimes are male, and most male multiples have a fairly small number of alters. It is thus more likely than I once believed that all the alters will have acquiesced in the crime. Indeed, in my experience in consulting on some cases involving MPD, I have now come across several cases of male multiples who are probably guilty on my standard.

6. See Brickey 1990, 26, citing United States v. American Radiator & Standard Sanitary Corp. (1970, 204–5).

7. One court, reporting in dictum on the view of the court below, suggested a fourth view: "In its decision, the district court found it unnecessary to determine whether Halcomb had multiple personality disorder at the time the crimes were committed because whether acting under the personality named 'Oman' or some other, the person who committed these crimes was in fact Anthony Halcomb" (State v. Halcomb 1993, 347). If the "person who committed these crimes was in fact Anthony Halcomb" because the body was, this is a most implausible view; it completely does away with any mental state requirement. This view must become one of the other views — probably the first. I do not consider it further in its own right.

8. Another court held that a conviction for murder was not supported by the evidence. Because the defendant had established the affirmative defense of extreme emotional disturbance, the conviction would be reduced to manslaughter. The "evidence showed that defendant suffered from a multiple personality disorder and one of the 'alter' personalities manifested itself at the time of the shooting." Moreover, the "rebuttal testimony . . . was unavailing and equivocal" (People v. Owens 1994, 67–68). Another court has found that it was error not to instruct on diminished capacity in a death penalty case involving a possible multiple. See State v. Moore (1988). Still other courts sustain findings of Guilty But Mentally Ill. See, e.g., *Kirkland* (1983) and *Kirby* (1991), discussed below.

9. The Court of Appeals of Georgia subsequently rejected an argument that *Kirkland* should be overruled and found that a GBMI finding was appropriate in the case at bar for the same reasons as in *Kirkland*. See Kirby v. State (1991).

10. There are other cases in which an expert's theory of the case supposes that the issue is whether the alter in control meets the insanity defense. See, e.g., Alley v. State

(1994, 813) (expert had planned to testify that "a personality other than the personality known as 'Sedley' was in control and that the controlling personality was legally insane"; later became unsure that a "psychotic personality" was in control at time of killing); State v. Bonney (1991, 151) (expert's theory that when defendant shot victim, Demian was in control and "believed he was shooting the defendant's father who had abused him in childhood"); United States v. Howard (1994) (expert's theory will be that personality in control at time made applications for loans yet was unaware that she had made previous applications under different names). Two further cases contain evidence that the courts subscribe to this theory but also contain evidence which suggests that the courts subscribe to the second theory as well. See discussion of *Rodrigues* (1984) and *Darnall* (1980) below.

11. In other cases, too, experts sometimes testify about the sanity of all of the alters, thus suggesting that they subscribe to this theory. See, e.g., United States v. Hopkins (1958, 193) (expert testified defendant was "sane and responsible for his acts in both personalities"); State v. Darnall (1980, 123) (experts testify about both personalities, although the theory of the case seems to be that the alter in control is the relevant one).

12. See State v. Wheaton (1993).

13. United States v. Denny-Shaffer (1993, 1006 n.4), citing Braun 1986.

14. United States v. Denny-Shaffer (1993, 1006 n.4), citing Braun 1986.

15. I disagree with Jennifer Radden (1996) insofar as she concludes that we must find multiples guilty because their case does not fit into the insanity and involuntariness defenses as currently formulated. Given the formulation of these rules with the cases of ordinary mental illnesses in mind, we should formulate a *new* rule for MPD based on our view of the best disposition in these cases; the law is not lifeless and unchanging. Indeed, as I show later, the case of MPD can be fit into current formulations of the insanity defense if we must; why Radden is satisfied to end her analysis by showing that MPD does not fit into the standard understandings of the defenses is not clear. If, moreover, Radden thinks the moral disposition is to treat the innocent alters as innocent, does not hospitalizing the patient in a psychiatric hospital best accommodate her views — however we accomplish that doctrinally?

16. See, e.g., Wexler and Winick 1991, 1996; Winick 1996.

17. Beahrs 1994; Coons 1991; Halleck 1990.

18. Radden (1996) is correct to argue that we should assess the responsibility of multiples according to our purposes and the context, whether the court or the therapist's office. She and I come to exactly opposite conclusions, however, on when to find multiples nonresponsible. Radden would hold multiples nonresponsible in the therapeutic context and responsible in the criminal law context. I would do the reverse.

NOTES TO CHAPTER 7

1. The converse question is apposite too: Why concern ourselves with criminal responsibility if multiples turn out to be incompetent to stand trial? The answer is clear: even if incompetent to stand trial, multiples are likely to be restored to competency in a reasonable time, and thus the issue of their criminal responsibility will inevitably arise.

2. See Reisner and Slobogin 1990, 890–91.

3. See Pate v. Robinson (1966).

4. When a defendant may refuse psychotropic medication in the trial competency process is still an open question in many important circumstances. See Riggins v. Nevada (1992).

5. I do not address the problem of when certain alters wish to cooperate and others do not. In this case it would seem unfair to burden the alters who wish to go to trial in a competent state by trying them when they are incompetent (or even perhaps to hold charges over their heads indefinitely, see above). Such an alternative may, however, be less a burden than imprisoning an innocent alter. Thus, administrative convenience may favor going forward with the trial. In any case, uncooperative alters will probably not, on their own, be able to render a multiple incompetent; at most, they will probably be able only to cause disagreement among alters, which we have allowed to toll trial for at most six months. Thus, the problem of unfairly burdening cooperative alters in this manner may not be such a problem after all.

6. Woodson v. North Carolina (1976, 304).

7. Zant v. Stephens (1983, 877).

8. Barefoot v. Estelle (1983, 884).

9. ALI 1985, sec. 210.6(4)—sections (f), (b), (g), and (d), (respectively).

10. Barefoot v. Estelle (1983, 884).

11. See Ford v. Wainwright (1986, 409).

12. Hazard and Louisell (1962) mention such statutes but comment, as noted, that in practice such laws apply only in the context of executions.

NOTES TO CHAPTER 8

1. "Derealization . . . is experienced as the sense that the external world is strange or unreal." APA 1994, 488.

2. The sole exception to a finding of responsibility in this case arises when a generalized amnesia is coupled with a profound personality change such that, for all intents and purposes, the former individual ceases to exist and a new person comes into being. This would obviously be an extremely rare — if even extant — contingency, one the law nevertheless should provide for. The upshot would be that, should the former person, who committed the crime, reappear, he would be responsible for the crime. The nonresponsibility of the person following amnesia is a provisional status, valid only as long as the former person is not present.

3. For this reason I differ with Jennifer Radden (1996), who argues that responsibility requires memory. Belief that one committed a crime, as opposed to memory of the actual event, is sufficient. Perhaps more significantly, memory (as well as belief) is important for *acknowledging* one's responsibility, not for *being* responsible. Acknowledging one's responsibility is a precondition for competency to be punished, which is different from criminal responsibility. As I suggested earlier in the text, virtually everything postdating a crime speaks to competency to be punished, rather than to criminal responsibility.

4. That is, the question is not whether person x did the act but whether I am indeed person x.

5. I mean by "crimes" acts that would be crimes were there no defense like insanity. The clinicians who deny that generalized amnesiacs can commit crimes mean that they cannot commit such acts.

6. The reader will appreciate how this discussion relates to the discussion in Chapter 5 of why dissociation may vitiate responsibility: because significant parts of the person are not brought to bear on the act. Here I deepen the analysis by suggesting what sorts of parts must play a role in the decision to act — e.g., dispositions may be important, but not mere items of information. There is also a question whether dispositions retained, but inaccessible to consciousness, play a part in an act. With a multiple we have supposed that the answer can be no, while with a generalized amnesiac we have wondered whether the answer might not be yes. With the multiple the "characters," as it were, that are not coconscious may be supposed to be entirely dormant.

7. But why could one not say in these two categories that the person's earlier dispositions were not available to be brought to bear on the act, and that he is therefore nonresponsible? The answer, perhaps, is that in these two scenarios he has formed a new character, and thus become a different person; and that person is fully responsible. Should his old character return — should his amnesia be reversed — this case would be like that of a fugue, and should be analyzed accordingly. See below.

8. *SCID-D interview, unpublished transcript.*

9. These, of course, are in addition to serious proof problems.

10. If DDNOS flowers into MPD, the scenario would become more complicated, and might call for a finding of nonresponsibility in cases where alters other than the offending alter come into existence and appear to fit our criteria of personhood. If, however, the original personality-configuration returned, the person would be responsible. His nonresponsibility, then, might be only temporary, as in the case of certain fugue states.

NOTES TO THE APPENDIX

1. Instruments are also being studied for testing child and adolescent dissociation. See the CDC and the A-DES. Armstrong et al. 1996; Putnam and Peterson 1994; Putnam, Helmers, and Trickett 1993.

2. See also North et al.'s (1993, 101) table of median DES scores across a large number of studies; the results are roughly the same.

3. See, e.g., Sandberg and Lynn 1992; Sanders and Giolas 1991; and Strick and Wilcoxon 1991.

4. Carlson et al. 1993; Murphy 1994.

5. Waller 1995, cited in Carlson and Armstrong 1994, 165.

6. See, e.g., Carlson et al. 1993, cited in Hacking 1995, 107; Ray et al. 1992, cited in Hacking 1995, 107–8; Ross, Joshi, and Currie 1991; Sanders and Green 1994.

7. See, e.g., North et al. 1993. The F score indicates faking.

8. See also Armstrong 1991b. Early studies of the Rorschach produced scoring rules that have not been supported by later research. Carlson and Armstrong (1994, 168), cite Wagner and Heise 1974 and Wagner, Allison, and Wagner 1983 for the early studies, and Lovitt and Lefkof 1985 for the later.

9. The DDIS has an overall interrater reliability of only .68, which indicates a certain

amount of difficulty in scoring. The DDIS has been used in a number of studies, often in conjunction with the DES. See, e.g., Anderson, Yasenik, and Ross 1993; Berger et al. 1994; Heber 1989; Hughes 1992; Murphy 1994; Ross 1991; Ross, Ryan, et al. 1991.

10. Steinberg, Rounsaville, and Cicchetti 1990, cited in Steinberg et al. 1993, 4–5.

11. See, e.g., Steinberg, Rounsaville, and Cicchetti 1990; Steinberg et al. 1989–92.

12. See, e.g., Goff et al. 1992; Boon and Draijer 1991, 1993. See Steinberg 1995.

13. Applications of the SCID-D in research to date have been varied. See, e.g., Boon and Draijer 1991; Goff et al. 1992; Hall and Steinberg 1994; Steinberg 1994b; Steinberg and Steinberg 1994.

14. Many of the reports are purely anecdotal but are striking nonetheless. See, e.g., Braun 1983b (only one alter nonallergic to citrus; if that alter ate an orange, no allergic reaction was noted; if switched, would develop rash; if nonallergic personality returned, itching would cease and blisters reabsorb more quickly). See also Packard and Brown 1986 (alters with different types of headaches). Some early studies were somewhat more quantitative. See, e.g., Condon, Ogston, and Pacoe 1969 (one of Eve's alters exhibited transient microstrabismus, a movement disorder involving the eyes, five times as often as did two other personalities).

15. For another early report of a variety of tests, see Thigpen and Cleckley 1954 (Rorschach, EEG, and handwriting analysis).

16. One of the few other studies including intelligence tests was Cutler and Reed's, which found results consistent with the character of the personalities (one being a child), and different from what would be expected if the patient were simulating. See Cutler and Reed 1975.

17. See also Brandsma and Ludwig 1974, a later report of the psychological and memory testing of the same patient. Once again, the alters were reported to be very different on the psychological tests, in ways consistent with the clinical data; the authors thought these test results could not be malingered by this patient.

18. Lovitt and Lefkof 1985, 289. See also Battle 1985; Danesino, Daniels, and McLaughlin 1979.

Instead of measuring psychological differences among alter personalities, others do psychological testing to attempt to determine a typical profile of a multiple on, for example, the MMPI or Rorschach test. See, e.g., Armstrong and Loewenstein 1990; Bliss 1984b; Coons and Sterne 1986; Labott et al. 1992; Solomon 1983; Wagner, Allison, and Wagner 1983; Wagner and Heise 1974. See also Coons and Fine 1990 (authors blindly rated sixty-three MMPIs as being either multiple personality or not, achieving an overall hit rate of 71.4 percent, and a hit rate for patients with MPD of 68 percent).

19. See, e.g., Lovitt and Lefkof 1985, 292.

20. Another interesting study (hard to classify in my tripartite schema) is a handwriting analysis. See Yank 1991 (MPD patients showed significantly more variability in handwriting in different alters than would be expected from different samples produced by the same person over time, but less than the differences found among different people in most cases).

21. An earlier fragment-completion test had yielded contrary results. That test, however, contained only one correct response, as opposed to the ten possible correct responses in the test where no priming effect occurred. The task that yielded no priming effect was more similar to a free-association task. In the words of the authors, "Alternate

personalities would be likely to give different free associations, and any priming effects might not be strong enough to overcome these associative biases." Nissen et al. 1988, 131.

22. For comprehensive reviews of psychophysiological aspects of MPD, see Coons 1988; Miller and Triggiano 1992; and Putnam 1991. These sometimes include reports of studies presented at conferences, and not yet published. I limit myself to published reports.

23. Although how we should construe alter personalities is, as I have argued in the text, an open question. See Chapter 4.

24. See also Saxe et al. 1992 (study of four alters of one patient; authors found increased cerebral blood flow in the left temporal lobe — on average, 10.7 percent vs. 2.5 percent. The authors speculated this may mean MPD is mediated by temporal lobe activity).

25. See also Brende 1984 (EDR measurements of alters of one subject showed differences suggesting hemisphere dissociation). For an early use of galvanic skin responses to demonstrate the effect of subconscious ideas, see Prince and Peterson 1908.

26. For an interesting study of the relation of dissociative phenomena to levels of cerebrospinal fluid monoamine metabolites and beta endorphin in patients with eating disorders, see Demitrack et al. 1993. They found evidence that neurochemical changes in dopaminergic, serotonergic, and opioid systems may be associated with the clinical expression of dissociation in patients with anorexia nervosa and bulimia nervosa during the acute phase of their illness. I mention this study only in a footnote because it deals with dissociation in general, not MPD in particular.

27. See Braun 1983a, 88, utilizing one of the same measures and methods of analysis as Coons, Milstein, and Marley 1982, whose results were to the contrary.

28. See also Putnam 1984, 35, reporting on a study of visual evoked potentials of eleven multiples and controls: "The multiple personality patients had significantly lower intraclass correlation coefficients for amplitude and latency components across alternate personalities than did the normal controls who were attempting to simulate an alternate personality. These results suggest that normal control subjects are not able to simply 'fake' this condition." Putnam (1984, 36) also reported on another study in progress: "Topographical power spectral electroencephalographic studies currently in progress at NIMH suggest that differences in electroencephalographic power four certain frequency bands may vary across alternate personalities in a manner that cannot be matched by simulating control subjects." See also Herbert 1982 (reporting results of Putnam's studies, showing that the brain patterns of the alters were as different as one would expect from two normal human subjects).

29. As noted, F scores measure the level of faking on the MMPI. For the claim that MMPI studies show a large percentage of multiples as having high F scores, see, e.g., Bliss 1984b, 199; Coons and Sterne 1986, 47; Larmore, Ludwig, and Cain 1977, 37; Solomon 1983.

30. For a recent review of the ability of evaluators to detect malingering on the Rorschach, see Perry and Kinder 1990. For an earlier review, see Stermac 1988. For reviews of the literature on the ability to detect malingering on psychological tests in general, see, e.g., Rogers 1984; Ziskin 1984.

31. Skeptics will point out that affectively laden material, for that very reason, is easy to remember, and hence easy to feign forgetting.

32. For some examples, see, e.g., Braun 1983a. One physician reported the hypnotic treatment of a boy with allergies, who regained his allergies after amnesia for the previous antiallergic suggestions was hypnotically induced, and regained his immunity — and lost his hives — when the suggestions were hypnotically restored. Braun 1983a, 126. Similarly, the "treatment of warts can be done with hypnosis, blisters can be raised through memories of burns, and warts can be created by autosuggestion with or without hypnosis." Braun 1983a, 128.

33. Many therapists recommend concomitant adjunctive treatments as well. Perhaps the most common adjunct to therapy is hypnosis. See, e.g., Braun 1984b; Howland 1975; Kluft 1982; Smith 1993 for more recent recommendations. Amytal is also used for interviews (deVito 1993). While often medication is used for anxiolytic and antipsychotic purposes, as well as to treat concurrent illnesses, there is no medication that treats the MPD itself (Loewenstein 1991b). Other recommendations include occupational therapy (Richert and Bergland 1992; see also Fike, "Special Issue: Multiple Personality Disorder" in *American Journal of Occupational Therapy* 44, no. 11 [1990]); movement and dance therapy (Kluft, Poteat, and Kluft 1986; Volkman 1993); family and marital therapy (Benjamin and Benjamin 1994a, 1994b, 1994c; Chiappa 1994; Karpel 1995; Porter, Kelly, and Grame 1993; Sachs, Frischholz, and Wood 1988); as well as group therapy Buchele 1993; (Caul 1984; Coons and Bradley 1985; Hogan 1992). Techniques specific to dissociative disorders and MPD include the "dissociative table technique" (Fraser 1991), the use of sand trays (Sachs 1993), and hypnoplay with child alters (Shapiro 1991a, 1991b, and responses). Rosik (1992) recommends integrating the church in the treatment of MPD patients, while Hyde and Weinberg (1991) believe that study groups can be enormously beneficial. More controversial are the uses of electroconvulsive therapy (Bowman and Coons 1992) and mechanical restraints (see, e.g., Lamberti and Cummings 1992; Young 1986b; Young, Young, and Lehl 1991).

34. See also Levin and Spauster 1994. Ross's approach also tends toward the cognitive.

35. See also Loewenstein and Ross's (1992, 26–28) interesting discussion of conceptualizing MPD treatment as occurring on two levels, the abstract and the concrete.

36. See also Comstock 1991; Fink 1992; Perlman 1993; Roth 1992; Saakvitne 1995; Schwartz 1994.

37. See also Marmer's (1991, 680) caution that "simple remembering of the traumatic events is not sufficient to bring about lasting change" in MPD patients. He urges therapists to keep in mind that trauma, conflict, and defense *all* play a contributing role in the genesis of MPD: the "operation of the defenses is just as important as the discovery of what is being defended against" (678).

38. See, e.g., Dunn 1992; Putnam 1989, 297–98.

Bibliography

Abrams, Stanley. 1983. The multiple personality: A legal defense. *American Journal of Clinical Hypnosis* 25:225–31.

Ahern, Geoffrey L., Anne M. Herring, Julie Tackenberg, Joachim F. Seeger, Kalarickal J. Dommen, David Labriner, and Martin E. Weinard. 1993. The association of multiple personality and temporolimbic epilepsy. *Archives of Neurology* 50:1020–25.

Aldridge-Morris, Ray. 1993. Professional skepticism towards multiple personality disorder. *British Journal of Psychiatry* 162:569–70.

Allen, Jon G. 1993. Dissociative processes: Theoretical underpinnings of a working model for clinician and patient. *Bulletin of the Menninger Clinic* 57:287–308.

Allison, Ralph B. 1981. Multiple personality and criminal behavior. *American Journal of Forensic Psychology* 2:32–38.

———. 1982–83. The multiple personality defendant in court. *American Journal of Forensic Psychiatry* 3:181–91.

Alpher, Victor S. 1991. Assessment of ego functioning in multiple personality disorder. *Journal of Personality Assessment* 56:373–87.

American Law Institute (ALI). 1985. *The Model Penal Code.* Philadelphia: American Law Institute.

American Psychiatric Association (APA). 1980. *Diagnostic and statistical manual of mental disorders.* 3d ed. *(DSM-III).* Washington, D.C.: American Psychiatric Association.

——. 1994 *Diagnostic and statistical manual of mental disorders.* 4th ed. (*DSM-IV*). Washington, D.C.: American Psychiatric Association.

Anderson, Geri, Lorri Yasenik, and Colin A. Ross. 1993. Dissociative experiences and disorders among women who identify themselves as sexual abuse survivors. *Child Abuse and Neglect* 17:677–86.

Anderson, Susan L. 1976. Coconsciousness and numerical identity of the person. *Philosophical Studies* 30:1–10.

Andorfer, Joseph C. 1985. Multiple personality in the human information processor: A case history and theoretical formulation. *Journal of Clinical Psychology* 41:309–24.

Annas, George J. 1987. Siamese twins: Killing one to save the other. *Hastings Center Report* 17:27–29.

Appelbaum, Paul S., and Alexander Greer. 1994. Who's on trial? Multiple personalities and the insanity defense. *Hospital and Community Psychiatry* 45:965–66.

Arbetter, Sandra. 1992. Multiple personality disorder: Someone else lives inside me. *Current Health 2* 19:17–19.

Arlow, Jacob A. 1992. Altered ego states. *Israel Journal of Psychiatry and Related Sciences* 29:65–76.

Armstrong, Judith G. 1991a. Keeping one's balance in a moving system: The effects of the multiple personality disordered patient on the cognitive development of the therapist. In *Bridging paradigms: Positive development in adulthood and cognitive aging,* edited by Jan D. Sinnott and John C. Cavanaugh. New York: Praeger.

——. 1991b. The psychological organization of multiple personality disordered patients as revealed in psychological testing. *Psychiatric Clinics of North America* 14:533–46.

——. 1993. Is anything consistent over time?: Comment. *Journal of Nervous and Mental Disease* 181:601–3.

Armstrong, Judith G., and Richard J. Loewenstein. 1990. Characteristics of patients with multiple personality and dissociative disorders on psychological testing. *Journal of Nervous and Mental Disease* 178:448–54.

Armstrong, Judith G., Frank W. Putnam, Eve M. Carlson, Deborah Libero, and S. Smith. 1996. Initial validation of an adolescent dissociation scale. Paper presented at the meeting of the Society for Personality Assessment, Denver, Colorado, March.

Barach, Peter M. 1991. Multiple personality disorder as an attachment disorder. *Dissociation* 4:117–23.

Barratt, Deidre. 1994. Dreaming as a normal model for multiple personality disorder. In *Dissociation,* edited by Steven Jay Lynn and Judith W. Rhue. New York: Guilford Press.

Barton, Charles. 1994a. Backstage in psychiatry: The multiple personality disorder controversy. *Dissociation* 7:167–72.

———. 1994b. More from backstage: A rejoinder to Merskey. *Dissociation* 7:176–77.

Battle, Allen O. 1985. Rorschach evaluations of two personalities in a patient. *British Journal of Projective Psychology and Personality Study* 30:11–23.

Beahrs, John O. 1994. Why dissociative disordered patients are fundamentally responsible: A master class commentary. *International Journal of Clinical and Experimental Hypnosis* 42:93–96.

Benjamin, Lynn R., and Robert Benjamin. 1994a. A group for partners and parents of MPD clients. Part I: Process and format. *Dissociation* 7:35–43.

———. 1994b. A group for partners and parents of MPD clients. Part II: Themes and responses. *Dissociation* 7:104–11.

———. 1994c. A group for partners and parents of MPD clients. Part III: Marital types and dynamics. *Dissociation* 7:191–96.

Benner, David G., and Brenda Joscelyne. 1984. Multiple personality as a borderline disorder. *Journal of Nervous and Mental Disease* 172:98–104.

Benson, D. Frank, Bruce L. Miller, and Stephen F. Signer. 1986. Dual personality associated with epilepsy. *Archives of Neurology* 43:471–74.

Berger, Douglas, S. Saito, Y. Ono, I. Tezuka, J. Shirahase, T. Kuboki, and H. Suematsu. 1994. Dissociation and child abuse histories in an eating disorder cohort in Japan. *Acta Psychiatrica Scandinavica* 90:274–80.

Berman, Emanuel H. 1981. Multiple personality: Psychoanalytic perspectives. *International Journal of Psycho-Analysis* 62:283–300.

Bernstein, Eve M., and Frank W. Putnam. 1986. Development, reliability, and validity of a dissociation scale. *Journal of Nervous and Mental Disease* 174:727–35.

Blackstone, Sir William. 1897. *Commentaries on the laws of England.* St. Paul, Minn.: West Publishing Co.

Bliss, Eugene L. 1980. Multiple Personalities: A report of 14 cases with implications for schizophrenia and hysteria. *Archives of General Psychiatry* 37:1388–97.

———. 1983. Multiple personalities, related disorders and hypnosis. *American Journal of Clinical Hypnosis* 26:114–23.

———. 1984a. Spontaneous self-hypnosis in multiple personality disorder. *Psychiatric Clinics of North America* 7:135–48.

——. 1984b. A symptom profile of patients with multiple personalities, including MMPI results. *Journal of Nervous and Mental Disease* 172:197–202.

Bliss, Eugene L., and E. Alan Jeppsen. 1985. Prevalence of multiple personality among inpatients and outpatients. *American Journal of Psychiatry* 142:250–51.

Boon, Suzette, and Nel Draijer. 1991. Diagnosing dissociative disorders in the Netherlands: A pilot study with the Structured Clinical Interview for DSM-III-R Dissociative Disorders. *American Journal of Psychiatry* 148:458–62.

——. 1993. Multiple personality disorder in the Netherlands: A clinical investigation of 71 patients. *American Journal of Psychiatry* 150:489–94.

Bowers, Kenneth S. 1991. Dissociation in hypnosis and multiple personality disorder. *International Journal of Clinical and Experimental Hypnosis* 39:155–76.

Bowman, Elizabeth S., and Philip M. Coons. 1992. The use of electroconvulsive therapy in patients with dissociative disorders. *Journal of Nervous and Mental Disease* 180:524–28.

Brandsma, Jeffrey M., and Arnold M. Ludwig. 1974. A case of multiple personality: Diagnosis and therapy. *International Journal of Clinical and Experimental Hypnosis* 22:216–33.

Branscomb, Louisa P. 1991. Dissociation in combat-related post-traumatic stress disorder. *Dissociation* 4:13–20.

Braude, Stephen E. 1991. *First person plural: Multiple personality and the philosophy of mind.* London: Routledge.

——. 1996. Multiple personality and moral responsibility. *Philosophy, Psychiatry, and Psychology* 3:37–54.

Braun, Bennett G. 1983a. Neurophysiologic changes in multiple personality due to integration: A preliminary report. *American Journal of Clinical Hypnosis* 26:84–92.

——. 1983b. Psychophysiologic phenomena in multiple personality and hypnosis. *American Journal of Clinical Hypnosis* 26:124–37.

——. 1984a. Towards a theory of multiple personality and other dissociative phenomena. *Psychiatric Clinics of North America* 7:171–93.

——. 1984b. Uses of hypnosis with multiple personality. *Psychiatric Annals* 14:34–40.

——. 1986. *Treatment of multiple personality disorder.* Washington, D.C.: American Psychiatric Press.

———. 1990. Multiple personality disorder: An overview. *American Journal of Occupational Therapy* 44:971–76.

Brende, Joel O. 1984. The psychophysiologic manifestations of dissociation: Electrodermal responses in a multiple personality patient. *Psychiatric Clinics of North America* 7:41–50.

Brende, Joel O., and Donald B. Rinsley. 1981. A case of multiple personality with psychological automatisms. *Journal of the American Academy of Psychoanalysis* 9:129–51.

Brenner, Ira. 1994. The dissociative character: A reconsideration of "multiple personality." *Journal of the American Psychoanalytic Association* 42:819–46.

Brickey, Kathleen F. 1990. *Corporate and white collar crime: Cases and materials*. Boston: Little, Brown.

Bruce-Jones, William D., and Jeremy Coid. 1992. Identity diffusion presenting as multiple personality disorder in a female psychopath. *British Journal of Psychiatry* 160:541–44.

Buchele, Bonnie J. 1993. Group psychotherapy for persons with multiple personality and dissociative disorders. *Bulletin of the Menninger Clinic* 57:362–70.

Buck, Owen D. 1983. Multiple personality as a borderline state. *Journal of Nervous and Mental Disease* 171:62–65.

Bucy, Pamela H. 1992. *White collar crime: Cases and materials*. St. Paul, Minn.: West Publishing Co.

Cardeña, Etzel. 1994. The domain of dissociation. In *Dissociation,* edited by Steven Jay Lynn and Judith W. Rhue. New York: Guilford Press.

Carlson, Eve B., and Judith Armstrong. 1994. The diagnosis and assessment of dissociative disorders. In *Dissociation,* edited by Steven Jay Lynn and Judith W. Rhue. New York: Guilford Press.

Carlson, Eve Bernstein, Frank W. Putnam, Colin A. Ross, Moshe Torem, Philip Coons, Diana L. Dill, Richard J. Loewenstein, and Bennett G. Braun. 1993. Validity of the Dissociative Experiences Scale in screening for multiple personality disorder: A multicenter study. *American Journal of Psychiatry* 150:1030–36.

Carter, William R. 1990. Why personal identity is animal identity. *LOGOS: Philosophic Issues in Christian Perspective* 11:71–81.

Caul, David. 1984. Group and videotape techniques for multiple personality disorder. *Psychiatric Annals* 14:43–50.

Chande, Ann. 1992. Manufacture of multiple personality disorder. *British Journal of Psychiatry* 161:269.

Chiappa, Francis. 1994. Effective management of family and individual interventions in the treatment of dissociative disorders. *Dissociation* 7:185–90.

Chodoff, Paul. 1987. More on multiple personality disorder. *American Journal of Psychiatry* 144:124.

Chu, James A. 1991. On the misdiagnosis of multiple personality disorder. *Dissociation* 4:200–204.

———. 1994. The rational treatment of multiple personality disorder. *Psychotherapy* 31:94–100.

Clancy, Gerard P., William R. Yates, and Remi J. Cadoret. N.d. Characteristics of believers and non-believers in the diagnosis of multiple personality disorder. University of Iowa, College of Medicine, Department of Psychiatry. Duplicated.

Clary, William F., Kenneth J. Burstin, and John S. Carpenter. 1984. Multiple personality and borderline personality disorder. *Psychiatric Clinics of North America* 7:89–99.

Cocores, James A., Andrew Lee Bender, and Eugene McBride. 1984. Multiple personality, seizure disorder, and the electroencephalogram. *Journal of Nervous and Mental Disease* 172:436–38.

Cohen, Lewis M., Joan N. Berzoff, and Mark R. Elin, eds. 1995. *Dissociative Identity Disorder: Theoretical and treatment controversies*. Northvale, N.J.: Jason Aronson.

Comstock, Christine M. 1991. Counter-transference and the suicidal multiple personality disorder patient. *Dissociation* 4:25–35.

Condon, William S., William D. Ogston, and Larry V. Pacoe. 1969. Three faces of Eve revisited: A study of transient microstrabismus. *Journal of Abnormal Psychology* 74:618–20.

Confer, William N. 1984. Hypnotic treatment of multiple personality: A case study. *Psychotherapy* 21:408–13.

Coons, Philip M. 1986a. Child abuse and multiple personality disorder: Review of the literature and suggestions for treatment. *Child Abuse and Neglect* 10:455–62.

———. 1986b. Treatment progress in 20 patients with multiple personality disorder. *Journal of Nervous and Mental Disease* 174:715–21.

———. 1988. Psychophysiologic aspects of multiple personality disorder: A review. *Dissociation* 1:47–53.

———. 1990. More on multiple personality disorder. *British Journal of Psychiatry* 156:448–49.

———. 1991. Iatrogenesis and malingering of multiple personality disorder in the forensic evaluation of homicide defendants. *Psychiatric Clinics of North America* 14:757–68.

Coons, Philip M., and Elizabeth S. Bowman. 1993. Dissociation and eating. *American Journal of Psychiatry* 150:171–72.

Coons, Philip M., Elizabeth S. Bowman, Richard P. Kluft, and Victor Milstein. 1991. The cross-cultural occurrence of MPD: Additional cases from a recent survey. *Dissociation* 4:124–28.

Coons, Philip M., and Karen Bradley. 1985. Group psychotherapy with multiple personality patients. *Journal of Nervous and Mental Disease* 173:515–21.

Coons, Philip M., and Catherine G. Fine. 1990. Accuracy of the MMPI in identifying multiple personality disorder. *Psychological Reports* 66:831–34.

Coons, Philip M., and Jacqueline Kanovitz. 1994. Multiple personality disorder: Forensic aspects. In *Principles & practice of forensic psychiatry*, edited by Richard Rosner. New York: Chapman and Hall.

Coons, Philip M., and Victor Milstein. 1986. Psychosexual disturbances in multiple personality: Characteristics, etiology, and treatment. *Journal of Clinical Psychiatry* 47:106–10.

Coons, Philip M., Victor Milstein, and Carma Marley. 1982. EEG studies of two multiple personalities and a control. *Archives of General Psychiatry* 39:823–25.

Coons, Philip M., and Arthur L. Sterne. 1986. Initial and follow-up psychological testing on a group of patients with multiple personality disorder. *Psychological Reports* 58:43–49.

Coryell, William. 1983. Multiple personality and primary affective disorder. *Journal of Nervous and Mental Disease* 171:388–90.

Cutler, Brian, and John Reed. 1975. Multiple personality: A single case study with a 15 year follow-up. *Psychological Medicine* 5:18–26.

Danesino, Angelo, Joseph Daniels, and Thomas J. McLaughlin. 1979. Jo-Jo, Josephine, and Joanne: A study of multiple personality by means of the Rorschach test. *Journal of Personality Assessment* 43:300–313.

Dell, Paul F. 1988. Professional skepticism about multiple personality. *Journal of Nervous and Mental Disease* 176:528–31.

Demitrack, Mark A., Frank W. Putnam, David R. Rubinow, Teresa A. Pigott, Margaret Altemus, Dean D. Krahn, and Philip W. Gold. 1993. Relation of dissociative phenomena to levels of cerebrospinal fluid monoamine metabolites and beta-endorphin in patients with eating disorders: A pilot study. *Psychiatry Research* 49:1–10.

Dennett, Daniel C. 1976. Conditions of personhood. In *The identities of per-*

sons, edited by Amelie Oksenberg Rorty. Berkeley: University of California Press.

deVito, Robert A. 1993. The use of Amytal interviews in the treatment of an exceptionally complex case of multiple personality disorder. In *Clinical perspectives on multiple personality disorder,* edited by Richard P. Kluft and Catherine G. Fine. Washington, D.C.: American Psychiatric Press.

Dick-Barnes, Margaret, Rosemery O. Nelson, and Cheryl J. Aine. 1987. Behavioral measures of multiple personality: The case of Margaret. *Journal of Behavior Therapy and Experimental Psychiatry* 18:229–39.

Dinwiddie, Stephen H., Carol S. North, and Sean H. Yutzy. 1993. Multiple personality disorder: Scientific and medicolegal issues. *Bulletin of the American Academy of Psychiatry and the Law* 21:69–79.

Drake, Miles E., Jr., Ann Pakalnis, and Lena D. Denio. 1988. Differential diagnosis of epilepsy and multiple personality: Clinical and EEG findings in 15 cases. *Neuropsychiatry, Neuropsychology, and Behavioral Neurology* 1:131–40.

Dunn, Gary E. 1992. Multiple personality disorder: A new challenge for psychology. *Professional Psychology: Research and Practice* 23:18–23.

Elin, Mark R. 1995. A developmental model for trauma. In *Dissociative Identity Disorder: Theoretical and treatment controversies,* edited by Lewis M. Cohen, Joan N. Berzoff, and Mark R. Elin. Northvale, N.J.: Jason Aronson.

Ellsworth, Phoebe C. 1989. Are twelve heads better than one? *Law and Contemporary Problems* 52:205–24.

Erickson, Milton H., and David Rapaport. 1980. Findings on the nature of the personality structures in two different dual personalities by means of projective and psychometric tests. In *The Collected papers of Milton H. Erickson on hypnosis,* edited by Ernest L. Rossi. New York: Irvington Publishers.

Fahy, Thomas A. 1988. The diagnosis of multiple personality disorder: A critical review. *British Journal of Psychiatry* 153:597–606.

———. 1992. Manufacture of multiple personality disorder. *British Journal of Psychiatry* 161:268–70.

Fahy, Thomas A., Melanie Abas, and Jeremy C. Brown. 1989. Multiple personality: A symptom of psychiatric disorder. *British Journal of Psychiatry* 154:99–101.

Ferguson, Michael. 1990. Mirroring processes, hypnotic processes, and multiple personality. *Psychoanalysis and Contemporary Thought* 13:417–50.

Fike, M. Laurita, ed. 1990. Special Issue: Multiple personality disorder. *American Journal of Occupational Therapy* 44, no. 11.

Fine, Catherine G. 1993. A tactical integrationalist perspective on the treatment of multiple personality disorder. In *Clinical perspectives on multiple personality disorder,* edited by Richard P. Kluft and Catherine G. Fine. Washington, D.C.: American Psychiatric Press.

Fink, David. 1991. The comorbidity of multiple personality disorder and DSM-III-R Axis-II disorders. *Psychiatric Clinics of North America* 14: 547–66.

———. 1992. The psychotherapy of multiple personality disorder: A case study. *Psychoanalytic Inquiry* 12:49–70.

Fink, David, and Michael Golinkoff. 1990. Multiple personality disorder, borderline personality disorder and schizophrenia: A comparative study of clinical features. *Dissociation* 3:127–34.

Finkel, Norman J., and Steven R. Sabat. 1984. Split-brain madness: An insanity defense waiting to happen. *Law and Human Behavior* 8:225–52.

Fleming, Jonathan A. E. 1989. Multiple personality disorder. *British Journal of Psychiatry* 154:877.

Frankel, A. Steven, and Todd O'Hearn. In press. Similarities in responses to extreme and unremitting stress between east European ghettoes during World War II and DID patients: Cultures of communities under siege. *Psychotherapy: Theory, Research, Practice, Training.*

Frankfurt, Harry G. 1971. Freedom of the will and the concept of a person. *Journal of Philosophy* 48:5–20.

Fraser, George A. 1991. The dissociative table technique: A strategy for working with ego states in dissociative disorders and ego-state therapy. *Dissociation* 4:205–13.

———. 1992. Multiple personality disorder. *British Journal of Psychiatry* 161:416–17.

French, Alfred P., and Bryan R. Shechmeister. 1983. The multiple personality syndrome and criminal defense. *Bulletin of the American Academy of Psychiatry and the Law* 11:17–25.

Gabbard, Glen O. 1989. Splitting and dissociation, borderline personality and multiple personality: Reply. *American Journal of Psychiatry* 146:1236.

Garfinkle, Ely. 1989. Remembering and repeating in multiple personality. *Psychoanalytic Psychotherapy* 4:169–81.

Gelb, Jerome L. 1993. Multiple personality disorder and satanic ritual abuse. *Australian and New Zealand Journal of Psychiatry* 27:701–8.

Ghadirian, A. Missagh, Heinz E. Lehmann, Maurice Dongier, and Thomas Kolivakis. 1985. Multiple personality in a case of functional psychosis. *Comprehensive Psychiatry* 26:22–28.

Glass, James M. 1993. *Shattered selves: Multiple personality in a postmodern world*. Ithaca, N.Y.: Cornell University Press.

Goff, Donald C., Jonathan A. Olin, Michael A. Jenike, Lee Baer, and M. Lynn Buttolph. 1992. Dissociative symptoms in patients with obsessive-compulsive disorder. *Journal of Nervous and Mental Disease* 180:332–37.

Goff, Donald C., and Claudia A. Simms. 1993. Has multiple personality disorder remained consistent over time? A comparison of past and recent cases. *Journal of Nervous and Mental Disease* 181:595–600.

Greaves, George B. 1980. Multiple personality: 165 years after Mary Reynolds. *Journal of Nervous and Mental Disease* 168:577–96.

Grotstein, James S. 1984. A proposed revision of the psychoanalytic concept of primitive mental states: Part II. The borderline syndrome—Section 3: Disorders of autistic safety and symbiotic relatedness. *Contemporary Psychoanalysis* 20:266–343.

Gruenewald, Doris. 1977. Multiple personality and splitting phenomena: A reconceptualization. *Journal of Nervous and Mental Disease* 164:385–93.

———. 1984. On the nature of multiple personality: Comparisons with hypnosis. *International Journal of Clinical and Experimental Hypnosis* 32: 170–90.

Hacking, Ian. 1992 Multiple personality disorder and its hosts. *History of the Human Sciences* 5:3–31.

———. 1995. *Rewriting the soul: Multiple personality and the sciences of memory*. Princeton, N.J.: Princeton University Press.

Hall, Pamela E. 1989. Multiple personality disorder and homicide: Professional and legal issues. *Dissociation* 2:110–15.

Hall, Pamela, and Marlene Steinberg. 1994. Systematic assessment of dissociative symptoms and disorders using the SCID-D in a clinical outpatient setting: Three cases. *Dissociation* 7:112–16.

Halleck, Seymour L. 1990. Dissociative phenomena and the question of responsibility. *International Journal of Clinical and Experimental Hypnosis* 38:298–314.

Hart, H. L. A. 1968. *Punishment and responsibility*. Oxford: Clarendon Press.

Hayes, Jeffrey A., and Jeffrey C. Mitchell. 1994. Mental health professionals' skepticism about multiple personality disorder. *Professional Psychology: Research and Practice* 25:410–15.

Hazard, Geoffrey C., Jr., and David W. Louisell. 1962. Death, the state, and the insane: Stay of execution. *U.C.L.A. Law Review* 9:381–405.

Heber, A. Sharon, William P. Fleisher, Colin A. Ross, and Richard S. Stanwick. 1989. Dissociation in alternative healers and traditional therapists: A comparative study. *American Journal of Psychotherapy* 43:562–74.

Herbert, W. 1982. The three brains of Eve: EEG data. *Science News* 121:356.

Hersh, Mindy, and Jeffrey Atlas. 1993. Language in differential diagnosis of a teenage schizophrenic girl with aspects of multiple personality. *Psychological Reports* 73:691–98.

Hilgard, Ernest R. 1988. Commentary: Professional skepticism about multiple personality. *Journal of Nervous and Mental Disease* 176:532.

Hindley, Mark E. 1994. *United States v. Denny-Shaffer* and multiple personality disorder: "Who stole the cookie from the cookie jar?" *Utah Law Review* 2:961–97.

Hoff, Jeanne. 1987. Multiple personality disorder? *Journal of Clinical Psychiatry* 48:174.

Hogan, Lisa C. 1992. Managing persons with multiple personality disorder in a heterogeneous inpatient group. *Group* 16:247–56.

Horevitz, Richard P., and Bennett G. Braun. 1984. Are multiple personalities borderline? An analysis of 33 cases. *Psychiatric Clinics of North America* 7:69–87.

Horevitz, Richard, and Richard J. Loewenstein. 1994. The rational treatment of multiple personality disorder. In *Dissociation,* edited by Steven Jay Lynn and Judith W. Rhue. New York: Guilford Press.

Hornstein, Nancy L., and Frank W. Putnam. 1992. Clinical phenomenology of child and adolescent dissociative disorders. *Journal of the American Academy of Child and Adolescent Psychiatry* 31:1077–85.

Howe, Edmund G. 1984. Psychiatric evaluation of offenders who commit crimes while experiencing dissociative states. *Law and Human Behavior* 8:253–82.

Howland, John S. 1975. The use of hypnosis in the treatment of a case of multiple personality. *Journal of Nervous and Mental Disease* 161:138–42.

Huapaya, Luis V. M. 1994. More comments on supposed multiple personality disorder. *Canadian Journal of Psychiatry* 39:247.

Hughes, Dureen J. 1992. Differences between trance channeling and multiple personality disorder on structured interview. *Journal of Transpersonal Psychology* 24:181–92.

Hughes, John R., Donald T. Kuhlman, Christopher G. Fichtner, and Michael J. Gruenfeld. 1990. Brain mapping in a case of multiple personality. *Clinical Electroencephalography* 21:200–209.

Humphrey, Nicholas, and Daniel C. Dennett. 1989. Speaking for ourselves: An assessment of multiple personality disorder. *Raritan* 9:68–98.

Hyde, Rosalie, and Denise Weinberg. 1991. The process of the MPD therapist and the use of the study group. *Dissociation* 4:105–8.

Hyer, Lee A., J. William Albrecht, Patrick A. Boudewyns, M. Gail Woods, and Jeffrey Brandsma. 1993. Dissociative experiences of Vietnam veterans with chronic post-traumatic stress disorder. *Psychological Reports* 73: 519–30.

Jorn, Nancy. 1982. Repression in a case of multiple personality disorder. *Perspectives in Psychiatric Care* 20:105–10.

Karpel, Mark A. 1995. The role of the client's partner in the treatment of multiple personality disorder. In *Dissociative Identity Disorder: Theoretical and treatment controversies,* edited by Lewis M. Cohen, Joan N. Berzoff, and Mark R. Elin. Northvale, N.J.: Jason Aronson.

Kemp, Kristen, Alan D. Gilbertson, and Moshe S. Torem. 1988. The differential diagnosis of multiple personality disorder from borderline personality disorder. *Dissociation* 1:41–46.

Kenny, Michael G. 1981. Multiple personality and spirit possession. *Psychiatry* 44:337–58.

Kihlstrom, John, Martha L. Glisky, and Michael J. Angiulo. 1994. Dissociative tendencies and dissociative disorders. *Journal of Abnormal Psychology* 103:117–24.

Kim, Hyung I. 1981. *Fundamental legal concepts of China and the West: A comparative study.* Port Washington, N.Y.: Kennikat Press.

Kirsten, Markham. 1990. Multiple personality disorder and borderline personality disorder. *American Journal of Psychiatry* 147:1386–87.

Kline, Neal A. 1990. Multiple personality disorder: The new "royal road?" *American Journal of Psychiatry* 147:538–39.

Kluft, Estelle S., Janis Poteat, and Richard P. Kluft. 1986. Movement observations in multiple personality disorder: A preliminary report. *American Journal of Dance Therapy* 9:31–46.

Kluft, Richard P. 1982. Varieties of hypnotic interventions in the treatment of multiple personality. *American Journal of Clinical Hypnosis* 24:230–40.

———. 1984a. An introduction to multiple personality disorder. *Psychiatric Annals* 14:19–24.

———. 1984b. Treatment of multiple personality disorder: A study of 33 cases. *Psychiatric Clinics of North America* 7:9–29.

———. 1986a. First rank symptoms of schizophrenia, experiences within hypnosis, and multiple personality disorder. *American Journal of Clinical Hypnosis* 28:197–98.

———. 1986b. Personality unification in multiple personality disorder: A follow-up study. In *Treatment of multiple personality disorder,* edited by Bennett G. Braun. Washington, D.C.: American Psychiatric Press.

———. 1986c. The prevalence of multiple personality. *American Journal of Psychiatry* 143:802–3.

———. 1987a. An update on multiple personality disorder. *Hospital and Community Psychiatry* 38:363–73.

———. 1987b. First-rank symptoms as a diagnostic clue to multiple personality disorder. *American Journal of Psychiatry* 144:293–98.

———. 1988a. The phenomenology and treatment of extremely complex multiple personality disorder. *Dissociation* 1:47–58.

———. 1988b. The postunification treatment of multiple personality disorder: First findings. *American Journal of Psychotherapy* 42:212–28.

———. 1992. A specialist's perspective on multiple personality disorder. *Psychoanalytic Inquiry* 12:139–71.

———. 1994. Treatment trajectories in multiple personality disorder. *Dissociation* 7:63–76.

Kohlenberg, Robert J. 1973. Behavioristic approach to multiple personality: A case study. *Behavior Therapy* 4:137–40.

Kolodner, George, and Richard Frances. 1993. Recognizing dissociative disorders in patients with chemical dependency. *Hospital and Community Psychiatry* 44:1041–43.

Kroonenberg, Pieter M. 1985. Three-mode principal components analysis of semantic differential data: The case of a triple personality. *Applied Psychological Measurement* 9:83–94.

Labott, Susan M., Frank Leavitt, Bennett G. Braun, and Roberta G. Sachs. 1992. Rorschach indicators of multiple personality disorder. *Perceptual and Motor Skills* 75:147–58.

LaFave, Wayne R., and Austin W. Scott, Jr. 1986. *Criminal law.* 2d ed. St. Paul, Minn.: West Publishing Co.

Lamberti, J. Steven, and Sheila Cummings. 1992. Hands-on restraints in the treatment of multiple personality disorder. *Hospital and Community Psychiatry* 43:283–84.

Lampl-De Groot, Jeanne. 1981. Notes on multiple personality. *Psychoanalytic Quarterly* 50:614–24.

Larmore, Kim, Arnold M. Ludwig, and Rolene L. Cain. 1977. Multiple personality: An objective case study. *British Journal of Psychiatry* 131:35–40.

Lasky, Richard. 1978. The psychoanalytic treatment of a case of multiple personality. *Psychoanalytic Review* 65:355–80.

Leavitt, Frank, and Bennett Braun. 1991. Historical reliability: A key to differentiating populations among patients presenting signs of multiple personality disorder. *Psychological Reports* 69:499–510.

Leavitt, Harry C. 1947. A case of hypnotically produced secondary and tertiary personalities. *Psychoanalytic Review* 34:274–95.

Levin, Andrew P., Michael Kahan, Joshua B. Lamm, and Edward Spauster. 1993. Multiple personality in eating disorder patients. *International Journal of Eating Disorders* 13:235–39.

Levin, Andrew P., and Edward Spauster. 1994. Inpatient cognitive-behavioral treatment of eating disorder patients with dissociative disorders. *Dissociation* 7:178–84.

Lewis, Dorothy O., and Jennifer S. Bard. 1991. Multiple personality and forensic issues. *Psychiatric Clinics of North America* 14:741–56.

Li, David, and David Spiegel. 1992. A neural network model of dissociative disorders. *Psychiatric Annals* 22:144–47.

Locke, John. 1690. *An essay concerning humane understanding: In four books.* London: Printed for Thomas, Basset, and sold by Edward Mory.

Loewenstein, Richard J. 1991a. An office mental status examination for complex chronic dissociative symptoms and multiple personality disorder. *Psychiatric Clinics of North America* 14:567–604.

———. 1991b. Rational psychopharmacology in the treatment of multiple personality disorder. *Psychiatric Clinics of North America* 14:721–40.

———. 1993. Posttraumatic and dissociative aspects of transference and countertransference in the treatment of multiple personality disorder. In *Clinical perspectives on multiple personality disorder,* edited by Richard P. Kluft and Catherine G. Fine. Washington, D.C.: American Psychiatric Press.

———. 1994. Diagnosis, epidemiology, clinical course, treatment, and cost effectiveness of treatment for dissociative disorders and MPD. *Dissociation* 7:3–11.

Loewenstein, Richard J., Jean Hamilton, Sheryle Alagna, Nancy Reid, and Martin deVries. 1987. Experiential sampling in the study of multiple personality disorder. *American Journal of Psychiatry* 144:19–24.

Loewenstein, Richard J., and Frank W. Putnam. 1988. A comparison study of dissociative symptoms in patients with complex partial seizures, MPD, and post-traumatic stress disorder. *Dissociation* 1:17–23.

Loewenstein, Richard J., and Donald R. Ross. 1992. Multiple personality and psychoanalysis: An introduction. *Psychoanalytic Inquiry* 12:3–48.

Lovinger, Sophie L. 1983. Multiple personality: A theoretical view. *Psychotherapy: Theory, Research and Practice* 20:425–34.

Lovitt, Robert, and Gary Lefkof. 1985. Understanding multiple personality with the comprehensive Rorschach system. *Journal of Personality Assessment* 49:289–94.

Ludolph, Pamela S. 1985. How prevalent is multiple personality? *American Journal of Psychiatry* 142:1526–27.

Ludwig, Arnold M. 1984. Intoxication and sobriety: Implications for the understanding of multiple personality. *Psychiatric Clinics of North America* 7:161–69.

Ludwig, Arnold M., Jeffrey M. Brandsma, Cornelia B. Wilbur, Fernando Bendfeldt, and Douglas H. Jameson. 1972. The objective study of a multiple personality: Or, are four heads better than one? *Archives of General Psychiatry* 26:298–310.

Lyon, Kathleen A. 1992. Shattered mirror: A fragment of the treatment of a patient with multiple personality disorder. *Psychoanalytic Inquiry* 12: 71–94.

MacIlwain, Ian F. 1992. Multiple personality disorder. *British Journal of Psychiatry* 161:863–64.

Marcum, James M., Kenneth Wright, and William G. Bissell. 1986. Chance discovery of multiple personality disorder in a depressed patient by amobarbital interview. *Journal of Nervous and Mental Disease* 174:489–92.

Marmer, Stephen S. 1980. Psychoanalysis of multiple personality. *International Journal of Psycho-Analysis* 61:439–59.

———. 1991. Multiple personality disorder: A psychoanalytic perspective. *Psychiatric Clinics of North America* 14:677–93.

Marmer, Stephen S., and David Fink. 1994. Rethinking the comparison of borderline personality disorder and multiple personality disorder. *Psychiatric Clinics of North America* 17:743–71.

Martínez-Taboas, Alfonso. 1991. Multiple personality disorder as seen from a social constructionist viewpoint. *Dissociation* 4:129–33.

Martínez-Taboas, Alfonso, and M. Francia. 1992. Multiple personality disorder. *British Journal of Psychiatry* 161:417–18.

Mathew, Roy J., Robert A. Jack, and W. Scott West. 1985. Regional cerebral blood flow in a patient with multiple personality. *American Journal of Psychiatry* 142:504–5.

McInerney, Peter K. 1985. Person-stages and unity of consciousness. *American Philosophical Quarterly* 22:197–209.

Merskey, Harold. 1992. The manufacture of personalities: The production of multiple personality disorder. *British Journal of Psychiatry* 160:327–40.

Mesulam, Marek Marsel. 1981. Dissociative states with abnormal temporal-lobe EEG: Multiple personality and the illusion of possession. *Archives of Neurology* 38:176–81.

Miller, Scott D. 1989. Optical differences in cases of multiple personality disorder. *Journal of Nervous and Mental Disease* 177:480–86.

Miller, Scott D., Terrell Blackburn, Gary Scholes, George L. White, and Nick Mamalis. 1991. Optical differences in multiple personality disorder: A second look. *Journal of Nervous and Mental Disease* 179: 132–35.

Miller, Scott D., and Patrick J. Triggiano. 1992. The psychophysiological investigation of multiple personality disorder: Review and update. *American Journal of Clinical Hypnosis* 35:47–61.

Mindham, R. H. S., J. G. Scadding, and R. H. Cawley. 1992. Diagnoses are not diseases. *British Journal of Psychiatry* 161:686–91.

Modestin, Jiri. 1992. Multiple personality disorder in Switzerland. *American Journal of Psychiatry* 149:88–92.

Mollinger, Robert N. 1984. Self defense: Multiple personality and the fear of murder. *Current Issues in Psychoanalytic Practice* 1:35–45.

Moor, James. 1982. Split brains and atomic persons. *Philosophy of Science* 49:91–106.

Moore, Michael S. 1984. *Law and psychiatry: Rethinking the relationship.* Cambridge: Cambridge University Press.

———. 1993. *Act and crime: The philosophy of action and its implications for criminal law.* Oxford: Clarendon Press.

Moss, C. Scott, Mary Margaret Thompson, and John Nolte. 1962. An additional study in hysteria: The case of Alice M. *International Journal of Clinical and Experimental Hypnosis* 10:59–74.

Murphy, Patricia E. 1994. Dissociative experiences and dissociative disorders in a non-clinical university student group. *Dissociation* 7:28–34.

Nakdimen, Kenneth A. 1989a. Asking patients about symptoms of multiple personality disorder. *American Journal of Psychiatry* 146:682–83.

———. 1989b. Splitting and dissociation, borderline personality and multiple personality. *American Journal of Psychiatry* 146:1236.

———. 1990. Multiple personality. *Hospital and Community Psychiatry* 41:566–67.

Nissen, Mary Jo, James L. Ross, Daniel B. Willingham, Thomas B. MacKenzie, and Daniel L. Schacter. 1988. Memory and awareness in a patient with multiple personality disorder. *Brain and Cognition* 8:117–34.

Noll, Richard 1989. Multiple personality, dissociation, and C. G. Jung's complex theory. *Journal of Analytical Psychology* 34:353–70.

———. 1993. Multiple personality and the complex theory: A correction and a rejection of C. G. Jung's 'collective unconscious.' *Journal of Analytical Psychology* 38:321–23.

North, Carol S., Jo-Ellyn M. Ryall, Daniel A. Ricci, and Richard D. Wetzel. 1993. *Multiple personalities, multiple disorders: Psychiatric classification and media influence.* New York: Oxford University Press.

Novello, Paolo, and Alberto Primavera. 1992. Multiple personality disorder. *British Journal of Psychiatry* 161:415.

Ogata, Susan N., Kenneth R. Silk, Sonya Goodrich, Naomi E. Lohr, Drew Westen, and Elizabeth M. Hill. 1990. Childhood sexual and physical abuse in adult patients with borderline personality disorder. *American Journal of Psychiatry* 147:1008–13.

Ohberg, Hjordis G., Gene F. Haring, and Robert E. Marsh. 1982. A case of embezzlement and multiple personality. Abstract in *International Journal of Clinical and Experimental Hypnosis* 30:203.

Packard, Russell C., and Frank Brown. 1986. Multiple headaches in a case of multiple personality disorder. *Headache* 26:99–102.

Parfit, Derek. 1984. *Reasons and persons.* Oxford: Clarendon Press.

Perlman, Stuart D. 1993. Unlocking incest memories: Preoedipal transference, countertransference, and the body. *Journal of American Academy of Psychoanalysis* 21:363–86.

Perr, Irwin N. 1991. Crime and multiple personality disorder: A case history and discussion. *Bulletin of the American Academy of Psychiatry and Law* 19:203–14.

Perry, Glenn G., and Bill N. Kinder. 1990. The susceptibility of the Rorschach to malingering: A critical review. *Journal of Personality Assessment* 54:47–57.

Piper, August, Jr. 1994. Multiple personality disorder and criminal responsibility: Critique of a paper by Elyn Saks. *Journal of Psychiatry & Law* 22:7–49.

———. 1995. A skeptical look at multiple personality disorder. In *Dissociative Identity Disorder: Theoretical and treatment controversies,* edited by Lewis M. Cohen, Joan N. Berzoff, and Mark R. Elin. Northvale, N.J.: Jason Aronson.

Pitblado, Colin, and Jonathan Cohen. 1984. State-related changes in amplitude, latency and cerebral asymmetry of averaged evoked potentials in a case of multiple personality. Abstract in *International Journal of Clinical Neuropsychology* 6:70.

Pohl, Richard L. 1977. Multiple personality in a middle-aged woman. *Psychiatric Opinion* 14:35–39.

Porter, Sue, Kay A. Kelly, and Carolyn J. Grame. 1993. Family treatment of spouses and children of patients with multiple personality disorder. *Bulletin of the Menninger Clinic* 57:371–79.

Prasad, Ashoka. 1985. Multiple personality syndrome. *British Journal of Hospital Medicine* 34:301–3.

Pribor, Elizabeth F., and Stephen H. Dinwiddie. 1992. Psychiatric correlates of incest in childhood. *American Journal of Psychiatry* 149:52–56.

Price, Reese. 1988. Of multiple personalities and dissociated selves: The fragmentation of the child. *Transactional Analysis Journal* 18:231–37.

Prince, Morton. 1978. *The dissociation of a personality: The hunt for the real Miss Beauchamp.* 2d ed. Oxford: Oxford University Press.

Prince, Morton, and Frederick Peterson. 1908. Experiments in psycho-galvanic reactions from co-conscious (sub-conscious) ideas in a case of multiple personality. *Journal of Abnormal Psychology* 3:114–86.

Putnam, Frank W. 1982. Traces of Eve's faces. *Psychology Today* 16:88.

——. 1984. The psychophysiologic investigation of multiple personality disorder: A review. *Psychiatric Clinics of North America* 7:31–39.

——. 1989. *Diagnosis and treatment of multiple personality disorder.* New York: Guilford Press.

——. 1991. Recent research on multiple personality disorder. *Psychiatric Clinics of North America* 14:489–502.

——. 1992. Multiple personality disorder. *British Journal of Psychiatry* 161:415–16.

——. 1993. Diagnosis and clinical phenomenology of multiple personality disorder: A North American perspective. *Dissociation* 6:80–86.

Putnam, Frank W., and Eve B. Carlson. In press. Hypnosis, dissociation, and trauma: Myths, metaphors, and mechanisms. In *Trauma, memory and dissociation,* edited by J. C. Bremner and C. Marmar. Washington, D.C.: American Psychiatric Press.

Putnam, Frank W., Juliet J. Guroff, Edward K. Silberman, and Lisa Barban. 1986. The clinical phenomenology of multiple personality disorder: Review of 100 recent cases. *Journal of Clinical Psychiatry* 47:285–93.

Putnam, Frank W., Karin Helmers, and Penelope K. Trickett. 1993. Development, reliability, and validity of a child dissociation scale. *Child Abuse and Neglect* 17:731–41.

Putnam, Frank W., and Gary Peterson. 1994. Further validation of the Child Dissociative Checklist. *Dissociation* 7:204–11.

Putnam, Frank W., Theodore P. Zahn, and Robert M. Post. 1990. Differential autonomic nervous system activity in multiple personality disorder. *Psychiatry Research* 31:251–60.

Radden, Jennifer. 1996. *Divided minds and successive selves: Ethical issues in disorders of identity and personality.* Cambridge, Mass.: MIT Press.

Radwin, Jill O. 1991. The multiple personality disorder: Has this trendy alibi lost its way? *Law and Psychology Review* 15:351–73.

Rathbun, J. M., and P. K. Rustagi. 1990. Differential diagnosis of schizophrenia and multiple personality disorder. *American Journal of Psychiatry* 147:375.

Ray, William J., Kimberly June, Kristyn Turaj, and Richard Lundy. 1992. Dissociative experiences in a college age population: A factor analytic study of 2 dissociation scales. *Personality and Individual Differences* 13:417–24.

Reis, Bruce E. 1993. Toward a psychoanalytic understanding of multiple personality disorder. *Bulletin of the Menninger Clinic* 57:309–18.

Reisner, Ralph, and Christopher Slobogin. 1990. *Law and the mental health system: Civil and criminal aspects.* 2d ed. St. Paul, Minn.: West Publishing Co.

Richert, Gail Zehner, and Christy Bergland. 1992. Treatment choices: Rehabilitation services used by patients with multiple personality disorder. *American Journal of Occupational Therapy* 46:634–38.

Riley, Kevin C. 1988. Measurement of dissociation. *Journal of Nervous and Mental Disease* 176:449–50.

Robinson, Paul H. 1984. *Criminal law defenses.* 2 vols. St. Paul, Minn.: West Publishing Co.

Rogers, Richard. 1984. Towards an empirical model of malingering and deception. *Behavioral Sciences and the Law* 2:93–111.

——, ed. 1988. *Clinical assessment of malingering and deception.* New York: Guilford Press.

Rose, Gilbert J. 1987. *Trauma and mastery in life and art.* New Haven: Yale University Press.

Rosenbaum, Milton. 1980. The role of the term schizophrenia in the decline of diagnoses of multiple personality. *Archives of General Psychiatry* 37:1383–85.

Rosenstein, Leslie D. 1994. Potential neuropsychologic and neurophysiologic correlates of multiple personality disorder. *Neuropsychiatry, Neuropsychology, and Behavioral Neurology* 7:215–29.

Rosik, Christopher H. 1992. On introducing multiple personality disorder to the local church. *Journal of Psychology and Christianity* 11:263–68.

Ross, Colin A. 1989. *Multiple personality disorder: diagnosis, clinical features, and treatment.* New York: Wiley.

——. 1990a. Dr. Ross replies. *Canadian Journal of Psychiatry* 35:195–96.

——. 1990b. Twelve cognitive errors about multiple personality disorder. *American Journal of Psychotherapy* 44:348–56.

——. 1991. Epidemiology of multiple personality disorder and dissociation. *Psychiatric Clinics of North America* 14: 503–17.

——. 1995. The validity and reliability of Dissociative Identity Disorder. In *Dissociative Identity Disorder: Theoretical and treatment controversies,* edited by Lewis M. Cohen, Joan N. Berzoff, and Mark R. Elin. Northvale, N.J.: Jason Aronson.

Ross, Colin A., and Geri Anderson. 1988. Phenomenological overlap of multiple personality disorder and obsessive-compulsive disorder. *Journal of Nervous and Mental Disease* 176:295–99.

Ross, Colin A., and Pam Gahan. 1988. Cognitive analysis of multiple personality disorder. *American Journal of Psychotherapy* 42:229–39.

Ross, Colin A., Sharon Heber, Geri Anderson, Ron Norton, Brian A. Anderson, Martin del Campo, and Neelan Pillay. 1989. Differentiating multiple personality disorder and complex partial seizures. *General Hospital Psychiatry* 11:54–58.

Ross, Colin A., Sharon Heber, G. Ron Norton, and Geri Anderson. 1989. Somatic symptoms in multiple personality disorder. *Psychosomatics* 30:154–60.

Ross, Colin A., Shaun Joshi, and Raymond Currie. 1991. Dissociative experiences in the general population: A factor analysis. *Hospital and Community Psychiatry* 42:297–301.

Ross, Colin A., Scott D. Miller, Lynda Bjornson, Pamela Reagor, George A. Fraser, and Geri Anderson. 1991. Abuse histories in 102 cases of multiple personality disorder. *Canadian Journal of Psychiatry* 36:97–101.

Ross, Colin A., G. Ron Norton, and Kay Wozney. 1989. Multiple personality disorder: An analysis of 236 cases. *Canadian Journal of Psychiatry* 34: 413–18.

Ross, Colin A., Lynne Ryan, Harrison Voigt, and Lyle Eide. 1991. High and low dissociators in a college student population. *Dissociation* 4:147–51.

Ross, Colin A., and Michael Weissberg. 1991. MPD: Does it exist? A debate. Paper presented at American Psychiatric Association Institute on Hospital and Community Psychiatry. Los Angeles, California.

Roth, Sheldon. 1992. A psychoanalyst's perspective on multiple personality disorder. *Psychoanalytic Inquiry* 12:112–23.

Rubenstein, Felicia G. 1991. Committing crimes while experiencing a true dissociative state: The multiple personality defense and appropriate criminal responsibility. *Wayne Law Review* 38:353–81.

Saakvitne, Karen W. 1995. Vicarious traumatization: Countertransference responses to dissociative clients. In *Dissociative Identity Disorder: Theoretical and treatment controversies,* edited by Lewis M. Cohen, Joan N. Berzoff, and Mark R. Elin. Northvale, N.J.: Jason Aronson.

Sachs, Roberta G. 1993. Use of sand trays in the beginning treatment of a patient with dissociative disorder. In *Clinical perspectives on multiple personality disorder,* edited by Richard P. Kluft and Catherine G. Fine. Washington, D.C.: American Psychiatric Press.

Sachs, Roberta G., Edward J. Frischholz, and Joan I. Wood. 1988. Marital and family therapy in the treatment of multiple personality disorder. *Journal of Marital and Family Therapy* 14:249–59.

Saks, Elyn R. 1992. Multiple personality disorder and criminal responsibility. *U.C. Davis Law Review* 25:383–461.

———. 1993. Competency to refuse psychotropic medication: Three alternatives to the law's cognitive standard. *University of Miami Law Review* 47:689–761.

Sandberg, David A., and Steven J. Lynn. 1992. Dissociative experiences, psychopathology and adjustment, and child and adolescent maltreatment in female college students. *Journal of Abnormal Psychology* 101:717–23.

Sanders, Barbara, and Marina H. Giolas. 1991. Dissociation and childhood trauma in psychologically disturbed adolescents. *American Journal of Psychiatry* 148:50–54.

Sanders, Barbara, and James A. Green. 1994. The factor structure of the Dissociative Experiences Scale in college students. *Dissociation* 7:23–27.

Sanders, Shirley. 1986. The perceptual alteration scale: A scale measuring dissociation. *American Journal of Clinical Hypnosis* 29:95–102.

Sands, Michael S. 1981. The mad murderer in the courtroom: Paul and Jack — a case study. Paper presented at the American Psychiatric Association. New Orleans, Louisiana.

Satel, Sally L., and Frances C. Howland. 1992. Multiple personality disorder presenting as postpartum depression. *Hospital and Community Psychiatry* 43:1241–43.

Savitz, David B. 1990. The legal defense of persons with the diagnosis of multiple personality disorder. *Dissociation* 3:195–203.

Saxe, Glenn N., Gary Chinman, Robert Berkowitz, Kathryn Hall, Gabriele Lieberg, Jane Schwartz, and Bessel A. Van der Kolk. 1994. Somatization in patients with dissociative disorders. *American Journal of Psychiatry* 151:1329–34.

Saxe, Glenn N., Russell G. Vasile, Thomas C. Hill, Kerry Bloomingdale, and Bessel A. Van der Kolk. 1992. SPECT imaging and multiple personality disorder. *Journal of Nervous and Mental Disease* 180:662–63.

Schafer, Donald W. 1986. Recognizing multiple personality patients. *American Journal of Psychotherapy* 40:500–510.

Schenk, Laura, and David Bear. 1981. Multiple personality and related dissociative phenomena in patients with temporal lobe epilepsy. *American Journal of Psychiatry* 138:1311–16.

Schopp, Robert F. 1991. *Automatism, insanity, and the psychology of criminal responsibility: A philosophical inquiry.* Cambridge: Cambridge University Press.

Schwartz, Harvey. 1994. From dissociation to negotiation: A relational psychoanalytic perspective on multiple personality disorder. *Psychoanalytic Psychology* 11:189–231.

Scialli, John V. K. 1982. Multiple identity processes and the development of the observing ego. *Journal of the American Academy of Psychoanalysis* 10:387–405.

Shapiro, Marian Kaplun. 1991a. Bandaging a "broken heart": Hypnoplay therapy in the treatment of multiple personality disorder. *American Journal of Clinical Hypnosis* 34:1–10.

———. 1991b. Bandaging a "broken heart": Hypnoplay therapy in the treatment of multiple personality disorder: Rejoinder to invited discussion. *American Journal of Clinical Hypnosis* 34:20–23.

Silberman, Edward K., Frank W. Putnam, Herbert Weingartner, Bennett G. Braun, and Robert M. Post. 1985. Dissociative states in multiple personality disorder: A quantitative study. *Psychiatry Research* 15:253–60.

Simpson, Michael A. 1989. Multiple personality disorder. *British Journal of Psychiatry* 155:565.

Slovenko, Ralph. 1989. The multiple personality: A challenge to legal concepts. *Journal of Psychiatry & Law* 17:681–719.

Smith, William H. 1993. Incorporating hypnosis into the psychotherapy of patients with multiple personality disorder. *Bulletin of the Menninger Clinic* 57:344–54.

Solomon, Robert S. 1983. Use of the MMPI with multiple personality patients. *Psychological Reports* 53:1004–6.

Spanos, Nicholas P. 1994. Multiple identity enactments and multiple personality disorder: A sociocognitive perspective. *Psychological Bulletin* 116: 143–65.

Spanos, Nicholas P., John R. Weekes, and Lorne D. Bertrand. 1985. Multiple personality: A social psychological perspective. *Journal of Abnormal Psychology* 94:362–76.

Steele, Kathy. 1989. Looking for answers: Understanding multiple personality disorders. *Journal of Psychosocial Nursing and Mental Health Services* 27:4–10.

Steinberg, Annie, and Marlene Steinberg. 1994. Systematic assessment of Dissociative Identity Disorder in an adolescent who is blind. *Dissociation* 7:117–28.

Steinberg, Marlene. 1994a. *Interviewer's guide to the Structured Clinical Interview for DSM-IV Dissociative Disorders (SCID-D): Revised.* Washington, D.C.: American Psychiatric Press.

———. 1994b. Systematizing dissociation: Symptomatology and diagnostic assessment. In *Dissociation: Culture, mind and body,* edited by David Spiegel. Washington, D.C.: American Psychiatric Press.

———. 1995. *Handbook for the assessment of dissociation: A clinical guide.* Washington, D.C.: American Psychiatric Press.

———. 1996. The psychological assessment of dissociative disorders. In *Handbook of Dissociation,* edited by Larry K. Michelson and William J. Ray. New York: Plenum Press.

Steinberg, Marlene, Jean Bancroft, and Josephine Buchanan. 1993. Multiple personality disorder in criminal law. *Bulletin of the American Academy of Psychiatry and the Law* 21:345–56.

Steinberg, Marlene, Domenic V. Cicchetti, Josephine Buchanan, Pamela E. Hall, and Bruce J. Rounsaville. 1989–92. *NIMH field trials of the Structured Clinical Interview for DSM-IV Dissociative Disorders (SCID-D).* New Haven, Conn.: Yale University School of Medicine.

———. 1993. Clinical assessment of dissociative symptoms and disorders: The Structured Clinical Interview for DSM-IV Dissociative Disorders (SCID-D). *Dissociation* 6:3–15.

Steinberg, Marlene, Domenic Cicchetti, Josephine Buchanan, Jaak Rakfeldt, and Bruce Rounsaville. 1994. Distinguishing between multiple personality disorder (Dissociative Identity Disorder) and schizophrenia using the Structured Clinical Interview for DSM-IV Dissociative Disorders. *Journal of Nervous and Mental Disease* 182:495–502.

Steinberg, Marlene, Bruce J. Rounsaville, and Domenic V. Cicchetti. 1990. The Structured Clinical Interview for DSM-III-R Dissociative Disorders: Preliminary report on a new diagnostic instrument. *American Journal of Psychiatry* 147:76–82.

Stermac, Lana. 1988. Projective testing and dissimulation. In *Clinical assessment of malingering and deception,* edited by Richard Rogers. New York: Guilford Press.

Sternlicht, Harold C., James Payton, Gerhardt Werner, and Michael Rancurello. 1989. Multiple personality disorder: A neuroscience and cognitive psychology perspective. *Psychiatric Annals* 19:448–55.

Stoller, Robert J. 1973. *Splitting: A case of female masculinity.* New York: Quadrangle.

Strick, Frances L., and S. Allen Wilcoxon. 1991. A comparison of dissociative experiences in adult female outpatients with and without histories of early incestuous abuse. *Dissociation* 4:193–99.

Szasz, Thomas S. 1974. *The myth of mental illness.* New York: Harper and Row.

———. 1969. Interview. *New Physician* 18:453–55.

Thigpen, Corbett H., and Hervey M. Cleckley. 1954. A case of multiple personality. *Journal of Abnormal and Social Psychology* 49:135–51.

———. 1957. *The three faces of Eve.* New York: McGraw-Hill.

———. 1984. On the incidence of multiple personality disorder: A brief communication. *International Journal of Clinical and Experimental Hypnosis* 32:63–66.

Torem, Moshe S. 1990. Covert multiple personality underlying eating disorders. *American Journal of Psychotherapy* 44:357–68.

Toth, Ellen L., and Andrea Baggaley. 1991. Coexistence of Munchausen's syndrome and multiple personality disorder: Detailed report of a case and theoretical discussion. *Psychiatry* 54:176–83.

Tozman, Seymour, and Roman Pabis. 1989. MPD: Further skepticism (without hostility . . . we think). *Journal of Nervous and Mental Disease* 177:708–9.

Van der Hart, Onno, and Suzette Boon. 1989. Multiple personality disorder. *British Journal of Psychiatry* 154:419.

Volkman, Stephanie. 1993. Music therapy and the treatment of trauma-induced dissociative disorders. *The Arts in Psychotherapy* 20:243–51.

Wagner, Edwin E., Ralph B. Allison, and Carol F. Wagner. 1983. Diagnosing multiple personalities with the Rorschach: A confirmation. *Journal of Personality Assessment* 47:143–49.

Wagner, Edwin E., and Marion R. Heise. 1974. A comparison of Rorschach records of three multiple personalities. *Journal of Personality Assessment* 38:308–31.

Waller, N. G. 1995. The Dissociative Experiences Scale. In *Twelfth mental measurements yearbook,* edited by Jane C. Conoley and James C. Impara. Lincoln, Neb.: Buros Institute of Mental Measurement.

Watkins, John G. 1976. Ego states and the problem of responsibility: A psychological analysis of the Patty Hearst case. *Journal of Psychiatry and Law* 4:471–89.

———. 1978. Ego states and the problem of responsibility II: The case of Patricia W. *Journal of Psychiatry and Law* 6:519–35.

Weissberg, Michael. 1993. Multiple personality disorder and iatrogenesis: The cautionary tale of Anna O. *International Journal of Clinical and Experimental Hypnosis* 41:15–34.

Wetsman, Howard. 1992. Obesity and multiple personality disorder. *American Journal of Psychiatry* 149:1612.

Wexler, David B., and Bruce J. Winick. 1991 *Essays in therapeutic jurisprudence.* Durham, N.C.: Carolina Academic Press.

———. 1996. *Law in a therapeutic key: Developments in therapeutic jurisprudence.* Durham, N.C.: Carolina Academic Press. Forthcoming.

Wilbur, Cornelia B. 1984. Treatment of multiple personality. *Psychiatric Annals* 14:27–31.

———. 1988. Multiple personality disorder and transference. *Dissociation* 1:73–76.

Wilbur, Cornelia B., and Richard P. Kluft. 1989. Multiple personality disorder. In *Treatments of psychiatric disorders: A task force report of the American Psychiatric Association.* Vol. 3. Washington, D.C.: American Psychiatric Association.

Wilkes, Kathleen V. 1981. Multiple personality and personal identity. *British Journal for the Philosophy of Science* 32:331–48.

———. 1988. *Real people: Personal identity without thought experiments.* Oxford: Clarendon Press.

Williams, Bernard. 1973. *Problems of the self.* New York: Cambridge University Press.

Williams, Glanville. 1978. *Textbook of criminal law.* London: Stevens & Sons.

Winick, Bruce J. 1996. *Therapeutic jurisprudence applied: Essays in mental health law.* Durham, N.C.: Carolina Academic Press. Forthcoming.

Yank, Jane R. 1991. Handwriting variations in individuals with multiple personality disorder. *Dissociation* 4:2–12.

Young, Walter C. 1986a. Multiple personality and modern childhood folklore. Paper presented at the Third International Conference on Multiple Personality-Dissociative States, Chicago, Illinois.

———. 1986b. Restraints in the treatment of a patient with multiple personality. *American Journal of Psychotherapy* 40:601–6.

———. 1987. Emergence of a multiple personality in a posttraumatic stress disorder of adulthood. *American Journal of Clinical Hypnosis* 29:249–54.

———. 1988. Psychodynamics and dissociation: All that switches is not split. *Dissociation* 1:33–38.

Young, Walter C., Linda J. Young, and Kelly Lehl. 1991. Restraints in the treatment of dissociative disorders: A follow-up of twenty patients. *Dissociation* 4:74–78.

Zalewski, Christine. 1991. Review of *Multiple personality: An exercise in deception,* by Ray Aldridge-Morris. *Contemporary Psychology* 36:624–25.

Zerbe, Kathryn. 1993. Selves that starve and suffocate: The continuum of eating disorders and dissociative phenomena. *Bulletin of the Menninger Clinic* 57:319–27.

Ziskin, Jay. 1984. Malingering of psychological disorders. *Behavioral Sciences and the Law* 2:39–49.

Table of Cases

Index